SAINT-SIMON AT VERSAILLES

By Lucy Norton
FIRST LADY OF VERSAILLES

Translated by Lucy Norton
THE JOURNAL OF EUGÈNE DELACROIX

Edited and translated by Lucy Norton
LETTERS FROM A PORTUGUESE NUN
THE HISTORICAL MEMOIRS OF THE DUC DE SAINT-SIMON

SAINT-SIMON AT VERSAILLES

Edited and translated by

LUCY NORTON

HARMONY BOOKS/NEW YORK

To Keith and Betty

Inquiries should be addressed to Harmony Books, a division of Crown Publishers, Inc., One Park Avenue, New York, New York 10016

First American Edition

Library of Congress Catalog Card Number: 80–28021

The major portion of the text was first published, with an introduction by Nancy Mitford, in 1958 by Hamish Hamilton Ltd Garden House, 57–59 Long Acre, London WC2E 9JZ

This edition published in Great Britain 1980 by Hamish Hamilton Ltd Printed in Great Britain

Design by Patrick Leeson

Picture Research by Joy Law

ISBN: 0-517-544334

10 9 8 7 6 5 4 3 2 1

TITLE PAGE ILLUSTRATION
The arms of Louis de Rouvroy, Duc de Saint-Simon, Pair de France, taken from the binding of the *Mémoires*.

Contents

List of Illustrations

Acknowledgments

Illustration VI is reproduced by gracious permission of Her Majesty the Queen; V by kind permission of His Grace the Duke of Marlborough (photo: Jeremy Whitaker); VII by kind permission of the Greater London Council as Trustees of the Iveagh Bequest, Kenwood; A, 1, 5b, 8, 11, 14, 15, 18, 21, 22, 23, 25, 28, 30, 31, 39, 40, 43, 44, 45, 46, 47, 49, 51, 61, 62, 63, 64, 68, 72, 74, 75, 76, 77, 84, 86, 91 and 99 by kind permission of the Bibliothèque Nationale, Paris; 2, 6, 10, 12, 35, 55, 70, 81, 93 and 98 by kind permission of Giraudon, Paris; I, II, III, IV, 3, 16, 17, 26, 29, 33, 37, 52, 54, 58, 60, 67, 71, 73, 78, 79, 83, 85, 88, 90, 92, 94 and 96 by kind permission of the Musée de Versailles (photos: Documentation Photographique, Paris); 4, 9, 24, 56 and 97 by kind permission of Roger-Viollet, Paris; 5c, 7, 50, 65 and 66 by kind permission of the National Museum, Stockholm; 5a, 19, 20 and 69 by kind permission of Musée du Louvre, Paris (photos: Documentation Photographique, Paris); 13, 36, 38, 41, 82, 87, 89 and 95 by kind permission of Bulloz, Paris; 27 by kind permission of Brompton Studios; 32, 59 and 80 by kind permission of Archives Nationales, Paris; 34 by kind permission of the Brighton Art Gallery; 42 by kind permission of the Ashmolean Museum, Oxford; 53 by kind permission of the Trustees, The Wallace Collection, London; 57 by kind permission of Musée de Mobilier National, France (photo: Documentation Photographique, Paris).

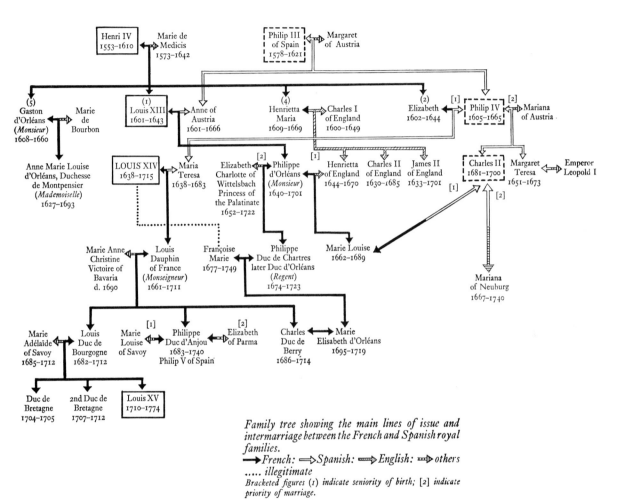

Henri IV
1553–1610

Marie de
Medicis
1573–1642

Philip III
of Spain
1578–1621

Margaret
of Austria

(5)
Gaston
d'Orléans
(*Monsieur*)
1608–1660

Marie
de
Bourbon

(1)
Louis XIII
1601–1643

Anne of
Austria
1601–1666

(4)
Henrietta
Maria
1609–1669

Charles I
of England
1600–1649

(2)
Elizabeth
1602–1644

[1]

Philip IV
1605–1665

[2]

Mariana
of Austria

Anne Marie Louise
d'Orléans, Duchesse
de Montpensier
(*Mademoiselle*)
1627–1693

LOUIS XIV
1638–1715

Maria
Teresa
1638–1683

Elizabeth
Charlotte of
Wittelsbach
Princess of
the Palatinate
1652–1722

[2]

Philippe
d'Orléans
(*Monsieur*)
1640–1701

[1]

Henrietta
of England
1644–1670

Charles II
of England
1630–1685

James II
of England
1633–1701

Charles II
1681–1700

Margaret
Teresa
1651–1673

Emperor
Leopold I

[1]

[2]

Marie Anne
Christine
Victoire of
Bavaria
d. 1690

Louis
Dauphin
of France
(*Monseigneur*)
1661–1711

Françoise
Marie
1677–1749

Philippe
Duc de Chartres
later Duc d'Orléans
(*Regent*)
1674–1723

Marie Louise
1662–1689

Mariana
of Neuburg
1667–1740

Marie
Adélaïde
of Savoy
1685–1712

Louis
Duc de
Bourgogne
1682–1712

Marie
Louise
of Savoy

[1]

Philippe
Duc d'Anjou
1683–1740
Philip V of Spain

[2]

Elizabeth
of Parma

Charles
Duc de
Berry
1686–1714

Marie
Elisabeth d'Orléans
1695–1719

Duc de
Bretagne
1704–1705

2nd Duc de
Bretagne
1707–1712

Louis XV
1710–1774

*Family tree showing the main lines of issue and
intermarriage between the French and Spanish royal
families.*
→ *French:* ⇒*Spanish:* ⇛*English:* ⇝*others*
..... *illegitimate*
*Bracketed figures (1) indicate seniority of birth; [2] indicate
priority of marriage.*

11

Claude Duc de Saint-Simon,
Pair de France and Master of
the Wolf-hounds. Father of
the Memoirist.

1691

Childhood

I was born on the night of January 15th, 1675, son of Claude, Duc de Saint-Simon, Peer of France, by his second wife, Charlotte de l'Aubespine, the only child of that marriage. By my father's first wife, Diane de Budos, he had had no sons but one daughter, whom he had married to the Duc de Brissac, the only brother of the Duchesse de Villeroy. She died without issue in 1684, and in her will she made me her residuary legatee.

I bore the title of Vidame de Chartres, and much care and thought was lavished on my upbringing, for my mother, a most virtuous lady, vastly sensible and intelligent, took endless pains over my education. She did not want me to share the fate of many young men who think their fortunes made, when they become independent too soon, and my father, who had been born in 1606, seemed unlikely to live long enough to spare me that misfortune. She therefore constantly reminded me that I urgently needed to train myself for some position since I should be entering the world alone and unprotected, the son of Louis XIII's favourite, whose friends were dead or in no position to aid me. As for her, she had been brought up in the house of her kinswoman, the old Duchesse d'Angoulême, and had married an elderly man. Thus she had made no friendships with people of her own age, and, what is more, had no uncles, aunts, or cousins. I should therefore be thrown entirely upon my own resources, which made it doubly necessary to make the best possible use of myself, for I could expect no other support.

My mother accordingly did her utmost to encourage me to overcome this major handicap, and she succeeded in giving me a great desire to do so, although the fact that I cared little for learning did not assist her. I had, however, a natural love for reading and history, and I improved my mind by trying to emulate the great men of whom I read, which made up for my dislike of the classics. Indeed, I have sometimes thought that had I made the former my serious study and wasted less time upon the latter, I might perhaps have become something.

My reading of history, especially the memoirs of my own times and the period immediately after the reign of François I, gave me the idea of writing down my own observations, in the hope that by learning all I could of current affairs I might fit myself for some high position. I foresaw the dangers of such a course, but a firm resolve to keep my undertaking secret seemed to meet all

possible objections. In July 1694, therefore, I began my Memoirs, being at that time colonel of a cavalry regiment in my own name, encamped at Guinsheim in the Vieux-Rhin, part of the army commanded by the Maréchal Duc de Lorges.

In 1691, I had been studying philosophy and equitation at the Académie des Sieurs de Mesmont et Rochefort, but was beginning to be tired of masters and study. I became very eager to enter the army, for the King himself had commanded at the siege of Mons in the early spring of that year, and most of the young men of my own age were serving in their first campaign. What moved me most, however, was that M. le Duc de Chartres[1] was there also. He was my elder by eight months; we had been brought up together, as it were, and, if youth will excuse the expression between men so unequal in rank, we were friends. Such considerations determined me to extricate myself from the schoolroom, but I shall not enlarge upon all the ruses I used in order to succeed. I first spoke to my mother; but soon realized that she would only laugh at me; I then went to my father and managed to persuade him that as the King had laid one great siege that year he would rest in the next; I deceived my

[1] Later, Duc d'Orléans. Became Regent of France, 1715.

14

mother, who only discovered my plot on the eve of its execution, and I worked upon my father so that he should not weaken.

The King always insisted that everyone who entered his service, except the Princes of the Blood and his bastards, should spend a year in one of his two companies of musketeers. Then, before they were allowed to buy a regiment, they had to go for training, for a varying period, either as captains of cavalry, or as junior officers in his own artillery regiment. My father therefore took me with him when he went to Versailles. He made his bow, and presented me as wishing to become a musketeer, on St. Simon and St. Jude's Day, at half-past noon, at the time when the King was leaving the Council.

His Majesty did him the honour of embracing him three times, but when it came to me, he thought me puny and delicate-looking and said that I was still exceedingly young. My father answered that I should have all the longer to serve him. Then the King asked in which company my father wished to place me, and he chose the first, because his friend Maupertuis was captain, and he knew that I should be well looked after. He also knew that the King always questioned the two captains minutely, and especially Maupertuis, about the young men of quality in their companies, and that their reports influenced his first impressions, on which so much depended. As it turned out, my father was not mistaken, for I have reason to attribute the King's early good opinion of me to Maupertuis' kind offices.

1692

Marriage of M. le Duc de Chartres

The King had been busy providing establishments for his bastards, whom every day he advanced in rank and honours. Two of his illegitimate daughters he had already married to Princes of the Blood. Mme la Princesse de Conti, his only daughter by Mme de la Vallière, was a widow without children, the other, his eldest daughter by Mme de Montespan, had married Monsieur le Duc. For a long time past Mme de Maintenon, even more than the King, had thought of nothing but their further aggrandisement. Now, both wished to marry Mlle de Blois, the King's second daughter by Mme de Montespan, to M. le Duc de Chartres, his only legitimate nephew, far above even the Princes of the Blood, by his rank as a Grandson of France and by the Court of Monsieur, his father.

The King well knew the shocking scandal that had been created by the marriages of the Princes of the Blood, and he could imagine the effect of one which society would consider infinitely more improper. Nevertheless, he had been turning the matter over in his mind during the past four years and had already begun to make the first moves. These he had found all the more difficult because Monsieur was inordinately proud in anything that touched his rank, and Madame came of a nation that abhorred bastardy and misalliances.

In this dilemma he consulted his crony, Monsieur le Grand,[1] desiring him to win over his brother the Chevalier de Lorraine, an exceedingly good-looking man who ruled Monsieur in everything. Indeed, the latter, who had no taste for women (a fact which he did not even try to disguise), had taken the Chevalier for his master and remained true to him for the rest of his life. These two brothers asked for nothing better than to please the King in a matter that touched him so closely, and, like the clever men that they were, they turned it to their own advantage. The first move was made in the summer of 1688. Only about a dozen chevaliers of the Order[2] still remained, and everyone knew that promotions could not be long delayed. The two brothers now demanded the honour for themselves and claimed to be given precedence of the dukes. The King, who had never yet given the Order to any Lorrainer on such an assumption, was reluctant to agree, but the brothers stood firm. They triumphed; and thus, having received payment in advance, the Chevalier de Lorraine answered for Monsieur's consent and the means to bring Madame and the Duc de Chartres to agree to the marriage.

Now the young Duc de Chartres when he left the nursery had been placed in the care of Saint-Laurent, a man of no standing, an assistant to the head of the protocol in Monsieur's household, of humble appearance, but for all that a gentleman and well-fitted to educate a prince and form a great King. He was a friend of the curé of Saint-Eustache, who had a valet named Dubois,[3] a most intelligent man, whom he had encouraged to study the classics and even history. This Dubois had been no more than a servant in the curé's employ, but he had pleased his master, who passed him on to Saint-Laurent to act as a secretary in the education of M. le Duc de Chartres. They made him take orders to rub off his rough corners and gradually introduced him into the prince's schoolroom to help in preparing his lessons, copying his essays, looking up words for him in the dictionary, and generally making his work easier. I used often to see Dubois when I went to play with M. le Duc de Chartres. Later, when Saint-Laurent grew old, Dubois set the lessons and did it very well and at the same time managed to make himself agreeable to the young prince. After Saint-Laurent's sudden death he was temporarily appointed to the post of tutor.

The Chevalier de Lorraine and the Marquis d'Effiat, Monsieur's first equerry, had become interested in Dubois when he was training for the priesthood, and they now tried to have him confirmed in the appointment. This they were not able to achieve at first, but by obstructing all other nominations they finally managed to stampede him into the post. Never have I seen a man so happy as Dubois, nor with better reason. Gratitude and a desire to keep his job made him loyal to his patrons, and it was therefore to him that the Chevalier applied when they wished to persuade M. le Duc de Chartres to accept the marriage.

[1] Court name for the Master of the Horse (le Grand Ecuyer de France) who was at that time Louis de Lorraine, Comte d'Armagnac.

[2] Always refers to the Ordre du Saint-Esprit.

[3] The Abbé, later Cardinal, Dubois, First minister of France, 1722.

'Monsieur', Philippe Duc d'Orléans, the King's brother. French School, 17thC.

Dubois, as I have explained, was in the prince's confidence; it was not hard for him to teach one so young and inexperienced to dread the anger of the King and Monsieur and to regard any alternative as heaven itself. None the less, in spite of all his efforts, the best he could do was to prevent a flat refusal, but that was enough to ensure success. Monsieur's consent had already been gained, and as soon as the King received the word he made haste to dispose of the business. A day or two earlier, however, Madame had got wind of it, and with the forcefulness which she never lacked she had spoken to her son and had extracted a promise that he would never agree. Thus, M. de Chartres, weak with his tutor and weak with his mother, hating the one course and fearing the other, found himself utterly discomfited.

17

One afternoon, very early, as I was passing through the upper gallery, I saw M. le Duc de Chartres come out of the back door of his apartment looking monstrously wretched and harassed, attended by an officer of Monsieur's guard. As I happened to be in his way, I asked him where he was going in such a hurry, to which he replied that the King had sent for him. I did not think it politic to accompany him, so I turned to my tutor and said that there might be some question of his marriage and that the news would soon break. There had been rumours of angry scenes for some days past, and my curiosity made me very watchful and attentive.

M. de Chartres found the King alone with Monsieur in his study, where he had little expected to see the latter. His reception was most loving, for the King said that he wished to provide an establishment for him, and that since the war deprived him of suitable foreign princesses and there were no Princesses of the Blood of his own age, he could show him no greater love than to give him his own daughter, both of whose sisters were already married to Princes of the Blood. Such a marriage, said the King, would make him a son-in-law as well as a nephew, but, although he was eager to arrange it, he would not compel him, but would leave him full liberty to decide for himself. This proposal, delivered with the terrifying majesty that was the King's natural manner, and addressed to a prince who had no answer ready, upset M. de Chartres completely. He tried to shirk the question by putting the responsibility upon Monsieur and Madame, stammering out that the King was master, but that his own wishes depended on his parents. 'That is very right and proper,' replied the King, 'and since you have no objection, your father and mother will not stand in your way.' Then, turning to Monsieur, he continued, 'Is that not true, brother?' Thereupon Monsieur agreed, as had already been arranged between them, and the King immediately sent for Madame, saying that only she remained to be consulted. He then began a conversation with Monsieur and both of them pretended not to notice M. de Chartres's nervousness and low spirits.

As soon as Madame made her appearance, the King said that he felt sure she would not oppose an arrangement which Monsieur welcomed and M. de Chartres approved, namely his marriage to Mlle de Blois. He admitted that he himself was most anxious for it and shortly repeated what he had been saying to M. de Chartres. All this was done with a commanding air, yet as though he never doubted that she would be otherwise than delighted, which he very well knew was not the case. Madame, who had counted on her son's refusal because he had given his promise (and he had really done his best to keep it by hesitating and looking embarrassed), was left speechless and cornered. Darting two furious glances at Monsieur and M. de Chartres, she said that since they were determined, she had nothing further to say and, dropping a very brief curtsey, she returned to her apartments. Her son followed her instantly, but she did not give him a moment to explain and drove him from the room with a torrent of tears and abuse.

Shortly afterwards, Monsieur went to her, but except that she did not

Design for a chandelier by Charles Le Brun.

The King's knife, fork and spoon, designed by Nicolas de Launay, the King's silversmith.

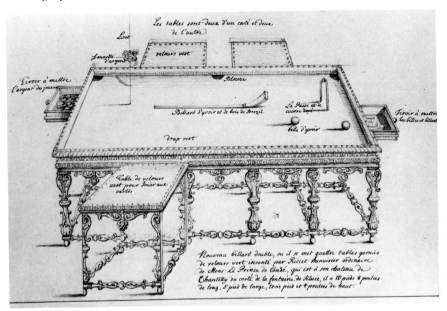

The Prince de Condé's billiard table, with a velvet-covered card-table, one of four designed by Riccet.

actually turn him out, she spared him no more than her son, and he came out looking abashed, not having had the chance to utter a single word. The entire scene was over by four in the afternoon, and that evening there was 'Appartement', as used to happen three times a week in wintertime. On the other three evenings there was a play, and on Sundays, nothing.

What they called 'Appartement' was a reception for the entire Court in the great suite of rooms that runs from one end of the long gallery to the ante-chamber of the chapel. It lasted from seven until ten in the evening, when the King sat down to supper. At first there was music, and then tables were prepared for all kinds of games. There was one for lansquenet, which Monseigneur and Monsieur always played, and another for billiards; in a word there was freedom to do as one pleased, to make up card-parties and to call for more tables when necessary. Beyond the room used for billiards there were refreshments, and each room was beautifully illuminated. In the beginning, the King used to appear and played for a time, but latterly he ceased to come, although he liked others to attend regularly, and everyone went because they were anxious to please him. He used to spend his own evenings in Mme de Maintenon's apartments working with the different ministers, one after another.

That evening, shortly after the end of the concert, the King sent for Monseigneur and Monsieur, who had already sat down to lansquenet; for Madame, who had taken up her position by a game of hombre but was scarcely giving it a glance; for M. de Chartres, who was gloomily playing chess, and for Mlle de Blois. The latter [aged 15] had only just begun to appear in society, and was marvellously over-dressed, although she knew nothing of what was happening. Being naturally timid and horribly frightened of the King, she thought she was being sent for to receive a scolding, and trembled so violently as she entered, that Mme de Maintenon took her upon her lap and held her in her arms, but even so could not entirely calm her.

After all this bustle of the royalty being summoned to Mme de Maintenon's apartments and Mlle de Blois with them, rumours of a marriage spread through the Appartement at the same time that the King was announcing it to his family. The commotion lasted only a few minutes and the news was made public as soon as the royal persons returned. That was the moment at which I arrived to find the Court all in a huddle together, and astonishment pictured on every face. I soon learned what was the matter, but was not surprised because of my encounter with M. de Chartres earlier in the day.

In the long gallery, Madame was marching up and down with Châteautiers, her favourite. She strode about handkerchief in hand, weeping unrestrainedly, speaking rather loud, gesticulating, and looking for all the world like Ceres after the rape of Proserpine. Everyone made way for her respectfully, and only passed her when they wished to reach the Appartement. Monseigneur and Monsieur went back to their lansquenet. The former appeared quite as usual, but no one has ever looked more ashamed of himself than Monsieur, nor more embarrassed, and he remained in this condition for several weeks. M. de Chartres looked utterly miserable, and his intended was in a state of great distress and unhappiness. She was very young and the marriage a marvellous one for her, yet she could see and feel the effects of it and dreaded the consequences. Indeed, the dismay was pretty general, except amongst a few. As for the Lorraines, they triumphantly rejoiced in their success, and, having no shame, they had good reason.

On the surface, that Appartement seemed duller than usual, on account of the situation, but in reality it was very lively and interesting and, to me, it seemed shorter than usual. It ended with the King's supper, where I resolved to let nothing escape me. The King seemed perfectly composed. Madame sat next M. de Chartres, but never so much as glanced at him, nor at Monsieur. Her eyes were full of tears, which fell from time to time, and every now and then she wiped them away, looking around all the while to see how others were affected. M. de Chartres's eyes also were very red, and neither he nor his mother ate much. I observed how courteously the King offered Madame the dishes that were placed before him and how ungraciously she refused, which did not in any way disturb his air of polite attention. It was much remarked that after they had left the table, the King made Madame a particularly low and impressive bow, at which she performed a pirouette so neat and swift that all he could see as he straightened himself, was her back retreating towards the door.

Next day, the entire Court called upon Monsieur, Madame, and M. le Duc de Chartres, but nothing was said. People merely made their bows and everything passed off in perfect silence. Afterwards, everyone waited as usual in the long gallery for the Council to rise and the King to pass on his way to mass. Madame was there too, and when her son came up to her to kiss her hand, she dealt him such a resounding box on the ear that it could be heard some distance away. Receiving this, as he did, in the presence of the whole Court, the poor prince was covered with embarrassment and the vast crowd, myself included, were prodigiously amazed. On that same day the details of the bride's enormous dowry were announced, and on the following, the King visited

Courtiers in the Galerie des Glaces at Versailles, by Sébastien Le Clerc.

Monsieur and Madame. It was all very unhappy. After that, no one thought of anything but the wedding.

On Shrove Sunday, the King gave a state ball. That is to say, one that began with a *bransle*[1] after which everyone danced. I paid a call on Madame in the morning, and she could not resist telling me in a sour disagreeable voice that I seemed delighted about the balls but that was because I was young; for her part, she was older and wished that they were over. Monseigneur le Duc de Bourgogne danced that evening for the first time, and opened the *bransle* with Mademoiselle. This was also the first time that I danced at a state ball, and I led out the provost marshal's daughter, Mlle de Sourches, who danced exceedingly well. Everyone was vastly fine.

On Shrove Monday, all the royal party and the bride and bridegroom in splendid attire went to the King's study and thence to the chapel, which was arranged as it usually is for the King's mass, except that they had placed two cushions between his stool and the altar for the bridal pair, who thus had their backs turned to the King. Cardinal de Bouillon came out of the sacristy wearing his vestments, and said mass after performing the wedding ceremony. After this, they all went at once to dinner. There was a horseshoe table. The Princes and Princesses of the Blood sat to right and left according to precedence, ending with the King's two bastards, and next them, for the first time, the widow of the Duc de Verneuil (the bastard of Henri IV), who thus, long after his death, became a Prince of the Blood, which he would certainly never have expected. This the Duc d'Uzès thought so comical that he marched up and down in front of her, crying, 'Room, room, for Mme Charlotte Séguier!'[2] No duchesses paid their court at this dinner, except the Duchesse de Sully and the Duchesse du Lude, the daughter and daughter-in-law of Mme de Verneuil, which all the others thought so improper that they dared not return afterwards.

In the afternoon the King and Queen of England[3] came to Versailles with their suites. There was a gala concert and cards, with the King present nearly all the time, vastly delighted and very magnificent, wearing his blue ribbon over his coat, as he had done on the previous evening. Supper was like dinner, King James having his Queen on his right hand and the King on his left, and each with their *cadenas*.[4] Later the bridal pair were led to the apartments of the new Duchesse de Chartres. The Queen of England presented the shift to her, and the King of England gave the one to the Duc de Chartres, but he refused it at first, saying that he felt too miserable. Cardinal de Bouillon performed the rite of blessing the bed. He kept them waiting for a quarter of an hour, which everyone thought unbecoming in a man who had just returned from a long period of exile (he had been disgraced for refusing to pronounce the nuptial blessing over Madame la Duchesse without being invited to the royal banquet).

On Shrove Tuesday, there was a full dress reception in Mme de Chartres's apartments, with the King and Queen of England present, and the King and the entire Court. Mass followed, and then dinner, as on the previous day. Mme de

[1] A processional dance, performed by the highest-ranking guests.

[2] Maiden name of the Duchesse de Verneuil, whose father Pierre Séguier, the Chancellor, had died in 1672.

[3] James II and his second wife, Mary of Modena.

[4] Cases containing forks and spoons.

22

A *Cadena*, the locked case containing the knife, spoon and fork of a great noble. Drawing by A. N. Cousinet, 1702, probably designed for Louis XIV. The platform is the place for the napkin and plates. The pepper pot and salt cellar are shown at the side.

Verneuil was sent back to Paris that morning. It was considered that there had been enough of her. After dinner, the King was closeted with the King and Queen of England, and later a gala ball was held like the earlier one, except that the new Duchess was led out by Mgr le Duc de Bourgogne. Everyone wore the same coat and danced with the same partner as before.

1695

Marriage of Saint-Simon

The day of my marriage was now fast approaching. During the previous year, there had been some talk of an alliance with the eldest daughter of the Maréchal de Lorges, but the idea had been dismissed almost as soon as entertained. Now, on both sides, there were great hopes of renewal. The Maréchal had been ruined in the wars, his only reward having been his marshal's bâton. As soon as he had received it, however, he had married the daughter of Frémont, the keeper of the King's jewels, who amassed a vast fortune under M. Colbert and was considered the ablest and most consulted financier of his day. Immediately after his marriage, the Maréchal had been appointed captain of the bodyguard, a post left vacant by the death of the Maréchal de Rochefort. He had in all his service earned a great reputation for honour, courage, and ability.

The Maréchal de Lorges's integrity and candour had much pleased me when I had had the opportunity of observing him closely during the campaign which I fought under his command. The love and esteem in which he was held by the whole army, his high reputation at Court, his magnificent establishment and extremely noble birth, his distinguished connections that offset the inferior marriage which he was first of his line to be obliged to contract, all made me earnestly desire the match. His eldest brother, moreover, was greatly esteemed and, by a strange coincidence, held similar honours, offices, and establishments. The devoted affection between them and, indeed, throughout the entire large family, most of all, the goodness and sincerity of the Maréchal himself, so rare, so real in him, made me very eager. I hoped to find everything that I lacked to sustain me and advance my interests and to enable me to live agreeably amid noble connections and a pleasant family.

What is more, in the irreproachable virtue of the Maréchal's wife, and her sagacity in reconciling her husband with M. de Louvois and thus gaining him a dukedom, I found everything that I could desire for training a wife whom I wished to appear at Court. There the Maréchale was universally praised and respected for the elegant, wise, and dignified manner in which she kept open house to the highest society, without admixture, conducting herself with perfect modesty, yet never forgetting the position due to her husband's rank. By this means she had made her inferior birth forgotten by the Maréchal's family, the Court, and society in general, where her character had earned her general esteem. Nevertheless, she existed only for her husband, who trusted her in everything and lived with her and all her relations in a mutual affection and respect that did him much credit.

They had one son, a boy of twelve whom they loved to distraction, and five daughters. The two eldest had spent their childhood with the Benedictines, at Conflans, and for the past three years had been living with their grandmother, Mme Frémont, whose house communicated with that of the Maréchale de Lorges. The eldest girl was seventeen, the second, fifteen years old. They had never been allowed out of their grandmother's sight, for she was a woman of great good sense and perfect virtue, who, in her youth, had been exceedingly handsome and still retained some traces of her former beauty. She was a most pious lady, active in good works, and entirely devoted to the upbringing of her two granddaughters. For a long time past her husband had been afflicted by paralysis and other diseases, but his mind was clear and he managed his own affairs. The Maréchale lived with them all, busy with all manner of duties and charities, and they respected her and loved her dearly.

Mme Frémont secretly preferred Mlle de Lorges, whereas the Maréchale's favourite was the second daughter, Mlle de Quintin. Indeed, had it depended only on her mother's wishes, the elder would have been sent to a convent in order to give her sister the chance of a better marriage. The latter had dark hair and beautiful eyes; Mlle de Lorges, on the other hand, was fair, with a perfect figure and complexion. She had a most pleasing expression, was very modest, yet stately in her bearing, and there was something about her that I thought very gracious because it came from natural goodness and gentleness. I liked her infinitely the better of the two when I first saw them together; there was no

House of Saint-Simon's father-in-law, the Maréchal–Duc de Lorges, in the Rue Neuve-Saint-Augustin.

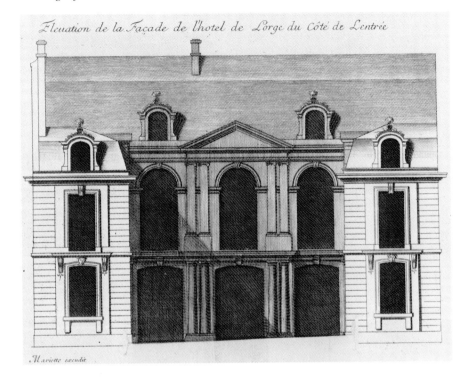

Elevation de la Façade de l'hotel de Lorge du Côté de l'entrée

Mariette excudit

[1] They had issue, two dreary sons, known at the Court as 'the dachshunds' (les bassets) and a daughter who was deformed.

comparison for me, and I hoped that she would make my life's happiness, as she has done, solely and absolutely. As she is now my wife, I shall abstain from saying more, except that she has proved far above all that was promised me and beyond my own fondest hopes.[1]

My mother and I were informed of all the necessary details by Mme Frémont's sister-in-law, a fine handsome woman, on excellent terms with them all and better used to good society than is usual with people of such inferior birth. She negotiated the marriage contract, and skilfully but honestly steered matters to a successful conclusion, in spite of the obstacles that invariably beset life's most important occasions. Finally, however, all the difficulties were smoothed away for a consideration of four hundred thousand livres, cash down (with no concessions), and living expenses for an indefinite period at Court and with the army.

When the arrangements were at last completed, the Maréchal de Lorges spoke to the King, on my behalf as well as his own, to avoid trouble. His Majesty was gracious enough to say that he could not do better for his daughter, and went on to speak most kindly of me—the Maréchal enjoyed telling me of this.

Thus it was that on the Thursday before Palm Sunday we signed the preliminary articles. Two days later, however, after we had taken the contract to the King and I was beginning to visit the Hôtel de Lorges every evening, the match was suddenly broken off on an ill-defined pretext, which everyone

25

persisted in interpreting after his own fashion. Luckily, just as we had reached a deadlock, with everyone pulling in a different direction, d'Auneuil the Maître des Requêtes, the Maréchale's only brother, arrived from the country where he had been on circuit and removed the obstacle at his own expense. (This is an obligation which I must repay and for which I shall ever be deeply grateful). God sometimes uses the most unexpected means to carry out His will. The whole venture thus almost miscarried, but the marriage was at last celebrated at the Hôtel de Lorges on April 8th, which I have always regarded, and with good reason, as the happiest day of my life. My mother behaved like the best of mothers. We proceeded to the Hôtel de Lorges on the Thursday before Low Sunday, at seven in the evening. The contract was signed and a grand banquet was given for the nearest relations on both sides of the family. At midnight, the curé of Saint-Roche said mass, and we were married in the private chapel. On the previous evening, my mother had sent forty thousand livres' worth of jewels to Mlle de Lorges, and I a corbeille containing six hundred louis and the elegant trifles usually given on such occasions.

We slept that night in the state bedroom, and on the following day M. d'Auneuil, who lodged over the way, gave a great dinner for us, after which the bride received in her bed at the Hôtel de Lorges. The highest society of France came in great numbers out of civility and curiosity, and the first to arrive was the Duchesse de Bracciano and her two daughters. My mother was still in half-mourning, her apartments were draped with grey and black, which was why we preferred to receive the company at the Hôtel de Lorges. Only one

LEFT Louis de Rouvroy, Duc de Saint-Simon, Pair de France. (Wedding portrait)

ABOVE Marie Gabrielle de Lorges, Duchesse de Saint-Simon. (Wedding portrait)

day was devoted to these visits, and on the following, we went to Versailles. In the evening the King graciously asked to see the bride in Mme de Maintenon's apartments, where she was presented by my mother and by hers. The King joked with me about my marriage on the way, and was so obliging as to receive the ladies with much praise and distinction.

Afterwards they attended the King's supper, and the new duchess had her tabouret.[1] As he came to the table, the King said to her, 'Madame, pray be seated'. He looked up as his napkin was being unfolded, and seeing all the duchesses and princesses still standing, he half-rose from his chair and said to Mme de Saint-Simon, 'Madame, I have already asked you to be seated', whereupon all those who had the right sat down, and Mme de Saint-Simon sat between my mother and hers, who came after her in order of rank. Next day, she received the entire Court, in her bed,[2] in the apartments of the Duchesse d'Arpajon, as being most convenient because they were on the ground floor. The Maréchal de Lorges and I were present only for the visit of the royal family. On the day after, they went to Saint-Germain and on to Paris, where I gave a grand dinner at my house for the whole wedding party. On the following day I gave a private supper to those remaining of my father's old friends, to whom I had been careful to announce my marriage before it was made public, and whom I always took great pains to cultivate until the day of their death.

[1] Folding stools on which duchesses might sit in the King's presence.

[2] At that time it was fashionable for ladies to receive in bed.

1695

The Duc du Maine at the Front

[*The accession to the English throne of the Prince of Orange, in 1688, had destroyed Louis XIV's carefully built-up alliance with England, a corner-stone of his foreign policy. In 1695 Louis was at war with the Empire, Holland, Spain, England, and Sweden. In spite of such a formidable alliance against her, France won all the battles on her northern front until the death of the Maréchal de Luxembourg (1695). He was replaced by the Maréchal de Villeroy (irresistible to women, but not the enemy) who was greatly hampered by the presence, as one of his commanders, of the Duc du Maine.*

The opposing general was an illegitimate scion of the House of Lorraine called Vaudémont. Saint-Simon himself was serving with the French army during the events which he describes. The war terminated in 1697 with the Treaty of Ryswick by which Louis XIV was obliged to acknowledge the heretic William as King of England.]

The Maréchal de Villeroy was pressing M. de Vaudémont as closely as he could, and the latter and by the far the weaker was using every endeavour to escape. Both commanders felt that the entire campaign was in their hands.

Vaudémont believed that the success or failure of the siege of Namur depended upon the safety of his army, and Villeroy that victory for him would seal the fate of the Low Countries, bring peace with glory, and all the personal consequences of so great an event. He therefore made the preliminary moves with the greatest care, and by the evening of the 13th [of July] was so near to M. de Vaudémont that the latter seemed to have no possible hope of escaping on the 14th. He then sent a courier to inform the King to that effect.

By dawn of the 14th everything was ready. Monsieur le Duc commanded the right wing, M. du Maine the left, M. le Prince de Conti all the infantry, and M. le Duc de Chartres the cavalry. It fell to the left to open the battle because that wing was nearer to the enemy. Vaudémont, in an exposed position and with the French so close, had not dared to retreat during the night, for his enemies were far superior in numbers and quality, and all his best troops were engaged at the siege. Neither had he dared to give battle without cover of any kind. Thus the only course that remained for him was to march by daylight, taking every precaution against being attacked on the march, but with the prime object of moving forward towards the broken wooded country that lay three good leagues ahead.

At the first ray of light, the Maréchal de Villeroy sent orders for M. du Maine to attack and open the engagement. He intended to bring up the entire army in support, but needed time for that operation and relied on the left wing to delay the enemy and prevent him from beginning his march. When nothing resulted from this order, he grew impatient and sent again to M. du Maine, five and even six times. M. du Maine wished to reconnoitre, then to confess, then to reorganize his wing, although that had been ready for a long time and the men were burning to be off. During this delay, Vaudémont was marching away as quickly as caution would permit. The general officers on our left wing were fuming, and Montrevel, the senior lieutenant-general, could no longer restrain himself as he saw what was happening. He pressed M. du Maine, reminding him of the repeated orders he had received from the Maréchal de Villeroy, the sure and easy victory, the consequence to his reputation and to the siege of Namur, the glorious outcome of success there, and the resulting panic and defencelessness of the Low Countries, when the only army capable of succouring them had been defeated. He spoke to him as man to man. He could not withhold his tears. Nothing was refused or denied, but all his efforts were useless. M. du Maine stammered and procrastinated, and continued in this way for so long that the chance was lost and M. de Vaudémont was allowed to escape from the most perilous situation in which any army could be placed. He would have been utterly destroyed had his enemy, who could see and count every man, made the slightest movement to attack him.

The French army were in despair, and no man attempted to withhold the words that patriotism, anger, and the evidence suggested to their minds. Even the common soldiers and mounted troopers said what they thought; in a word, the officers and men were even more outraged than astounded. The best that

The Siege of Namur, 1692, at which the Duc du Maine was present. Illumination from a missal.

the Maréchal de Villeroy could do was to detach three regiments of dragoons to attack the enemy's rear. They captured one or two flags and created some slight disorder among the last troops, who formed the rearguard of all that army.

No one was more outraged than the Maréchal himself, but he was too good a courtier to shift the blame to another's shoulders. Relying upon the support of the entire army, upon all that the soldiers had seen and heard, and the outcry which they had not attempted to suppress, he sent an officer to the King to report that contrary to his almost certain expectations, Vaudémont's swiftness in retreat had saved him. He entered into no details, but resigned himself to take the consequences, whatever those might be.

The King had been counting the hours throughout the past day and night as he waited for news of a great victory. He was therefore more than astonished to see only this private gentleman come with dispatches, instead of some high dignitary, and was deeply concerned when he learned how quietly the day had passed. The Court, anxious for news of sons, husbands, and brothers, was left in suspense, and the friends of the Maréchal de Villeroy felt intensely embarrassed. So general and brief a dispatch, making so little of a grave and crucial situation, disquieted the King considerably, but he decided to wait until time should bring an explanation.

In the meanwhile he made it his business to see all the gazettes from Holland. In the very first that appeared, he read of a great battle on the left flank and fulsome praise for the courage of M. du Maine, whose wounds were said to have prevented a victory and allowed M. de Vaudémont to escape. It was added that M. du Maine had been borne off the field on a stretcher. The King was irritated by this colossal piece of irony, but was still more annoyed when the next copy of the gazette retracted its previous description, saying that M. du Maine had not received so much as a scratch. All of which, with the total silence that had reigned since the day of battle, and the Maréchal de Villeroy's terse dispatch offering no excuses, combined to make him nervous and suspicious.

Vienne, a highly fashionable bathing attendant of Paris, who was taken into the King's personal service at the period of his love-affairs, had gained credit by prescribing various drugs which gave the King opportunities of greater satisfaction, and by this road, had risen to become one of the four head-valets.[1] He was a very good honest fellow, but a peasant, coarse and plain-spoken to a degree, and because of this very quality in a truthful man, the King had fallen into the habit of asking him things which other people would not tell him, always provided that the matter lay within his compass. The events mentioned above led to a visit to Marly, where Vienne was questioned. He looked intensely embarrassed, because, being taken unawares, he was unable to hide his feelings, which increased the King's curiosity until finally he issued commands. Then Vienne dared no longer hold back. He told the King that which he would gladly have gone through his life without knowing and which drove him to the verge of despair, for he had overcome so many difficulties and jealousies, had taken so much pleasure in giving M. de Vendôme[2] command of an army, solely because it meant advancement for M. du Maine. His entire object had been to hasten that promotion by using the rivalry between the Princes of the Blood as an excuse to be rid of them. The Comte de Toulouse[3] was already an admiral; his future was assured. It was therefore upon the Duc du Maine that the King's whole mind was fixed. At that moment he saw all his hopes dashed, and his distress was more than he could bear. He felt the weight of the army's contempt for that much cherished son, and the mockery in the gazettes taught him what was being said abroad. His chagrin was unbearable.

On this one occasion, Louis XIV, that prince who appeared so equable, who was always master of his smallest movements, even in moments of crisis, succumbed to his emotions. As he was leaving the table at Marly, with all the ladies and in the presence of the Court, he happened to notice one of the dessert-waiters in the act of pocketing a sweet biscuit. That instant, forgetting his royal dignity, cane in hand, for it had just been returned to him with his hat, he rushed at the footman who, like those whom the King thrust out of his way, expected anything but that, beat him, abused him, and ended by breaking the cane across his shoulders. As a matter of fact, it was bamboo and very brittle. Then still holding the broken end and cursing at the footman, who was well away by that time, he crossed the little salon and another ante-room into Mme de Maintenon's apartment, where he spent nearly an hour, as he often did after dinner at Marly. On leaving there to go to his own rooms he happened to meet Père de la Chaise,[4] and directly he perceived him standing among the

[1] 'He rendered services of a most intimate nature to Louis XIV, as Saint-Simon describes in decent language.' *Mémoires*, Pléiade, Paris 1950. He was also a fashionable ladies' hairdresser.

[2] The Duc de Vendôme, son of a bastard of Henri IV.

[3] The younger son of Louis XIV and Mme de Montespan.

[4] The King's confessor. The famous cemetery of Père Lachaise in Paris was built on land belonging to him.

30

Louis Auguste de Bourbon,
Duc du Maine, elder of the
King's two sons by Madame
de Montespan. By François
de Troy.

courtiers, he exclaimed in a loud voice, 'Mon Père, I have beaten a rascal soundly and have broken my stick on his back, but I do not think that God will be displeased', and then and there he described the so-called crime. All those present were still shaking with fright at what they had seen or learned from onlookers, and their terror increased at this fresh bout. Some of the more intimate began to murmur against the fellow, and the unhappy priest made noises of approval through his closed teeth, so as to prevent the King from becoming even angrier in public. You may imagine all the talk to which this gave rise, and the general consternation because no one could guess the cause, although all were aware that this provoking incident could not be the real matter. At last the truth became known, as word was gradually spread from one friend to another that it was Vienne, at the King's command, who had been the reason for this unparalleled and most unseemly display.

To cut a long story short, let me end by relating the witticism of M. d'Elbeuf. Good courtier though he was, he must have been nauseated by the sudden rise of the bastards, for when the campaign drew to a close and the princes were leaving he asked M. du Maine before the whole company where he meant to serve in the next campaigning season, for wherever he

The Château de Marly begun in 1679. The pavilions for courtiers round the King's house symbolised satellites circling the sun.

View of the Château de Versailles from beyond the Orangery by Jean-Baptiste Martin

Cartoon for a tapestry by Cotelle, of Mansart's colonnade in the gardens of Versailles

should go he meant to accompany him. When he was quizzed to give his reasons, he answered that anyone who stayed close to the duke could be sure of preserving his life. This devastating remark provoked a great stir. M. du Maine stared at the floor and dared not say anything. No doubt he remembered it against M. d'Elbeuf for a long time to come; but the latter and all his family were on excellent terms with the King, and that would have caused him no disquiet.

1695

Much Bickering among the Princesses

A few days later, we were included in a Marly excursion (the first for me, as it happened), during which a most extraordinary scene took place. Morning and evening, the King and Monseigneur each had their tables set at the same time and in the same room. The ladies divided impartially between the two, except that Mme la Princesse de Conti always went to Monseigneur's table, and her two sisters to that of the King. In a corner of that same room, five or six other tables were laid, where, in the same way, people might sit at random, but no one sat at the head. The King's table stood nearest to the large drawing-room, the other near the windows by the door through which the King went to Mme de Maintenon's apartments after dinner. At that period she often ate at the King's table, sitting opposite to him, for the tables were round. She never dined except at that table and supped alone in her own room. It was necessary to describe this scene in order to explain what followed.

The Princesses were only just on speaking terms, as I have already said, and Mme la Princesse de Conti was boiling inwardly at Monseigneur's partiality for Mlle Choin, whom she could not ignore and dared not snub. At dinner one day when Monseigneur was out hunting and his table was headed by Mme la Princesse de Conti, the King was pleased to amuse himself with Madame la Duchesse and, to the huge surprise of the assembled company, forsook that immense dignity which he almost never relaxed, and began to play at olives with her.[1] This pastime caused Madame la Duchesse to drink several glasses of wine, the King pretended to take one or two, and the game lasted until dessert was over and they left the room. As the King passed Mme la Princesse de Conti, he must have been annoyed by her disapproving look, for he said rather tartly that her sobriety hardly matched their drunkenness. The princess, more than a little piqued, let the King go, and turning to Mme de Châtillon in that moment of chaos, when everyone is rinsing out his mouth, said that she would prefer to be a sobersides than a chronic boozer. She was referring to certain somewhat prolonged repasts which her sisters had lately enjoyed together.

[1] Presumably to see who could furthest spit the stones.

33

This remark was overheard by Mme la Duchesse de Chartres, who retorted loudly in her slow, quavering voice, that for her part she would sooner be called a wine-skin than a tart, referring to the many guards officers who had been dismissed or banished on that princess's account. There was no answering this monstrous piece of cruelty, which soon spread all over Marly and on to Paris and elsewhere. Madame la Duchesse, so witty and clever, so brilliant in writing comic verses, made up some terrible rhymes in the same vein, and Mme la Princesse de Conti was driven to despair, for she had not the same skill and did not know how to extricate herself. Monsieur, ordinarily the king of mischief-makers, intervened when he thought that things had gone far enough, and Monseigneur assisted him. He gave a dinner-party for them at Meudon, to which Mme la Princesse de Conti went by herself and arrived first. Then the other two were brought by Monsieur. They said very little to each other, the atmosphere was frigid, and they returned to their homes in exactly the same mood as they had come.

The end of that year was very stormy at Marly. One evening, Mme la Duchesse de Chartres and Madame la Duchesse, who had been brought together by the enmity of Mme la Princesse de Conti, settled down to an impromptu meal after the King's *coucher*, in Mme de Chartres's room at the château. Monseigneur was playing cards very late in the salon. On his way up to bed, he went into the princess's room and found them both smoking pipes, which they had sent for from the Swiss Guards. Monseigneur, realizing the consequences if the smell of tobacco were to spread, told them to stop that experiment at once, but the smoke had already betrayed them. Next morning the King gave them a harsh reprimand, which made Mme la Princesse de Conti exultant. But the bickering continued, and the King, who had hoped that it would end of itself, finally grew vexed. That evening at Versailles, when they were all assembled in his study after dinner, he spoke very severely to them and ended by threatening that he would have no more of their nonsense. They each had country-houses where he would send them for a very long time and think himself well quit of them. This threat had its effect, for calm and decorum returned, and good manners took the place of mutual affection.

1696–1697

The Little Princess of Savoy

I returned to Paris on the evening before the King brought the little princess[1] from Montargis to Fontainebleau and I attended him at his carriage door. In this way, I hoped to conceal the fact that I had been absent for a short time.

The princess's new French household waited for nearly three weeks at

[1]Marie-Adélaide of Savoy, a granddaughter of Monsieur by his first wife, Henrietta of England, was nearly eleven years old at that time. She came to France in order to be married to the Duc de Bourgogne, eldest son of the Grand Dauphin. Their wedding was celebrated a year later.

Lyons, until she was taken to Pont-Beauvoisin, where she received them. She arrived there early on the morning of Tuesday, October 16th, accompanied by the Princesse de la Cisterne and Mme de Noyers, of the Court of Savoy. The Marquis de Dronero had been responsible for her journey, and to him and to the rest of her old household many valuable presents were distributed on behalf of the King.[1] A house had been prepared for her on the Savoy side of the town, and there she rested and dressed. She then went to the bridge that belongs

[1] Among the presents were a diamond rose, a box containing fifty diamonds, a set of bracelets, and silver-plate for the officers and servants of her household.

A secret smoking party. The King did not approve of ladies smelling of tobacco or snuff.

35

1696. The little Princess of Savoy arrives in France.

solely to France, received her new household at the entrance, and was escorted to her lodgings on the French side. She remained there for two days, after which she bade farewell to her Italian household without shedding a tear. Only one of her tiring women and her doctor remained with her; but they were not intended to stay long in France and were, in fact, sent back almost immediately.

On Sunday, November 4th, the King, Monseigneur, and Monsieur went separately and early to Montargis, so that when the princess arrived at six o'clock, the King was ready to receive her at the door of her coach. He led her to the apartments that had been prepared for her in the house where he was lodged, and presented Monseigneur, Monsieur, and M. le Duc de Chartres. They say that everyone was surprised by her graciousness, her pretty, lively remarks, and her easy, yet respectful manner, and that the King was charmed from the first. He did nothing but pet and praise her and sent off a courier in great haste to Mme de Maintenon to tell her of his delight. Afterwards he dined with the ladies of the suite and had the little princess placed between himself and Monseigneur.

Next day the King called for her to go to mass, dined as he had supped on the previous evening, and straightway got into his coach. The King and Monsieur sat on the back seat, Monseigneur and the little princess in front, and the Duchesse du Lude by the door on his side. The Duc de Bourgogne met them at Nemours and was made to take the door-seat on the other side. At four o'clock in the evening they all arrived at Fontainebleau, in the Cour du Cheval Blanc. The entire Court was assembled waiting to receive them on the horseshoe staircase, with the crowd standing below, a magnificent sight. The King led in the princess, so small that she seemed to be emerging from his pocket, walked very slowly along the terrace and then to the Queen-Mother's apartments, which had been allotted to her, where Madame and her ladies were waiting. He himself presented the first of the Princes and Princesses of the Blood, asked Monsieur to name the others and to be sure to see that she was kissed by all who had that right; and then went to rest. He and Monseigneur went out together, the former to Mme de Maintenon's apartments, the latter to Mme la Princesse de Conti, who was not dressed, because a wen had been removed from above her eye, which she had come near to losing.

Monsieur was thus left with the princess, both standing. He presented to her all those, men and women, who had come to kiss the hem of her dress, and told her whom she should kiss, that is to say, Princes and Princesses of the Blood, dukes and duchesses and other tabourets, and Marshals of France and their

Marie-Adélaïde of Savoy, Duchesse de Bourgogne, aged 11. Attributed to Pierre Gobert.

wives. This ceremony lasted a good two hours, after which the princess dined alone in her apartments, where Mme de Maintenon and Mme la Princesse de Conti visited her privately. On the following day, she called on Monseigneur and Mme la Princesse de Conti, and received many presents of jewellery and precious stones. The King sent all the crown jewels to Mme de Mailly,[1] her lady-in-waiting, so that she might wear as many as she wished.

The King gave a ruling that she should be styled simply 'La Princesse'; that she should dine alone attended by the Duchesse du Lude; that she should hold no courts as yet, and that Mgr le Duc de Bourgogne should visit her only once a fortnight and MM. his brothers[2] only once a month. On November 8th, the Court returned to Versailles, where the princess was allotted the late Queen's apartments, and afterwards, those of Madame la Dauphine. When she arrived, everyone of importance who had stayed in Paris was presented to her in the same way as at Fontainebleau. The King and Mme de Maintenon made a pet of her, for her pretty, coaxing ways and good manners pleased them vastly, and she gradually became familiar with them, in a way that none of the royal children dared to attempt. M. de Savoie must have informed himself very thoroughly about the ways of our Court, for he had instructed his daughter well, but the marvel was that she understood his teaching so perfectly and was so graceful in everything that she did. Nothing ever equalled the charm with which she bewitched Mme de Maintenon. She called her '*ma tante*', and showed her as much respect and obedience as though she were her mother and a queen, and all with such an air of freedom and affection that Mme de Maintenon was enchanted and the King also.

His Majesty delighted more and more in the princess, who was incomparably more intelligent and agreeable than is usual at her age, and he fixed the day of the marriage for December 7th [1697], which fell on a Saturday, being determined to lose no time after her twelfth birthday. He let it be known that he wished the Court to be very magnificent on that occasion and he himself, who for a long time past had dressed most simply, ordered some more resplendent coats. This was enough for all who were not priests or lawyers to disregard questions of means, or even of rank. Each one tried to surpass the rest in magnificence and originality. There was scarcely enough gold and silver to go round and the shops were emptied in a very few days. In short, the wildest extravagance reigned throughout the Court, and in the town as well, for there was an immense crowd of spectators. Things went to such a pitch that the King was sorry he had ever made the suggestion, and said that he failed to understand how husbands could be so foolish as to allow themselves to be ruined for their wives' clothes—or for their own, he might have added. But he had loosened the reins and there was no time to remedy matters. Indeed, I believe that in his heart of hearts the King would not have wished it otherwise, for he thoroughly enjoyed seeing the fine clothes. One could see that the display of rich materials and curious workmanship pleased him vastly and that he delighted in praising the most sumptuous and tasteful of the costumes. He

[1] Mme de Mailly was Mme de Maintenon's first cousin.

[2] The Dukes of Anjou and Berry.

38

had put in his word for the sake of policy, but was enchanted to find that it went unheeded.

This was not the first time that such a thing had happened, for he loved magnificence of any kind, especially on state occasions, and anyone who had listened to his dissuasions would not have been wise. In any event, there was no possibility of being wise in the midst of such extravagance, for so many new clothes were required. As for Mme de Saint-Simon and myself, it cost us twenty thousand francs between us. There were not enough embroiderers to have everything finished in time.

On Saturday morning, December 7th, the entire Court went early to the apartments of Mgr. le Duc de Bourgogne, after which the duke went to visit the princess. She was already dressed, but very few of her ladies were there, for most had gone to the tribunes and stands erected for spectators in the chapel. The royal family had already seen her and were waiting in the King's study, where the bridal pair presented themselves shortly after noon. The King immediately led the way to the chapel. The procession and all the details were just as they were for M. le Duc de Chartres, except that Cardinal de Coislin began with the betrothal and everybody knelt during the pause between the betrothal service and the marriage.

It was a dull day on the whole. The King and Queen of England came to dinner and the Queen sat between the two Kings. On leaving the table, the ladies went to see the bride's *coucher*, but the men were rigidly excluded by the King's command. The ladies remained with her and the Queen of England presented the nightgown, which was handed by the Duchesse du Lude. Mgr le Duc de Bourgogne undressed in the ante-room, seated on a folding stool, attended by the King and all the princes. The King of England presented the shirt, which was handed by the Duc de Beauvilliers.

When Mme la Duchesse de Bourgogne was in bed, Mgr le Duc de Bourgogne entered and got into bed on the right-hand side, in the presence of the King and the entire Court. Immediately afterwards the King and Queen of England departed, the King retired to bed, and everyone left the chamber except Monseigneur, the princess's ladies, and the Duc de Beauvilliers, who stayed with his pupil, while the Duchesse du Lude stood at the other side. Monseigneur remained chatting for about a quarter of an hour, after which he made his son get up, telling him to kiss the princess, in spite of the Duchesse du Lude's objections. It turned out that she was right, for the King thought it very bad, saying that he did not wish his grandson to kiss so much as the tip of his wife's little finger until the time came for them to live together. He dressed again in the anteroom because of the cold, and went back to sleep in his own bedroom in the usual way. The little Duc de Berry, so naughty and bold, thought very ill of his brother's meekness in this respect. He said that he should have remained in bed.

Wedding of the Duc de Bourgogne and Princess Marie-Adélaide of Savoy, 7 December, 1697, by Antoine Dieu. Cartoon for a tapestry.

1 'Monseigneur', Le Grand Dauphin
2 Louis XIV
3 The Duc d'Anjou
4 The Duc de Berry
5 The Duc de Bourgogne
6 Marie-Adélaide of Savoy
7 Cardinal Coislin
8 'Monsieur', Philippe I Duc d'Orléans
9 'Madame', Duchesse d'Orléans
10 The Duc de Chartres

Madame de Castries

When we returned from the army, we found the Marquise de Castries established as lady-in-waiting to Mme la Duchesse de Chartres in place of Mme de Mailly.

Mme de Castries was a scrap of a woman, a kind of *biscuit manqué*,[1] well-proportioned, but so extremely tiny that you might have passed her through a ring of medium size; no bottom, no bosom, no chin, monstrously plain, always looking anxious and bewildered, yet, withal, a face sparkling with intelligence and giving even better than its promise. She knew everything—history, philosophy, mathematics, the dead languages—yet she never appeared to do more than speak good French, which she did with eloquence, grace, and aptness, even in the most everyday matters, and with that unique turn of phrase which only the Mortemart family possess. Agreeable, diverting, grave, or gay, she could be all things to all men, fascinating when she wished to please, genuinely droll, brilliantly and apparently quite unconsciously witty, and delivering her sallies in a manner that made them unforgettable. She was imperious; liable to be shocked at a thousand things in a plaintive tone that would bring the house down. She could be cruelly cutting when she chose, but was a very good friend, cultivated, kind, always ready to oblige, not a coquette, but sensitive, and delighting in other people when she found them to her liking. She had a charming talent for story-telling, and when she pleased to invent some impromptu romance, everyone was amazed by her inspiration, variety; and humour. For all her pride, she thought herself well-married because she was fond of her husband. She expatiated on everything concerning him and was quite as vain about him as about herself. He returned the compliment and treated her with every care and consideration.

[1] A *biscuit manqué* is an innocent-looking sponge cake, strongly flavoured with rum – Tipsy Cake, in fact.

The King and the Prince of Orange

I perceive that I have not mentioned the private reasons which made it so bitter for Louis XIV to recognize the Prince of Orange as King of England. These are they.

The King was very far, when he first had bastards, from wishing to give them high rank, as he increasingly did in later years. The Princesse de Conti's birth, however, was the least distasteful,[1] she was also the eldest, and the King decided that she would make a splendid match for the Prince of Orange. He proposed it at a time when the prince's prospects and position in Europe had persuaded him that the marriage would be viewed as an honour and a great advantage. He was wrong. The Prince of Orange was the son of a daughter of King Charles I of England, and his grandmother had been the daughter of an Elector of Brandenburg. The prince recalled this fact with considerable haughtiness and added shortly that the Princes of Orange were accustomed to marry the rightful daughters of great kings, not their bastards. Louis XIV was so nettled by this remark that he never forgave it, and took peculiar pains, even against his own interests, to show that the insult had cut him to the quick.

The prince did everything possible to appease him. Respect, concessions, peace-offerings, patience under insults and personal injuries, renewed overtures, all were treated with contempt. The French ministers in Holland were given express instructions to thwart him at every turn, not only in affairs of state, but in all personal and private matters, to incite as many burghers as possible against him, to lavish money at elections so as to return opposing magistrates, to protect openly his declared enemies, in short, to do him all the harm and show him all the discourtesy that they could devise. Never, until the beginning of the war, did the prince cease, both in public and private, in his efforts to allay the King's anger, and never once did the King soften towards him. Finally, in despair, hoping that his departure to England and the formidable League which he had made against France would have their effect, he said openly that all his life he had tried in vain to win the King's friendship, but that he hoped now to be more successful in gaining his respect. You may imagine his triumph when he had compelled the King to recognize him as King of England, and what it cost Louis XIV to do so.

[1] Because her mother, Mlle de La Vallière, was unmarried, she was not the issue of double adultery, like the children of the King and Mme de Montespan.

1698

An Envoy from England

King William of England was gratified beyond measure when at last he had received recognition from King Louis and was in peace upon the throne. Nevertheless, usurpers are never truly satisfied nor in peace, and this one bitterly resented the fact that the rightful King and his family were still living at Saint-Germain. It was too close to the King of France and to England for his comfort. At Ryswick, he had made every effort to have them banished from the country or at least from the Court, but he had found the King inflexible. He now decided to stake everything on one throw and see whether by making no conditions (he had already won so much), but showering Louis XIV with

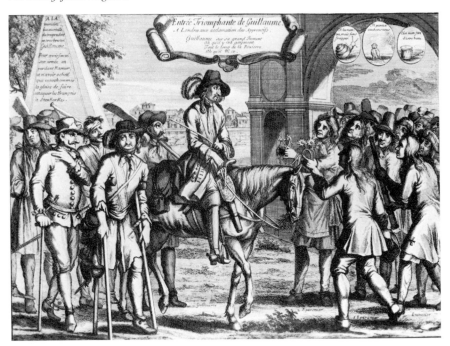

French caricature of William of Orange, hailed by the rabble on his entry into London.

proofs of his regard and respect, he could not gain his point by sweetness.

With this end in view he sent a Knight of the Garter, the Duke of St. Albans, as a special envoy to convey his congratulations on the marriage of Mgr le Duc de Bourgogne. He could hardly have chosen a greater man for so unimportant a mission and, indeed, it was a wonder that the duke accepted, for as the bastard of Charles II, the elder brother of King James, he would have had an excellent reason for refusing. As a matter of fact, he did try to obtain ambassadorial privileges on account of his rank, but the authorities were politely determined to treat him as an ordinary envoy from England. Dukes of that country have no ranking over here and French dukes have none in England. Our King did indeed make the Duchess of Portsmouth and her son, the Duke of Richmond, a duke and duchess of France, and he did casually grant a tabouret to the Duchess of Cleveland, the mistress of his friend, Charles II, but these were special cases and had no bearing on the general rule.

The Duke of St. Albans was the precursor of a new English ambassador, the Earl of Portland, after whose arrival he left. No one more splendid could possibly have been nominated. He was attended by a vast and magnificent suite, and his expenditure on his table, horses, liveries, carriages, furniture, dress, and silver was most princely and all in exquisite taste. Everything then seemed to happen at once, for no sooner was the earl in his coach, on his way from Calais, receiving all manner of military and civil honours, than a great fire broke out at Whitehall, during the course of which the biggest and most hideous palace in the whole of Europe was burned almost to the ground. It has not yet been rebuilt, and the Kings are now lodged pretty miserably in St. James's Palace.

Portland's first audience with the King was on February 4th, and he remained in France for four months. His arrival was an immense personal triumph, for people were overcome by his exquisite courtesy, his perfect bearing at Court and in society, his gallantry and amiability. Moreover, he was exceedingly dignified, even haughty, but tactful, very sound in all his judgements, and doing nothing rash. The French, who love novelty, good food, and magnificence, were delighted with him. He wooed them with discretion, like one who had studied the ways of our Court and desired only the best and most exclusive society. Soon it became the fashion to visit him, to give entertainments in his honour and be received at his house. What was most astonishing was that the King, who at heart was still greatly vexed with King William, should also have welcomed him, for he gave splendid fêtes and did more for Portland than he had done for any previous ambassador. He may perhaps have wished to compensate him for the disappointment which he must have felt on realizing that his mission was doomed to failure from the beginning.

Portland spoke of the expulsion of King James and his family at his very first meeting with Torcy, the secretary for foreign affairs, even before he had been to Versailles. Torcy very wisely cut him short once and for all, saying that the point had been discussed often and thoroughly during the conferences at Ryswick and that the subject was closed and done with. He said further that he knew that the King would never change his mind and would be exceedingly vexed if the matter were mentioned again. Portland, he said, might rest assured that King Louis was ready to play his part fully and sincerely in the alliance that was forming between himself and King William, and would treat the ambassador with every mark of distinction, but one word on the subject of Saint-Germain might ruin everything and render Portland's mission a sad and sorry affair. If he might offer a word of advice, added Torcy, it would be to say nothing whatsoever on the matter, either to the King or his ministers, for the King's mind was finally made up. Portland listened and complied, but as you shall see he was not best pleased. On the other hand, the King thoroughly approved of Torcy for having silenced him from the start. Great pains were taken to prevent any of the English at Saint-Germain from coming to Versailles or Paris, or within range of the ambassador, and it was all arranged most carefully.

Portland went hunting with Monseigneur, and twice went from Paris to Meudon for the wolf-hunting. On both occasions Monseigneur kept him to supper. One evening the King called him to hold the candlestick at his *coucher*, which was a signal favour, only granted to the most distinguished people. Ambassadors are scarcely ever on terms of sufficient intimacy to come to Court at such times, and even when they do they are rarely granted this honour. Thus, laden with favours, fêtes, and courtesies of every kind, Portland had his

RIGHT James II of England and his wife Mary of Modena, in 1694, with their children (the old Pretender and Princess Louisa, born 1688 and 1692).

44

farewell audience with the King on May 20th. The Maréchal de Villeroy then took him to Marly by the King's command and showed him the château, for he liked to see everything of interest and was especially pleased with Fontainebleau, which he said he preferred to all the other royal houses. After his formal audience, he went back to pay his court to the King, who happened to be taking physic. He was allowed in after the King had taken it, which was a monstrously great honour, and to cap everything he was admitted inside the balustrade, where no foreigner, no matter how distinguished, ever penetrates, except at the state audiences for the corps of ambassadors.

After leaving the King, Portland again attended Monseigneur out hunting and was invited for the third time to sup with him at Meudon. Monsieur himself wished to show him Saint-Cloud and Madame especially absented herself for the occasion. He was given a great banquet which Monseigneur attended with a vast number of guests. This was an honour indeed.

Nevertheless, amid all these roses strewn in his path, he did find a few thorns, chief amongst which was the continued presence of the rightful King of

England. Once, for instance, when he went to hunt at Meudon, just as they were about to start and Portland was drawing on his boots, Monseigneur was informed that the English King was coming to the meet. He at once explained the situation to Portland, asking him to wait for another day, whereupon the Earl was forced to remove his boots and return to Paris.

Portland was a keen huntsman, and whether because he really wished to ride after the King's hounds, or because he was vexed with the Duc de La Rochefoucauld[1] (the master of the royal hunts) for showing him no civilities beyond a bow when they happened to meet, he repeated over and over again that he longed to go with the King's pack. He said this so often in the hearing of so many people that he felt certain it had reached the duke's ears; yet there was no response. At last, he could endure it no longer, and stopping M. de La Rochefoucauld as they left the King's *lever*, he asked him point-blank. La Rochefoucauld, not in the least put out, answered rather shortly that although he had the honour to be master of the royal hunts he did not make the arrangements. He took his orders, he said, from the King of England, who often hunted but never announced until the last moment whether or not he intended to come. A stiff bow followed immediately, and Portland was left

[1] Son of the author of the Maxims.

46

standing, very much annoyed, but with nothing about which to complain. M. de La Rochefoucauld was the only great nobleman who never pandered to Portland. His answer had been made purely out of chivalry towards King James, who did indeed have the disposal of the royal hounds, although he rarely hunted. M. de La Rochefoucauld could easily have granted Lord Portland's request, but he felt vexed because society was fawning upon the Earl in full view of the Court of Saint-Germain, and he would not deny himself the pleasure of snubbing the usurper's triumphant ambassador. None the less, everyone else was conquered by Portland, not excepting M. de Lauzan, in spite of the latter's promises and his attachment to the English King and Queen. Yet Lauzun gained nothing but contempt for slavishly following the fashion and trying to curry favour with King Louis.

Finally, laden with every honour, Portland made up his mind to go home. Indeed, he was anxious to do so because the Duke of Albemarle was increasingly popular in England. On his way back, Monsieur le Prince invited him to stay at Chantilly and gave him a magnificent fête, in that perfect taste which is so typical of the Condés. He then continued his journey by way of Flanders, where the King not only granted him permission to inspect the fortifications, but sent engineers to explain them. Everywhere he was received with full honours and a captain and fifty guardsmen were always in attendance. He returned to England after this scintillating mission to find himself supplanted at the Court by a new and younger rival; he had no comfort but in the memory of past favours, and many regrets that his absence had allowed a new favourite to take his place.

Before leaving Paris, he most carefully spread it abroad that so long as King James remained at Saint-Germain, the Queen would not receive the dowry granted her by the Peace of Ryswick, and he kept his word.

1698

Manoeuvres at Compiègne

People talked of nothing but Compiègne, where sixty thousand men were assembled under canvas. In one way, it was the marriage of Mgr le Duc de Bourgogne all over again, for the King let it be known that he expected the regiments to be very splendidly equipped and that they should compete against one another. This was enough to provoke a rivalry among the individual officers which they had good reason to repent of later. Not only were all the troops very fine in themselves, indeed it would have been hard to distinguish any particular corps for excellence, but their commanders added to their military lustre, arms, horses, harness, and all the splendours of the Court, while

Reveuë general de toute Larmée faite par le Roy au Camp de Coudun pres Compiegne le 9.e Septembre.

The manoeuvres at
Compiègne, 1698:
The King takes the salute.

the junior officers ruined themselves still further by purchasing uniforms grand enough to suit a state occasion.

The colonels and many of the captains gave free meals to all who came, of the most abundant and delicious refreshments. Six lieutenant-generals and fourteen brigadiers were particularly noticeable for their open-handed expenditure, but the Maréchal de Boufflers astounded everyone by his spending, his perfect organization of the ample provisions, his exquisite taste, his magnificence, and his supreme courtesy during all the time that the camp lasted, day and night, at all hours, so that he gave an example to the King himself on how to give a really sumptuous entertainment. Monsieur le Prince was excellent in this line, but the Maréchal showed even him what true elegance, ingenuity, and perfect good taste could achieve. No spectacle has ever been more glorious nor, indeed, more grandiose, yet in the midst of it all, nothing could have surpassed the serenity of the Maréchal and all his household in distributing this universal hospitality. Nothing was ever more silent and smooth-running than this tremendous undertaking, or more easy, modest, and seemingly carefree than this great general, who made all the arrangements and continued to supervise, although to all appearance he was wholly concerned with commanding the army.

Innumerable tables were constantly replenished and meals were served as soon as people presented themselves. Officers, gentlemen of the Court, spectators, even the merest sightseers, were all received as honoured guests by the eager courtesy of his vast staff. All manner of hot and cold beverages were

le Manifique festin donné par Mr de Boufflers dans sa tente au Roy au Roy d'Angleterre et à toute la Cour au Camp de Coudun près Compiegne.

Universal hospitality offered by the Maréchal de Boufflers.

served, everything, in fact, that could possibly be included in a list of liquid refreshments. French and foreign wines and the choicest liqueurs were offered to everyone, and the arrangements were so perfect that immense quantities of game and venison continually arrived from all directions, and the seas around Normandy, Holland, England, Brittany, and even the Mediterranean furnished day after day all that was most costly and exotic, delivered in small post-chaises at exactly the right moment by a prodigious number of couriers. Even the very water, which, it was feared, might become exhausted or muddy with so many mouths to feed, was brought from Sainte-Reine, the Seine, and other famous sources. It is impossible to imagine anything not provided, for the poorest chance arrival as well as for the honoured and invited guest.

Wooden guest-houses had been built, furnished like the most comfortable Parisian mansions, all newly constructed with perfect taste to serve this very purpose, and vast tents were set up, sufficient to provide a camp in themselves. There were kitchens arranged, and butteries, and an innumerable staff of servants for the uninterrupted service of the tables, pantries, and cellars; and all this array provided a scene of such smooth-running order, serenity, punctuality, speed, and perfect decorum that it excited universal delight and admiration.

This camp was the first excursion on which the ladies overcame their natural fastidiousness in a way which no one would have liked to propose. So many of them wished to be of the party that the King relaxed his rule and allowed them all to go to Compiègne if they so desired. That, however, was not their ambition, for they all wished to be nominated and commanded, not merely permitted to make the journey, and that is why they played every trick in the pack to cram themselves into the princesses' carriages. Until then, the King had always chosen the ladies who followed the Queen or Madame la Dauphine in the carriages of the 'first princesses', as the King's bastards were called. They, however, had friends of their own, to whose presence they made the King consent, and these ladies travelled in their personal carriages, which they thought a fine thing, for they liked being placed on that footing. On this particular occasion, however, anything served provided that they went. There were no ladies in the King's coach, except the Duchesse du Lude, attending on the princesses. Monsieur and Madame remained at Saint-Cloud and Paris.

The gentlemen of the Court came in great numbers, and for the first time, dukes were billeted in couples. I shared with the Duc de Rohan a fine large house belonging to the Sieur de Chambaudon, where we and our servants were perfectly comfortable.

All the ambassadors were invited and going to Compiègne until old Ferreiro of Savoy put it into their heads to demand the privilege of the *pour*, which he insisted had been given to him on his first embassy to Paris. The Portuguese ambassador said that following the King's example, Monsieur had made the stewards give it to him when he had stayed at Montargis. The nuncio maintained that the Nuncio Cavallerini had had it before he was made a cardinal. All the masters of ceremonies protested that such a thing was impossible; that no ambassador had ever claimed it before, and that there was nothing about it in the records—but you know how much reliance should be placed on records. The fact of the matter was that the ambassadors realized the King's desire to impress them with the splendours of the camp and hoped to extract something for themselves in the shape of a new privilege. The King remained firm, however, so that the argument continued until the actual day of the journey, and in the end none of the ambassadors went. The King was so much vexed about it that I myself heard him say at supper—he, usually so silent and restrained—that he had a good mind to forbid their ever coming to Court except for audiences, as is the custom in other countries.

I am indeed ignorant of the origins of the *pour*, but as a distinction it is really utterly nonsensical. It consists in writing in chalk upon the doors of apartments, either '*pour* M. So and So', or merely 'M. So and So'. When the stewards of the King's household mark the rooms assigned to different people on such journeys, they add the *pour* for Princes of the Blood, cardinals, and foreign princes. M. de La Trémoille also had it, and the Duchesse de Bracciano (afterwards the Princesse des Ursins). I say that the distinction is foolish because it conveys no better nor more honourable lodging. Cardinals, foreign princes, and dukes are all lodged alike, without any distinction whatsoever. The whole matter is in the word *pour*, which has absolutely no significance.

The Court set out on Thursday, August 28th. The King went by way of Saint-Cloud, slept at Chantilly, stayed there for one day, and arrived at

Compiègne on the Saturday. The Maréchal de Boufflers's headquarters were in the village of Coudun, where houses had been erected as well as tents. The King had a wonderful meal there accompanied by Mgr le Duc and Mme la Duchesse de Bourgogne, and they viewed all the arrangements that I have mentioned with much wonder and admiration. When they reached Compiègne, the King told Livry (his high steward), that Mgr le Duc de Bourgogne must not dine as had been arranged, but that when he went to the camp he must dine with the Maréchal de Boufflers, for despite Livry's best endeavours, nothing could compare with what he had just seen.

During the reviews, an amusing trick was played on the Comte de Tessé, colonel-general of the dragoons. Two days earlier, M. de Lauzun had asked him in that friendly unassuming manner he so often adopted, whether he had everything proper to salute the King at the head of his dragoons. Thereupon the Comte had launched into a long description of his horse, uniform, and staff. After congratulating him, M. de Lauzun said guilelessly, 'But your hat? I did not hear you mention a hat.' 'Oh! no', said the other, 'I expect to wear a cap'. 'A cap!' exclaimed Lauzun, 'what can you be thinking of? Caps are all very well for the others; but a colonel-general in a cap! Monsieur le Comte, you cannot be serious!' 'What do you mean?' said Tessé. 'What else should I wear?' Lauzun kept him on tenterhooks, making him repeat the question again and again on the grounds that he must be joking. Finally, in response to entreaties, Lauzun said that he could not allow him to make such a terrible mistake. He knew the etiquette because the post had been created especially for him, and the most important rule was that the colonel-general should wear a grey hat when the king reviewed the dragoons. Tessé was dumbfounded, admitted his total ignorance and poured out his thanks to M. de Lauzun for the timely warning. He then hurried home and sent one of his servants to Paris to buy a hat. The Duc de Lauzun had been careful to draw Tessé on one side, for he did not wish to be overheard; he knew that Tessé would be too much ashamed of his ignorance to tell anyone, and he himself did not breathe a word.

On the morning of the review, I went to the King's *lever* and happened to notice that M. de Lauzun stayed in the room, although, having the *grande entrée*, he usually withdrew when the rest of the Court entered. I also noticed Tessé, strutting about and parading a grey hat, with a black plume and a vast cockade. What seemed to me most extraordinary was the colour of the hat, for the King had a particular aversion to grey and no one had worn it for several years past. It therefore struck me as odd and made me look at him attentively, for he was standing opposite me, and M. de Lauzun was fairly near him and a little behind. After the King had been given his shoes and had spoken to one or two people, he suddenly noticed the hat and in his astonishment asked Tessé where he had got it, to which Tessé smugly replied that he had sent for it to Paris. 'For what purpose?' said the King. 'Sire', said Tessé, 'Your Majesty does us the honour to review us today.' 'Well!' said the King, still more astonished. 'What has that got to do with a grey hat?' 'Sire', replied Tessé, beginning to feel embarrassed, 'it is the colonel-general's special privilege to wear a grey hat on review days'. 'A *grey* hat', said the King, 'where the devil did you learn that?' 'From M. de Lauzun, Sire; you created the post for him, and he told me.' At that moment M. de Lauzun burst out laughing and vanished. 'Lauzun was fooling you', said the King, rather crossly. 'Believe me, you had better send that hat at once to the prior-general of the White Friars.' Never have I seen a man more abashed than Tessé, as he stood with downcast eyes staring at the hat, looking so thoroughly miserable and ashamed of himself that he made a perfect spectacle. No one could help laughing, and those nearest and most intimate with the King said something smart, until at last Tessé pulled himself together sufficiently to leave the room. But the entire Court let him know what they thought, and asked him whether he had not yet learned to know M. de Lauzun, who chuckled whenever it was mentioned. Tessé did not dare to take offence and the incident passed as a joke, although it was really a bit steep; but he was tormented about it for a long time and was very much discomfited.

Nearly every day during the camp, the Sons of France dined with the Maréchal de Boufflers, and sometimes Mme la Duchesse de Bourgogne and the princesses and ladies-in-waiting accompanied them; but more often they picnicked. The quality and quantity of the silver services, enough for everyone and all marked with the Maréchal's crest, were wonderful, and even more so was the punctuality of the meals, not only to the hour, but to the very minute, everywhere. Nothing was ever wanting, nothing dragged. In serving the least of the bystanders, or even the lackeys, it was the same as for the greatest lords. There was something at all hours and for all comers. For ten miles around Compiègne, every village and farm was so full to overflowing with visitors, both French and foreign, that they could not have held another person; yet everything proceeded in orderly fashion. The gentlemen and servants belonging to the Maréchal were hosts in themselves, all most civil and obliging in their duty of welcoming all comers and serving them with whatsoever they needed, from five o'clock in the morning until ten or eleven at night, without stinting, and doing all the honours assisted by a vast staff and a great number of pages. I find that I repeat myself, but no one who witnessed it can ever forget that sight or cease to admire the abundance, splendour, and efficiency, which never failed for a single moment or at any point.

At Compiègne, the King wished to give an example of everything that happened in war, so that regular siege was laid to the town, with all the proper procedure, lines, trenches, batteries, mines, etc., but much simplified. An ancient rampart ran round the château on the side facing the open country; its top, raised on a level with the King's apartment, overlooked the entire plain. At its foot and stretching a little beyond stood an old wall and a windmill; the rampart, itself, had no buttress nor supporting wall.

Saturday, September 13th, was the day appointed for the assault. The King, followed by all the ladies and in the loveliest weather imaginable, went out on to

Design for a fan, depicting ladies accompanying the King on his Flemish campaign, *c.* 1692. Artist unknown.

the rampart, where crowds of people were assembled and all the distinguished foreigners. Standing there, one could see the entire plain and the disposition of all the troops. I was in the semi-circle, very close to His Majesty, not more than three paces away, and no one was in front of me. It was the most superb sight, that great army, and the crowds of spectators on foot and on horseback keeping at a proper distance so as to be out of the way. The movements of the attacking force and the defence were plain to see because there being no reason for the manoeuvres, except display, neither side needed to conceal themselves unless the precision of their movements required it. There was, nevertheless, one other spectacle which forty years hence I shall be able to describe as vividly as I do today, so forcibly did it strike me, and that was the spectacle which the King presented from the top of the rampart to his whole army, and to the enormous crowd of onlookers of every degree, both in the plain and on the rampart itself.

Mme de Maintenon[1] sat there facing the plain and the troops, in her sedan-chair, behind its three glass windows. On the front left-hand shaft sat Mme la Duchesse de Bourgogne, and standing behind her in a semi-circle were Madame la Duchesse, Mme la Princesse de Conti, and all the ladies, flanked by a group of courtiers. The King was by the right-hand window of the chair, standing, and behind him, a semi-circle of the most distinguished gentlemen. The King's hat was off for most of the time, and at every moment he bent down to speak to Mme de Maintenon through the window, explaining what she was seeing and the reason for every manoeuvre. Each time that he did so, she was polite enough to lower the glass four or five inches, but never as far as halfway, for I particularly noticed; and I must admit to having been far more interested in this scene than in the movements of the troops. She sometimes opened the window herself to ask the King a question, but it was nearly always he who bent down to inform her, without waiting for her to address him; and sometimes,

[1] Whom the King had secretly married in 1683 or 1684, soon after the Queen's death.

Duc et Maréchal de Boufflers. Astounded everyone by the perfect organisation of his magnificent hospitality.

when she was not paying attention, he rapped on the glass to make her open. He spoke to no one else, save to give orders, in a few words and very seldom, and occasionally to answer Mme la Duchesse de Bourgogne, who made efforts to persuade him to speak to her. Mme de Maintenon pointed things out to her and spoke in sign language from time to time through the front window, but without opening the glass, and the young Princess screamed back a few words in reply. I closely examined the faces of the onlookers. They all had expressions of ill-concealed nervous and shamefaced astonishment, and those in the semi-circles behind the chair gazed far more attentively at Mme de Maintenon than at the army, and all looked acutely alarmed and embarrassed. The King frequently laid his hat on the roof of the chair when he spoke into it, and the continual bending must have tired his back very considerably. Monseigneur was in the plain, on horseback, with his younger sons, and Mgr le Duc de Bourgogne was with the Maréchal de Boufflers, who commanded the entire operation. The time was five o'clock in the afternoon and the weather as fine as the heart could desire.

Directly in front of the sedan-chair, a steep path invisible from above led downhill, and an opening had been made at the end of the old wall, so that a messenger could come from below to take the King's orders, should it prove necessary. Such an event occurred when Crenan sent Canillac, the colonel of one of the defending regiments, to receive the King's commands on some detail or other, I know not what. Canillac came up the path, and had reached the point when his head and shoulders were beginning to appear above the level of the rampart (I see him now, as clearly as I saw him then). As his head gradually emerged, he suddenly perceived the chair, the King, and all the onlookers, whom he had hitherto neither seen nor suspected, because his post had been below, at the foot of the rampart, and he could not observe what was happening above. The sight completely bowled him over, so that he stopped short, staring, with mouth open and eyes glazed, and on his face an expression of the most utter astonishment. No one could have missed it, and the King saw it so plainly that he exclaimed with some heat, 'Come along, Canillac; hurry up!' Canillac stayed where he was, and the King said again, 'What is the matter, man? Come on up.' Canillac then did manage to come up and approached the King very slowly, trembling in every limb, and looking to right and left, thoroughly bewildered. I have already said that I was standing three paces from the King. Canillac passed directly in front of me and stammered out something in a very low voice. 'What's that?' said the King. 'Speak up, man!' He never managed to recover himself, but brought out some sort of mumble which the King failed to understand. Then, seeing that Canillac could do no better, he answered curtly, adding in a vexed tone, 'Go away, sir!' Canillac did not have to be told twice; he went back to his path and disappeared. 'I do not know what is wrong with Canillac', said the King, looking round as soon as the latter had gone, 'he seems to have taken leave of his senses; he has forgotten what he had to say to me'. Nobody answered.

Just before the surrender, it appeared as though Mme de Maintenon asked leave to withdraw, for the King cried out, 'Bearers for Madame!' and they came and carried her away. Less than a quarter of an hour afterwards the King retired, followed by Mme la Duchesse de Bourgogne and almost the entire company. Many of the spectators were eyeing and nudging one another as they went and whispering, but very low, for people could not get over the sight which they had just witnessed. It was the same with the spectators in the plain; even the soldiers were asking about the sedan-chair into which the King was continually bending, in fact it became necessary to silence the officers discreetly and stop the troops from asking questions. You may imagine the effect that it had on the foreigners and what they said about it. All Europe heard of it, and the incident was as much talked of as the camp itself, for all its pomp and splendour.

At other times Mme de Maintenon appeared very little at the camp, and always in a carriage with three or four intimate friends. She went once or twice to see the Maréchal de Boufflers and the marvels of his extraordinary lavishness. At last, after attacks on the trenches, displays of mimic warfare, and interminable reviews, the King finally left Compiègne on Monday, September 22nd, and travelled with the same people in his coach as far as Chantilly, where they spent the Tuesday night. On the Wednesday they arrived at Versailles, with as much relief on the part of the ladies as there had been eagerness to join the expedition at first. They had not eaten with the King at Compiègne, and had seen as little of Mme la Duchesse de Bourgogne as at Versailles. Nevertheless, they had been obliged to go to the camp every day and the fatigue had seemed to them greater than the pleasure, and far greater than any distinction which they might have hoped to gain.

The King was exceedingly pleased with the fine appearance of the troops, who had worn full-dress uniform with every embellishment that their officers could devise. As he left, he ordered six hundred francs to be given to each cavalry and dragoon captain, and three hundred to each infantry captain. He gave as much to the majors of every regiment, and distributed a few favours among his household. To the Maréchal de Boufflers, he presented one hundred thousand francs. Altogether, this must have cost him a good deal, but it was a drop in the ocean to the individuals concerned. There was not a single regiment that was not ruined for many years to come, both corps and officers. As for the Maréchal de Boufflers, I leave you to imagine how far one hundred thousand francs would go towards defraying the cost of a display so magnificent, so fantastic to those who saw it. All Europe trembled at the reports of the foreign observers, who day after day could scarcely believe their eyes.

RIGHT Versailles: View towards the gates and the stables from the Cour de Marbre. By J. B. Martin.

1699

Incredible Robberies

A most daring robbery was committed on the night of June 3rd in the great stables at Versailles, when the King himself was in residence. All the hammercloths and harness were taken to the tune of more than a hundred and fifty thousand francs' worth, and the thieves planned so well that although the house was full of people and the night a very short one, no one heard a sound. Everything was removed and nothing more was ever heard of it. Monsieur le Grand and his staff appeared in a fury, messengers were sent by all the roads, and searches were instituted in Paris and Versailles but without result.

Design for a horse-brass.

That reminds me of an even more outrageous theft that occurred shortly before I began to write my memoirs. The furniture in the state apartments, which ran from the gallery to the chapel, was upholstered in crimson velvet with gold braid and fringes. One morning, it was discovered that all this trimming had been cut off and removed, an incredible thing to have happened in a place where people were passing in and out all day long, and which was locked and guarded all night. Bontemps searched everywhere in desperation and had every possible inquiry made, but it was all quite useless.

Five or six days later, I attended the King's supper. There was no one but d'Aquin, the Royal physician, between me and the King, and no one at all between me and the table. Just as the entremets were being served, a monstrous big blackish object came sailing through the air over the table. It went so fast that I had no time to examine or point to it before it landed just in front of where Monsieur and Madame's covers were usually laid. On that day they happened to be in Paris, but they always sat at the end of the table, on the

57

King's left, with their backs to the window overlooking the courtyard. The noise it made was prodigious and the weight seemed likely to break the table. The plates jumped, but luckily nothing was upset, for the object fell upon the cloth and not among the dishes. The King half-turned his head at the sudden crash and said without the slightest trace of alarm, 'I expect those are my fringes.' And indeed, it was a package rather larger than a priest's hat with the edges flattened out, about two feet high, shaped like an ill-made pyramid.

It had been thrown from some distance behind where I was standing, through the middle door of the two ante-chambers, and a piece of fringe had become detached in mid-air and had fallen on the King's wig; but Livry, the high steward, who was on his left, noticed and removed it at once. Livry then went to the end of the table and verified that the object was indeed the fringes, done up into a bundle, and we all saw them at the same time and there was a hum of voices. He was just about to pick it up when he saw that there was a note attached, which he took, leaving the bundle where it was. At this, the King stretched out his hand, saying, 'Let me see'; but very rightly, Livry would not allow this. Taking a step backwards, he read it to himself and then passed it behind the King's back to d'Aquin, where I read it as he held it in his hand. The note was written in a disguised hand, long, like a woman's, and it read: 'Take back your fringes, Bontemps, they were not worth the trouble. Give my respects to the King.' It was folded, but not sealed.

The King again tried to take the paper from d'Aquin, but the latter drew back, smelt it, rubbed it, turned it over, and showed it to the King but would not let him handle it. The King then told him to read it aloud, and read it himself at the same time. 'This is most insolent!' he said, but in a calm almost bored voice. Then he told them to remove the package. It was so heavy that it was all Livry could do to lift it, and he quickly handed it to one of the blue-coated footmen. After that the King did not mention the incident again and no one else dared say anything, at least not aloud, and the rest of that supper passed as though nothing untoward had happened.

Apart from the incredible insolence of the theft, what an appalling risk to have taken! How could anyone, unless he were surrounded by accomplices, have hurled a package of that weight and size for such a distance, especially during the King's supper, when the crowd is so dense that one can scarcely move in the outer rooms? Even had there been a group of accomplices, how could the wide gesture needed to throw with such force possibly have passed unnoticed? It was the Duc de Gesvres's year of service, but until the King had risen, neither he nor anyone else thought of shutting the doors. You may imagine whether the culprits were likely to remain, when they were given three-quarters of an hour in which to escape. At last the doors were shut, but only one stranger was discovered, whom they immediately arrested. He said that he was a gentleman from Saintonge and acquainted with the Duc d'Uzès, the governor of that province. As the duke happened to be at Versailles, they sent to beg him to come, which he did, although he was about to go to bed. He

RIGHT Versailles: View of the *parterre* on the north side. By Etienne Allegrain.

58

recognized and vouched for the gentleman, who was set free with apologies. Nothing further has ever been discovered about this theft, and the strange manner of its return.

1700

Le Nôtre

[1] André Le Nôtre, the creator of French landscape gardening. The Avenue des Champs-Elysées and St. James's Park, London, were laid out by him.

Le Nôtre[1] died at about this time. He had lived in perfect health for eighty-eight years and retained his faculties, excellent taste, and capability until the last. He was celebrated for designing the fine gardens that adorn all France and have so lowered the reputation of Italian gardens (which are really nothing by comparison) that the most famous landscape architects of Italy now come to France to study and admire. Le Nôtre was honest, honourable, and plain-spoken; everybody loved and respected him, for he never stepped out of his place nor forgot it and was always perfectly disinterested, working for private patrons as for the King himself, and with the same care and industry. His only thought was to aid nature and reveal true beauty at as low a cost as possible.

There was an artlessness about him, a simple-hearted candour that was perfectly delightful. On one occasion, when the Pope had obtained the King's permission to borrow him for a few months, Le Nôtre entered his room, and instead of falling to his knees, ran towards him, and putting his arms round his neck kissed him on both cheeks, exclaiming, 'Ah! Holy Father, how well you look! How rejoiced I am to see you in good health!' The Pope, Clement X, Alfieri, laughed heartily. He thoroughly enjoyed this informal kind of greeting and treated Le Nôtre with much kindness.

After he returned, the King took him into the gardens of Versailles and showed him all that had been done in his absence. When they reached the colonnade, Le Nôtre did not utter a word until the King pressed him for his opinion. 'Well, Sire', said he, 'what would you have me say? You have turned a stone-mason into a gardener (he was referring to Mansard) and he has treated you to one of the tricks of his trade'. The King said nothing and everyone smiled, for indeed, although it pretends to be one, the colonnade has little resemblance to a fountain and is vastly out of place in a garden.

A month or so before he died, the King, who enjoyed seeing and talking to him, again took him into the gardens and because of his great age had him put into a chair, which a footman wheeled beside his own. Thereupon Le Nôtre exclaimed, 'Alas! my poor father,[1] had he but been alive to see this poor gardener, his own son, riding in a chair beside the greatest king on earth, his happiness would have been complete.'

[1] Jean Le Notre, designer and superintendent of the Tuileries and other Gardens.

He was superintendent of the royal residences and lived at the Tuileries, where he had charge of the palace and the gardens, which he had designed. All that he did is still considered far better than anything done since, although many have taken the greatest pains to imitate and follow him as far as they were capable. About ornamental flower-beds, he used to say that they were only

Tree-planting. From *Instructions pour les jardins fruitiers* by Jean de La Quintinie, the famous botanist who superintended the kitchen-garden at Versailles.

good for nursemaids who were tied to their charges and could look down upon them from second storey-windows. Nevertheless, he excelled in their design, as in the creation of all other parts of a garden; but he did not care for them, and he was right, because no one ever walks in those parts.

Death of Charles II of Spain, at three in the afternoon of 1 November 1700.

1700

The Duc d'Anjou becomes King of Spain

[1] Charles II King of Spain (1665–1700), bequeathed his throne to the Duc d'Anjou.

No sooner had the King of Spain[1] expired than there arose the question of opening his will. A council of state was held, at which all the grandees then in Madrid were present. Curiosity to witness so extraordinary a scene, affecting so many millions, drew all Madrid to the palace, where the crowds in the rooms adjoining that in which the will was read were so great that there was grave danger of suffocation. The foreign ministers thronged about the door in their anxiety to be the first to know the late King's choice and the first to inform their respective Courts. Blécourt (the French Ambassador) was there with the rest, knowing no more than they, and the Comte d'Harrach, the Emperor's envoy, who hoped and believed that the will would favour the Archduke,[2] stood next him by the door, wearing a look of triumph. Everyone grew impatient. Finally, the door opened and closed again. The Duc d'Abrantès, whose wit was lively though much to be dreaded, entered, apparently wishing to have the

[2] The Archduke Charles, second son of Leopold II, Emperor of Austria, who had a claim to the Spanish throne through his mother.

61

pleasure of announcing the successor as soon as the grandees and the council were agreed. He was instantly surrounded. Casting a glance around the assembly, he remained gravely silent. Blécourt stepped forward, at whom he looked fixedly, then turned away appearing to search among the bystanders, an action that surprised Blécourt, who thought that it boded no good for France. Suddenly the Duc d'Abrantès made as though he had just perceived the Comte d'Harrach. A look of joy came over his face, he flung his arms about his neck and said loudly in Spanish, 'Monsieur, it is with much pleasure . . .', then, after a pause for further embraces, 'Yes, Monsieur, it is with the greatest joy . . .' (still another pause for embraces) 'and satisfaction that I take leave of you for the remainder of my life and bid farewell to the Royal House of Austria'. He then made a dash through the crowd, who all ran after him to know the name of the successor. The Comte d'Harrach's surprise and indignation effectually stopped his mouth but fully appeared upon his countenance. He remained rooted to the spot for several minutes, allowed his underlings to inform him of the news when the council rose, and then went to his house in a state of confusion, all the greater from having been duped by the Duc d'Abrantès's embraces and the cruel mockery of his compliments.

Blécourt did not wait to hear more. He hurried home to write the news and dispatch his courier, and while he was so doing Ubilla[1] sent him an extract from the will itself, so that he had only to include it in the packet, which was carried straight to the King, at the Conseil des Finances, on the morning of Tuesday, November 9th.

The King had arranged to shoot on that day, but he countermanded the order and dined as usual *au petit couvert*, showing nothing by his expression, merely announcing the death of the King of Spain; that he should wear mourning, and that there would be no Appartement, plays, or other diversions at the Court during the whole of the winter. When he returned to his study, he summoned the ministers to assemble at three o'clock in Mme de Maintenon's room. By this time Monseigneur had returned from wolf-hunting, and he, too, went to Mme de Maintenon's room at three o'clock. That council lasted until seven in the evening, after which the King continued working until ten o'clock. Mme de Maintenon was present all the time that the council was sitting and during all the work that followed.

On the following day, the usual council of state was held in the morning in the King's study, and when he returned from hunting he held another in Mme de Maintenon's room, from six in the evening until ten. Although the Court had grown accustomed to the vogue for Mme de Maintenon, they were not used to see her openly taking part in state affairs, and there was great astonishment when two councils of state were held in her apartment on the gravest and most important matter that had come under discussion during that long reign or, indeed, in many others.

The King, Monseigneur, the Chancellor,[2] the Duc de Beauvilliers, and Torcy (no other ministers of state were present) were the only ones to debate

[1] Secretary of the Council.

[2] Pontchartrain.

'Monseigneur', Louis de
France—Le Grand Dauphin,
so-called because he was
taller than the King. By
Nicolas de Largillière.

this great matter, and Mme de Maintenon sat with them, but was silent out of modesty until the King asked for her opinion after all had expressed theirs with the exception of himself. The speakers were divided in their opinions; two were in favour of the Treaty of Partition,[1] the other two were for accepting the will.

These two opinions, of which I have given the barest summary, were much amplified by both sides and discussed at length many times over. Monseigneur, usually so deeply imbedded in fat and apathy, appeared a different man, to the

[1] By which the Spanish
Empire was to be divided
between France and Austria.

63

intense surprise of the King and his counsellors. When the time came for him to speak, he expressed himself strongly in favour of accepting the will, recapitulating some of the Chancellor's finest arguments, then, turning respectfully but firmly towards the King, he added that, having given his opinion like the rest, he took the liberty of claiming his inheritance, since he was in a position to accept it. The crown of Spain, he said, had been the rightful property of the Queen his mother, consequently it was now his, or, for the sake of the peace of Europe, that of his second son to whom he gladly ceded it. But, he added, he would not yield a single inch of that land to anyone else, for his claim was just, in conformity with the King's honour and the interests and majesty of the throne, and he hoped that it would not be rejected. All this he said, scarlet in the face, to the great astonishment of everyone present.

The King listened attentively and then said to Mme de Maintenon, 'And you, Madame, what is your opinion?' She made a show of reluctance but after being urged, even ordered, to speak her mind, produced a few words expressing becoming diffidence, a sentence or two in praise of Monseigneur, whom she both feared and detested (as he did her), and added that she advised acceptance.

The King ended the council without disclosing his own opinion. He said that he had listened well and understood that there were powerful arguments on both sides; it would be better therefore to sleep upon the matter and to wait for twenty-four hours, to see what might more come from Spain and whether the Spaniards were of the same mind as their late King. He then dismissed the counsellors, ordering them to assemble on the following evening at the same place. The next day, Thursday, between his *lever* and mass, the King gave an audience to the Spanish ambassador, at which Monseigneur and Torcy were present; the ambassador presented him with an authentic copy of the will, on behalf of the Queen[1] and the Junta. None of us doubted that the King, without committing himself, had then given the ambassador strong hopes of his acceptance, for after his departure Mgr le Duc de Bourgogne was sent for and let into the secret. The Chancellor went off to Paris and the other ministers were given leave of absence until the Court returned from Fontainebleau, so that everyone knew that the matter was decided one way or another.

The necessity of continuing so interesting a tale without breaking the thread has not allowed me to pause. Now, however, I must retrace some of my steps. At Madrid, Blécourt's amazement at a proposal which surprised him no less than it did the Comte d'Harrach, was unparalleled. That of King Louis and his ministers was inconceivable. Neither he nor they could believe what they read in Blécourt's dispatches, and several days were needed before they had recovered sufficiently to deliberate that vital matter. The news, when it was published, had the same effect upon the Court. Foreign ambassadors spent whole nights conferring together, meditating on the King's probable decision and the interests of their masters, yet externally preserving strict silence. The courtiers did nothing but argue, but nearly all favoured acceptance. The

[1] Mariana of Neuburg, the second wife of Charles II of Spain. His first wife had been Monsieur's daughter by Henrietta of England.

The Château and gardens of Marly by P. D. Martin

Louis XIV, surrounded by the royal princes, accepting reparations from the Doge of Genoa,
at Versailles on 15 May 1685

manner of so doing was much discussed in all the councils, and it was even proposed to spring a surprise upon the world by allowing the Duc d'Anjou to disappear and as suddenly to reappear in Spain under the auspices of the nuncio Gualterio. I heard of this plan and thought of being one of the party. But it would have been a shabby trick and was instantly rejected, partly from shame at so furtive an acceptance of the proffered crowns and partly because it was necessary to throw off the mask in order to support a Spain too weak to be left unprotected.

Since no one at Court talked of anything but the course to be followed, the King amused himself one evening by asking the Princesses for their advice. They answered that M. le Duc d'Anjou should be sent forthwith to Spain, and that such was the opinion which they heard from every side. 'I am sure', said the King, 'that plenty of people will blame me whatever I decide to do!'

This occurred on Saturday, November 13th. Next morning, the day before the Court left Fontainebleau, the King was closeted for a long time with Torcy, who then warned the Spanish ambassador to be at Versailles on the following evening. When this became generally known, it threw everyone into a state of ferment. Those in the know also discovered that on the preceding Friday the King had had a long conversation with M. le Duc d'Anjou in the presence of

The fountain-court and fishpond, in the gardens of Fontainebleau. Engraved by Aveline.

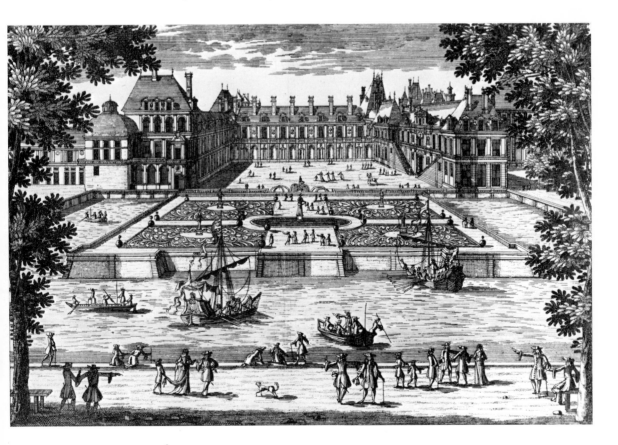

LE MARQUIS DE CASTEL DOS RIOS AMBASSADEUR D'ESPAGNE SALUE S.M. CATHOLI.
Philippe V. et luy presente ensuite son fils aîné et les Seign.^{rs} Espagnols qui l'accompagnoient
le 16. Novembre 1700.

The Spanish Ambassador,
the Marquis of Castel, salutes
the Duc d'Anjou as Philip V,
King of Spain.

Monseigneur and Mgr le Duc de Bourgogne, an event so extraordinary that
people were sure of an acceptance. On that very same Sunday, moreover, a
Spanish courier from the Comte d'Harrach had stopped at Fontainebleau on
his way to Vienna, had seen the King at his supper, and had said publicly that
they were waiting impatiently at Madrid for M. le Duc d'Anjou, and that four
grandees had been nominated to escort him to the capital. M. le Duc d'Anjou,
when approached, only expressed his gratitude to the late King, and behaved
so calmly that it appeared as though he neither knew nor expected anything
until the moment of his proclamation.

On Monday, November 15th, the King left Fontainebleau between nine and
ten in the morning, his coach containing only Mgr le Duc de Bourgogne, Mme
la Duchesse de Bourgogne, Mme la Princesse de Conti and the Duchesse du
Lude. He ate a morsel without leaving the coach and arrived at Versailles about
four o'clock. Monseigneur went to Meudon to dine and spend a few nights, and
Monsieur and Madame to Paris. The Spanish ambassador received another
courier while he was on the way, bringing fresh orders and urging him to be
zealous in asking for M. le Duc d'Anjou. The Court at Versailles was very
large, curiosity having brought them there even before the King's arrival.

On Tuesday, November 16th, immediately after his *lever*, the King
summoned the Spanish ambassador to his study, which the Duc d'Anjou had
already entered through the back way. The King then pointed to the Duke,
telling the ambassador that he might salute him as his King, at which he fell to

his knees in the Spanish fashion and made a longish address in that language, whereupon the King said that since the Prince, his grandson, did not yet understand Spanish, he would answer for him.

Immediately afterwards, against all custom, the King had the double doors of his study flung wide open, and commanded the company, which almost amounted to a crowd, to enter. Then casting a most majestic glance over that numerous assembly, he announced, pointing to the Duc d'Anjou, 'Messieurs! Behold the King of Spain! His birth has called him to that throne, also the will

Philippe de France becomes Philip V, King of Spain. He adopts the 'golilla', the stiff linen collar, jutting out beneath his chin, and wears black in the Spanish tradition. By Hyacinthe Rigaud, 1700.

of the late King. The entire nation desires him and claims him from me. This is Heaven's command, and I accede with pleasure.' Turning to his grandson, he continued, 'Be a good Spaniard, that is your first duty now; but remember that you were born a Frenchman and foster the unity between the two nations. That is the way to make them happy and to preserve the peace of Europe.' Then again pointing with his finger, he said to the ambassador, 'If he follows my advice, you will be a great noble, and that very soon. He cannot do better at present than be guided by you.'[1]

When the first excitement among the courtiers had subsided a little, the two other Sons of France stepped forward and all three embraced tenderly, again and again, with tears in their eyes. Zinzendorf, the Emperor's envoy (who has since amassed a vast fortune at Vienna), had asked for an audience at that time in complete ignorance of all that was happening, and was waiting below in the ambassadors' ante-room until the head of protocol should send for him to announce the birth of the Emperor's grandson.[2] He went upstairs knowing nothing of what had occurred. The King sent the King of Spain and the Spanish ambassador into one of the back offices, before summoning Zinzendorf, who learned only after his audience of the awkward moment that he had chosen. The King then went to mass, as usual, and the King of Spain walked beside him at his right hand. In the royal gallery, the whole royal family—that is to say, all down to and including the Grandsons of France, but no others—hurriedly arranged themselves in a row upon the King's foot-rug. Unlike the time of prie-dieu,[3] they all leaned with him upon the carpeted balustrade, but the King was the only one to have a hassock. The rest knelt on the same step, which was also covered with the rug, but there were no hassocks for them. When they entered the gallery, only one hassock was provided, which the King took, and offered to the King of Spain, and when he refused it, it was put on one side and both heard mass without hassocks. Afterwards, there were always two hassocks when they both attended the same mass, which happened very often.

On their return, the King stopped in the great bed-chamber of the state apartments, and told the King of Spain that that should henceforth be his room. He slept there that same night and received the whole Court, who came in crowds to pay their respects. Villequier, the first gentleman of the King's bedchamber, was given orders to wait on him, and the King gave up two rooms leading out of the state bedroom, so that he might be private, and communication uninterrupted between the two wings of the palace, for the only way was through the state rooms.

After that day, it became known that the King of Spain would leave on December 1st and that the two princes, his brothers,[4] would go with him to the frontier. M. le Duc de Beauvilliers was given authority over the princes and courtiers during the journey, and sole command over the troops, officers, and suite. He had the ordering of everything. The Maréchal the Duc de Noailles was appointed with him, not to interefere in any way, nor to give orders in his

[1] Voltaire states that this was the moment when Louis XIV exclaimed, 'There are no longer any Pyrenees!'

[2] Leopold Joseph, son of the Archduke Joseph. He died a few months later.

[3] The King's short prayer, said each day before leaving his bedroom.

[4] The dukes of Bourgogne and Berry.

presence, although he was a Marshal of France and Captain of the Bodyguard, but in case of his illness or absence from the princes. All the youth of the Court received permission to make the journey and many went, either in their own coaches or in those of the suite. We heard, too, that after the separation at Saint Jean-de-Luz, the princes would make a tour of Provence and the Languedoc, passing through part of the Dauphiné and returning by Lyons, and that their excursion would take four months. A hundred and twenty men of the guards, under a lieutenant and an ensign, and a number of police, were detailed to escort them, and MM. de Beauvilliers and de Noailles each had fifty thousand livres for their expenses.

Monseigneur, who knew the hour which the King had fixed for the proclamation, told those at Meudon. Monsieur was told the secret on leaving Fontainebleau and was so impatient to announce it that he stood under the clock for several minutes before the appointed time, and could not refrain from informing his Court that they were going to hear great news as soon as the hand touched the hour that allowed him to speak. Mgr le Duc de Bourgogne, M. le Duc d'Anjou, and the Spanish ambassador had known since the preceding Friday, but they guarded the secret so well that nothing appeared in their manner or expressions. Mme la Duchesse de Bourgogne had been told when she arrived at Fontainebleau, M. le Duc de Berry on the Monday morning. They were all delighted, but felt the sadness of the separation, for they were devoted to one another, and when youth and high spirits sometimes caused quarrels between the eldest and youngest brothers, it was always the second, with his calm, virtuous, reserved nature who patched them up again.

Immediately after the proclamation, the King sent word to the King and Queen of England, by the first equerry.[1] In the afternoon, the King of Spain called on Monseigneur at Meudon, who received him at the door and led him in. He made him walk in front, gave him 'Your Majesty', and everywhere in public with him remained standing. Monseigneur, indeed, appeared quite beside himself with joy, often repeating that no one had ever before been in a position to say, 'The King my father, and the King my son'. Had he, however, known the prophecy made at his birth, 'Son of a king, father of a king, never king himself', he might not have been so delighted. After the proclamation, the King of Spain was treated in the same manner as the King of England, with an armchair at dinner at the King's right hand, and his own cadenas. Monseigneur and the rest of the royal family had folding-stools, as usual, at the end and side of the table, a goblet and a covered glass to drink from, and a taster,[2] like the King's. They met in public only at chapel, on the way there and back, and at supper, after which the King accompanied him as far as the door of the great gallery. He saw the King and Queen of England at Versailles and Saint-Germain, and was treated in every way as an equal, but the three Kings never went anywhere together. In private, that is to say in the offices and in Mme de Maintenon's room, he behaved to the King as though he were still only Duc d'Anjou; indeed, at the first supper, he turned his head to the Spanish

[1] Jacques Louis, Marquis de Beringhen (1651–1723), Master of the Horse at Versailles; his Court name was M. le Premier.

[2] The wine and water was always tasted before it was offered to the King.

ambassador saying that he felt as though it had all been a dream. He made only one formal call on Mme la Duchesse de Bourgogne and on Messeigneurs her brothers-in-law, and received only one from them, the visit being like those paid to the King of England, and it was the same when he went to Paris to call on Monsieur and Madame. Whenever he went in or out the guards beat the general salute—in fact, complete equality with the King. When they passed through the state apartments together, going to or coming from mass, the King walked on the right, but when they reached the last chamber he ceded that position to the King of Spain, as being no longer on his own territory. The evenings were spent in Mme de Maintenon's apartments, in different rooms from that in which she sat with the King, and there he played all kinds of games, generally childish games like touch-last, with Messeigneurs his brothers, Mme la Duchesse de Bourgogne who worked hard to amuse him, and the small circle of ladies who were permitted to be present.

The nuncio and the Venetian ambassador broke through the crowd immediately after the proclamation and went to congratulate the King and the new monarch, a fact that was noted with great interest. The attitude of the other foreign ministers was much more reserved, indeed, embarrassed. As for Zinzendorf, who remained in the drawing-room for some time after his audience, his state of mind was vastly interesting and curious. I think that he would gladly have paid handsomely for prior information that would have kept him in Paris.

1700

Departure of Philip V

On Saturday, December 4th, the King of Spain went to the King before anyone else was admitted and stayed a long time. He then called on Monseigneur, with whom he was also a long time alone. They then all heard mass together, amidst a great throng of courtiers. After mass, they at once got into their coach, Mme la Duchesse de Bourgogne at the back between the two Kings, Monseigneur in front between Messeigneurs his two other sons, Monsieur by one door, and Madame by the other. They were surrounded by a far greater escort of guards than usual, as well as by mounted militiamen and light-horse. The whole road as far as Sceaux was lined with carriages and people. They arrived there shortly after midday, to find it full of ladies and courtiers and guarded by two companies of musketeers. When they left the coach, the King walked quickly through the lower apartments and entered the last room alone with the King of Spain, leaving the rest of the company in the salon. A quarter of an hour later he sent for Monsieur, and shortly afterwards for the Spanish ambassador to bid his royal master farewell. The King then summoned Mgr and Mme la Duchesse de Bourgogne, M. le Duc de Berry, Monsieur and Madame, all together, and, after a short interval, the Princes and Princesses of the Blood. The double doors were thrown wide open and from the salon they could be seen all weeping bitterly.

The King then said to the King of Spain, presenting the princes, 'Behold the princes of my blood and yours! From now onwards the two nations must regard themselves as one, their interests must be the same. I therefore desire that these princes shall be as closely attached to you as to myself, you could have no better nor more faithful friends.' This scene took up an hour and a half. At the close of it they were obliged to separate, the King conducted the King of Spain to the end of the state apartments and embraced him many times, holding him long in his arms, and Monseigneur did the same. It was a most touching sight.

The King then retired to recover his composure, Monseigneur got into his carriage alone, and the King of Spain, his brothers, and M. de Noailles drove away together and slept at Chartres. The King went for a drive in an open carriage with Mme la Duchesse de Bourgogne and Monsieur and Madame. Afterwards they all returned to Versailles. Various officers of the household followed on the journey to Spain, Desgranges, as master of ceremonies, as well as various secretaries and equerries. Hersent, keeper of the wardrobe and La Roche the head valet, were to remain in Spain with some servants and a few other people in the way of dentists and doctors.

M. de Beauvilliers, who had stuffed himself with quinine in the effort to check a persistent fever, accompanied by most distressing diarrhoea, took his wife, with Mmes de Cheverny and de Rasilly as her companions, for the King had absolutely insisted that he should start and attempt to make the journey.

Let them go, and let us marvel at the ways of Providence that so disposes of the thoughts of men and the fates of nations. What would Ferdinand and Isabella have thought, or Charles V, or Philip II, who so often attempted to invade France, and were accused of aspiring to world-monarchy? Or Philip IV himself, with all his precautions at the marriage of the King and the Peace of the Pyrenees? What would he have said at seeing a Son of France become King of Spain, by will of the last of his line and by the unanimous desire of all Spaniards, without French plots or intrigue, indeed, quite unknown to our King and his ministers, who felt only trouble in deciding and sorrow in acceptance? What deep, what grave thoughts such ideas provoke! But they would be out of place in these Memoirs. Let us now return to what was actually happening, for I am unwilling to interrupt so unusual and interesting a tale.

The Death of Monsieur

On Wednesday, June 8th, Monsieur came to Marly from Saint-Cloud to dine with the King, and entered the study as usual as soon as the council of state was over. He found the King exceedingly angry because M. de Chartres had been deliberately annoying his daughter and he did not care to take the matter up with him directly. The fact was that M. de Chartres had fallen in love with Mlle de Séry, one of Madame's maids of honour, and was pursuing the affair in a tactless, high-handed manner. The King took this occasion to heap bitter reproaches on Monsieur for the conduct of his son. Monsieur, in the state that he then was, needed no excuse to vex him and answered tartly that fathers who lived certain kinds of lives were in no position to issue reprimands. The King could not help seeing the point of this remark, but returned to his daughter's wounded feelings, saying that such things ought to be kept out of her sight. By this time, however, Monsieur had fairly got the bit between his teeth and reminded the King pretty sharply that he had paraded his own mistresses before the Queen, even going to the extent of making them sit beside her in his coach. Much incensed, the King returned the compliment, and they were soon at it hammer and tongs.

RIGHT View of the Château and gardens of Saint-Cloud, home of the Duc d'Orléans. By Etienne Allegrain.

At Marly, the four apartments on the ground floor were similar and each contained three rooms. The King's study opened out of a smaller drawing-room which, at that time of day, was always full of courtiers waiting to see him go to dinner. By one of those customs which, for no known reason, have developed differently in the different palaces, the door of the King's study at Marly was kept open, except during the council. There was nothing but a curtain which an usher drew back to allow entrance. This usher, when he heard the quarrel, went in and told the King that he was distinctly audible from the drawing-room, and Monsieur, too; then he immediately retired. The King's inner study opened out of the first, but with neither door nor curtain in between, and this room led into another small withdrawing-room, which had been reduced in width to make a place for the King's night-stool. The indoor footmen always stood in this inner drawing-room, so that they, too, must have heard the whole of the conversation as I have described it.

The usher's warning made them lower their voices but did not stop the recriminations, and at last, Monsieur, flying into a rage, told the King fairly that when the Duc de Chartres married he had promised him the moon and the stars and that so far all he had extracted had been a governorship. Monsieur said that he wished his son to have employment to divert him from love-affairs and that M. de Chartres also desired it keenly, as the King well knew, since he had again and again asked it as a favour. It had been refused him persistently,

72

however, and Monsieur did not intend to prevent the young man from finding consolation in his pleasures. He added that at the time of the marriage he had justly been warned that he would get nothing but shame and contempt and reap no profit whatsoever. The King, becoming more and more furious, retorted that the war would soon make him economize and that since Monsieur had shown himself so disobliging, his pensions should go before the King touched his own pocket.

At that point dinner was announced and they left the room to go to table. Monsieur was scarlet, his eyes sparkling with anger, so that some of the ladies remarked that he looked in great need of bleeding. Dinner passed off as usual, Monsieur eating prodigiously as he always did at his two meals, not to mention the copious draughts of chocolate every morning and all that he swallowed at other times of day in the way of fruit, sugar biscuits, and such titbits as filled his pockets and the drawers of the tables and cabinets. When they rose from

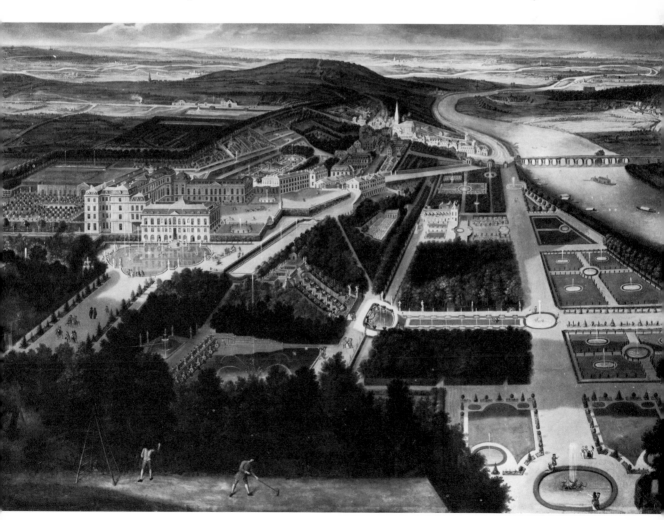

Still life of fruit. By Louise Moillon.

table, the King walked out alone, and Monsieur returned at once to Saint-Cloud.

After supper that evening, the King was still in his study, with Monseigneur and the princesses, when an attaché arrived from Saint-Cloud bearing a message from M. de Chartres. He was admitted to the study, where he told the King that Monsieur had been seized with acute exhaustion at supper, but that he had been bled and now felt better and that they had given him an emetic. It appeared that he had been supping as usual with the ladies and that when the entrées were being served he had poured a glass of wine for Mme de Bouillon, had seemed to stammer something, and had pointed with his finger. He used occasionally to speak Spanish, so that some of the ladies asked what he was saying, while others cried out in alarm. It was all over in a moment and he fell down in an apoplectic fit into the arms of M. de Chartres. They carried him to his bedroom, where they shook him, walked him up and down, bled him copiously, and gave him a strong emetic, without awakening more than the faintest signs of life.

The King, who usually rallied to Monsieur's side at the smallest provocation, went instead to Mme de Maintenon's apartments and had her woken up. After spending a quarter of an hour closeted with her, he returned to his own rooms at about midnight, ordered the horses to be harnessed, and sent the Marquis de Gesvres back to Saint-Cloud with instructions to return and wake him should Monsieur grow any worse. Then he went to bed. I think

74

that on account of the quarrel the King suspected a plot to relieve the tension between them, and that he had gone to consult with Mme de Maintenon because he preferred to fail in the proprieties rather than be duped.

Mme de Maintenon disliked and feared Monsieur. He seldom visited her and, in spite of his nervousness and more than deferential attitude, he sometimes allowed himself a sneer at her relations with the King, thus showing that he despised her and respected public opinion. She was therefore in no hurry to urge any sign of affection towards him. Still less was she ready to encourage the King to travel through the night, lose his sleep, and witness a pathetic scene that might touch his heart and cause him to examine his conscience. She may also have hoped that if all were quickly over the King might be spared some pain.

After the King had gone to bed, one of Monsieur's pages came to say that he was now better and had sent to ask M. le Prince de Conti for some Schaffeuse water, which is excellent in cases of apoplexy. About an hour and a half later, however, an officer arrived from M. de Chartres. He woke the King, to report that the emetic had had no effect and that Monsieur was now *in extremis*. Whereupon the King rose and left for Saint-Cloud, meeting M. de Gesvres upon the road.

It is impossible to describe the tumult and disorder of that night at Marly, or the horror that reigned in that pleasure-palace of Saint-Cloud. Everyone at Marly rushed as fast as they could to Saint-Cloud, taking any carriage that came to hand, without permission or any regard for good manners. Monseigneur travelled with Madame la Duchesse, in a great state of alarm because he, too, had lately been seriously ill with an attack of indigestion. It was as much as his equerry could do to half-drag, half-carry him trembling to his coach. The King arrived shortly before three in the morning to find that Monsieur had not regained consciousness for a single moment. There had been a glimmer of life when his confessor, le Père du Trévou, was about to say mass, but it had not lasted.

In the most awe-inspiring scenes there are often ridiculous incidents. Le Père du Trévou at that moment had turned round and shouted into Monsieur's ear, 'Monsieur, don't you recognize your own confessor? Don't you know dear old Père du Trévou?' which made those who were least moved laugh in rather a shocking manner.

The King himself appeared much affected. He was naturally prone to weep and therefore burst into tears. Indeed, he had never had cause to do other than love Monsieur, and although they had been on bad terms for the past two months, these sad moments must have reminded him of their old affection. It may be that he blamed himself for precipitating Monsieur's death by that morning's quarrel. Perhaps he may have felt uneasy because Monsieur was his junior by two years and had seemed as healthy as himself, if not more so. He remained at Saint-Cloud long enough to hear mass at eight o'clock, then, as his brother was past human aid, Mme de Maintenon and Mme de Bourgogne persuaded him to wait no longer and they all returned together to Marly. When he was about to leave, he said a few kinds words to M. de Chartres, both of them weeping bitterly; whereupon the young prince clasped his knees, crying, 'Alas, Sire, what will become of me?' The King, who was surprised and deeply touched, embraced him and spoke most affectionately.

After the King left, the crowd gradually melted away, so that Monsieur, dying upon the day-bed in his study, lay exposed to the view of the lackeys and lower servants, most of whom were much distressed, either out of love or self-interest. The upper servants and others who were about to lose their situations rent the air with their cries, while the women ran hither and thither shrieking, their hair loose, as wild as Bacchantes.

In the meantime, Madame, who never had much affection or regard for her husband but felt her loss of position most keenly, remained in her own apartments, crying out at the top of her voice, 'No convent for me! Let no one speak to me of convents! I will not go to a convent!' She was not out of her senses. She remembered that by the terms of her marriage contract she must choose between a convent and retirement to the Château de Montargis. It may well be that she saw better hope of escaping from the one than from the other, or else, knowing how much cause she had to dread the King,[1] although she did not yet know the whole matter and he had paid her the civilities usual on such occasions, she may well have feared a convent most. When Monsieur was dead, she immediately entered her coach with her ladies and drove to Versailles, followed by M. and Mme la Duchesse de Chartres and their entire households.

On the following morning, which was Friday, M. de Chartres went to the King, who was still in bed and who spoke very kindly, bidding him look henceforth on him as a father and promising to protect his honour and interests and to forget all the petty vexations of the past. He hoped that M. de Chartres also would forget, and that these protestations of affection would persuade him to return the love which the King offered. You may be sure that M. de Chartres knew how to answer in a proper spirit.

After so awe-inspiring a spectacle, such tears, such demonstrations of love, everyone believed that the remaining three days of that Marly excursion would be exceedingly dull. However, when the ladies went at midday to Mme de Maintenon's apartments on the morning after Monsieur's death, they found the King already there with Mme la Duchesse de Bourgogne, and heard them from the ante-room singing the prologues to several operas. Shortly afterwards the King perceived that Mme la Duchesse de Bourgogne was sitting in a corner of the room, looking very miserable. He seemed surprised, asked Mme de Maintenon what had upset her, and then tried to divert her by playing with her and some ladies whom he called for to entertain them. That was not all. When they came out from dinner, that is to say, shortly after two o'clock, only twenty-six hours after Monsieur's death, Mgr le Duc de Bourgogne invited the Duc de Montfort to play a hand of brelan. 'Brelan!' exclaimed Montfort in utter astonishment. 'You cannot have forgotten! Monsieur is not yet cold.' 'Indeed',

[1] In letters to her aunt, the Electress of Hanover, Madame had openly criticized the Government of France, and had sneered at Mme de Maintenon, all of which the King knew.

'Madame'. Elizabeth
Charlotte of Bavaria,
(miscalled 'of the Palatinate').
The second wife of Philippe
I, Duc d'Orléans. By Nicolas
de Largillière.

said the prince, 'I know it very well, but the King will have no one bored at
Marly. He has ordered me to start everyone playing and to set the example
myself.' They then sat down to a hand of cards and before long the drawing-
room was full of gaming tables. . . .

Although it would have been hard to find anyone meeker or more submissive
than Monsieur with the King, even down to flattering his ministers and
mistresses of former days, he took great pains to preserve, albeit with great
respect, the easy relationship of a brother when they were in private. Thus he
took many liberties, for instance he always sat boldly down in an armchair
without waiting to be invited, although, after the King's supper, no other
prince ever sat in the study, not even Monseigneur. Nevertheless, in public,
and when he approached or left the King, no subject ever showed more
profound deference, and his most casual gestures were naturally graceful and

dignified. At intervals he was assiduous in attendance on the King, but never for long, and when his gambling, and the upkeep of Saint-Cloud and his favourites, began to cost more money than the King allowed him, he gradually ceased to make an appearance. To Mme de Maintenon he could never bring himself to show respect, nor refrain from having a sly dig at her when speaking to the King, and an occasional sneer in public. It was not that he minded her being a favourite, but he could not tolerate the idea of La Scarron[1] being his sister-in-law.

He was intensely vain, not haughtily so, but exceedingly sensitive and proudly conscious of his rights and dignities. He was a little pot-bellied man, whose heels were so high that he seemed to walk on stilts. He decked himself out with rings, bracelets, and other jewellery like any woman, wore a long black and powdered wig, spread out in front, and ribbons everywhere. He covered himself with all manner of perfumes and was the very pattern of elegance. They said that he used a touch of rouge. A monstrous long nose, a fine mouth and eyes, a face plump, but very much on the long side; all his portraits are good likenesses. I used to be vexed at seeing them, for they reminded me of the portraits of his father Louis XIII, that great prince, whom in merit he so little resembled.

[1] Mme de Maintenon's first marriage was to the crippled poet Paul Scarron.

1702

Saint-Simon Leaves the Army

After the Peace of Ryswick, the reorganization of the army was exceedingly thorough and most strangely conducted, for no attention was paid to the varying excellence of the different regiments, their officers and colonels. Barbezieux, the war minister, was young and impulsive and the King gave him a free hand. I myself had no personal acquaintance with him. My regiment was reformed, and, because it was a very good one, parts were allocated to the Royals and the remnants to Duras' regiment; my own company was incorporated with that of the Comte d'Uzès, Barbezieux's brother-in-law. It was no consolation to me to know that others shared my fate, for colonels of the reformed companies were placed at the bottom of the list of their new regiments, and I had been seconded to that of Saint-Mauris, a gentleman of the Franche-Comté, whom I had never seen in my life.

After a time, some colonels junior to myself were given back their commands, but this seemed only reasonable, since they were all veterans, who had obtained their appointments through length of service. Rumours were current about a general promotion, but I attached little importance to them, for at this time birth and rank counted for nothing and special promotions were

Uniform of the Grey
Musketeers. Detail from a
painting by Van der Meulen
of Versailles in 1664.

given only for actions in the field; moreover, I had too many above me to
entertain any hopes of becoming a brigadier. My whole heart, therefore, was
set on having a regiment and commanding it in the campaign that was about to
open, so as to avoid the humiliation of acting as a kind of supernumerary aide-
de-camp to Saint-Mauris.

The general promotion was made at last and everyone was astonished at the
length of the list, for nothing had ever approached it in numbers. As I eagerly
searched through the names of the new cavalry brigadiers, vainly hoping to find
my own, I was humiliated to see five of my juniors included in the list. My
pride was so deeply hurt that I could never forget their names, Ourches,
Vendeuil, Streiff, the Comte d'Ayen, and Ruffey. Nevertheless, I kept silence,
for fear lest in my vexation I might say something foolish. The Maréchal de
Lorges was as indignant upon my account as upon his own, and his brother-in-
law[1] not less so, and they both insisted that I should leave the service. I myself
felt so angry that I was greatly disposed to do so; but my age, the opening of the
campaign, the thought of renouncing all ambition in my chosen profession, the
boredom of idleness, the sad summers when all conversation would be of war
and partings, the advancement of men who by distinguished conduct gained
high rank and reputation, were all powerful deterrents. I accordingly spent two
months in mental anguish, resigning from the army every morning, and every
night reversing my decision.

At last, driven to an extremity of doubt, I resolved to take the advice of
impartial judges, selected from different walks of life, and I chose the Maréchal

[1] The Maréchal de Duras.

79

Louis II Phélypeaux, Comte de Pontchartrain. Chancellor of France 1699–1714. French School, 18thC.

de Choiseul, M. de Beauvilliers, the chancellor [Pontchartrain], and M. de La Rochefoucauld. These gentlemen already knew how I was placed and were indignant at the injustice done to me; moreover, the last three were of the Court. This was just what I wished, for I was seeking to know what would be approved by the best people, the men of substance near to the King. Above all, I sought for the kind of advice that would not leave me a prey to uncertainty, rash impulses, or afterthoughts. The verdict, given unanimously and most forcibly, was that I should leave the service. They all said that it would be a shame and indefensible for a man of my rank, who had served with honour and distinction at the head of a fine regiment, to return to battle without regiment, troops, or even a company under his command, and with no other function than to act as aide-de-camp to Saint-Mauris. They added that no duke and peer of my condition should consent to serve as a mere soldier of fortune while other and lesser men gained employment and commands.

It was with no idea of pondering their advice that I had taken them as my arbiters. My course of action was now clear; but although I knew that they were right I still hesitated, and three months passed in a torment of doubt before I could bring myself to act. Finally, I did so, and when it came to procedure, I again followed the advice of the same judges. I was very careful not to display any personal feelings, for I was content to leave to public and especially to military opinion my omission from the list of promotions. The King's anger was inevitable; my friends warned me of it, and I fully expected it. Need I say that I dreaded it? He always took offence when people left his service, calling it desertion, especially where the nobility were concerned. What really nettled him, however, was that a man should leave him for a grievance, and anyone who did so felt his displeasure for a long time, if not for ever. My friends, nevertheless, allowed no comparison between the outcome of resignation which, after all, at my age, would eventually cease to affect me, and the disgrace of continuing to serve under such conditions. At the same time, they thought that respect and prudence demanded that I should act with all possible circumspection.

Accordingly, I wrote a short letter to the King, not in any way complaining, not mentioning my disappointment nor even hinting at regiments and promotions, but merely regretting that my health obliged me to leave his service. I added that my one consolation was my devotion to his person, for I now should have the opportunity of paying my court and attending on him more continuously. My friends approved my letter, and I gave it to the King myself, on the Tuesday in Holy Week, at the door of his study, as he returned from mass. I then went straight to see Chamillart,[1] with whom I was not then acquainted. He was just leaving to go to the council, but I stopped him and told my story, without allowing my disappointment to appear in any way. I then went to Paris, at once. I had already set several of my friends, both men and women, to discover anything, no matter how trivial, that might escape the King on the subject of my letter. For eight days I stayed in Paris and only returned on Easter Tuesday, when I learned that the Chancellor had found the King reading it when he went in and that he had called out angrily, 'Well, sir! Here is another deserter!' and thereupon had read my letter aloud, word by word. On that same evening of Holy Tuesday, as he came out from supper, I attended on him for the first time since he received my letter. I should indeed be ashamed of relating the following trifle were it not that, in the circumstances, it sheds light upon the King's character.

Although the dressing-room was extremely well lit, the chaplain for the day, who held the lighted candle at evening prayers, always handed it to the chief valet to carry before the King when he went to his chair. The latter would then look around the room and call out the name of one of those present and the chief valet would give him the candlestick. This was considered a favour of

[1] Michel Chamillart, Secretary for War. Louis XIV and Mme de Maintenon were devoted to him. Saint-Simon thought him honourable and patriotic but crassly stupid. He said, 'The extraordinary thing was that his very incapacity endeared him to the King who loved correcting and instructing him; so much so indeed that he thought of Chamillart's successes as his own, and forgave him every blunder.'

some importance, thanks to the King's skill in giving weight to the merest trifles. He usually presented the candlestick only to the noblest and most distinguished persons, and sometimes, but very rarely, to lesser men, when their age or position justified the honour. He often gave it to me, hardly ever to ambassadors, except to the nuncio and, latterly, to the Spanish ambassador on some occasions. One removed one's glove, one took a step forward, one held the candlestick during the time of the *coucher*, which was not long; then one handed it back to the chief valet, who selected some other person to take it for the *petit coucher*. On this particular evening, I had purposely kept in the background, and was therefore much astonished, as were the onlookers, to hear my name called. On the following days, I had the candlestick almost as often as before. It was not as though many other men of high rank were not present at that *coucher*; but the King was so much vexed with me that he did not wish others to perceive it.

That, however, was the only favour which I received from him for three consecutive years, and he never lost the smallest opportunity (for want of a greater one) to make me feel how much I had angered him. He never spoke to me nor looked at me, except by chance. He never mentioned my letter nor the fact that I had left his service. He no longer invited me to Marly, and after a few excursions I ceased to give him the satisfaction of refusing to see me there.

I must put an end to this sad tale. Fourteen or fifteen months later, he paid a

View of Paris looking towards the Pont Neuf.

82

visit to Trianon, where each of the Princesses was allowed to name two ladies to be present at his supper, and he never interfered with that privilege. After a time, however, he grew bored with constantly seeing new faces and took to making a list (a very short one it was) of the ladies whom he wished to see at his evening meal. Every day he sent the Duchesse du Lude to notify them.

This particular Trianon visit lasted from a Wednesday to a Saturday—thus three suppers—and Mme de Saint-Simon and I were doing as we usually did when we went to Marly, that is to day, dining with the Chamillarts at l'Étang, with the intention of driving on to Paris to sleep. Just as we were sitting down to table, Mme de Saint-Simon received a message from the Duchesse du Lude, to say that she was on the King's supper list for that day. We were much astonished and immediately returned to Versailles. Mme de Saint-Simon discovered that she was the only lady of approaching her own age at the King's table, although Mme de Chevreuse was there, with Mme de Beauvilliers and the Comtesse de Gramont, as well as three or four duenna kind of persons, the usual palace ladies, and no others. On the Friday, she was again summoned, and thereafter the King always sent for her on his rare visits to Trianon. I soon discovered the reason for this distinction and it struck me as comic. He never sent for Mme de Saint-Simon at Marly, because there husbands had the right to attend when their wives were invited. He intended to show me that his disfavour was for me alone and that my wife was not included.

None the less, we persevered in our usual attendance, but never sought an invitation to Marly. We lived among our friends pleasantly enough and Mme de Saint-Simon continued to enjoy all the entertainments to which the King and Mme la Duchesse de Bourgogne were in the habit of inviting her, although she might not share them with me.

I have chosen to deal with the entire subject here. It is of interest because it throws a light upon the King's nature.

1703

The Fuss over the Offertory

The year ended with another affair in which I played a more prominent role. On certain feast-days when the King went to high mass and vespers a lady of the Court always handed round the bag for the poor. The Queen, or when there was no longer a Queen, the Dauphine, nominated the ladies for each occasion, and in the interval between the two Dauphines, Mme de Maintenon took upon herself the duty of selecting somebody. So long as there were maids of honour, one of them was invariably chosen, but after these posts were abolished, one of the young ladies of the Court was appointed, as I have explained above.

The Lorraines, whose high rank was gained solely by the exploits of their family at the time of the League, and who had adroitly maintained and improved their position by constant care and intrigue, were ever on the watch to grasp the smallest opportunity. They began stealthily to avoid the duty of handing round the bag, so as to make it their right and privilege to abstain and thus, as in their marriages, to insinuate themselves onto the level of the Princesses of the Blood. A long time passed before anyone noticed or suspected what they were at, but at last the Duchesse de Noailles, her daughter, the Duchesse de Guiche, and the Maréchale de Boufflers discovered what was happening. Others gradually began to realize and then to speak of it, and they spoke to me also. Mme de Saint-Simon happened to be in full dress at the King's vespers one day during the Feast of the Conception, when there had been no high mass and Mme la Duchesse de Bourgogne had forgotten to appoint a lady. Mme la Duchesse de Bourgogne had accordingly thrown the bag to her and she had handed it round when it was time for the collection. At that moment, we had no idea that the Lorraine princesses would make it an excuse to abstain when their turns came.

After I had been warned, I determined that the other duchesses should be equally crafty until the occasion arrived to make things level. The Duchesse de Noailles spoke to the Duchesse du Lude, but she, being weak and frightened of everything, merely shrugged her shoulders. There was always some new, ignorant, or poor-spirited, duchess ready to collect from time to time. At last, the Duchesse du Lude was fairly hunted by Mme de Noailles until she agreed to speak to Mme la Duchesse de Bourgogne, who herself was resolved to see just how far the Lorraine princesses intended to go. Accordingly, at the next feast-day, she had the Princesse de Montbazon[1] notified. This lady was young, pretty, often at the Court, and in every way fit to give the lead, but she happened to be in Paris, where it was the fashion to go before the Christmas holidays. She sent her excuses, saying that she was ill, although in fact she was perfectly well, spent half a day in bed, and then went about as usual. After that, nothing more was needed to show the plot. The Duchesse du Lude dared not pursue the matter further, nor did Mme la Duchesse de Bourgogne, although she was piqued, but the result was that from that time onwards no duchess had either will or courage to collect. The other ladies of suitable rank then perceived what was on foot. They felt that the duty of collecting was being left entirely to them and they, too, began to avoid it, so that after a time it fell into all sorts of hands and was sometimes altogether omitted.

The matter was pushed until eventually the King grew so angry that he was on the point of making Mme la Duchesse de Bourgogne take the bag round herself. This I heard from the palace ladies, who wished to prevent us going to Paris, and tried to frighten me by saying that the King had not forgiven me for leaving the service and that the storm would break over my head. Indeed, I was still not going to Marly and was still in the same position regarding him as I have earlier described. They then flattered me by saying that this might well

[1] Her husband the Prince de Montbazon, was a Rohan, belonging to one of the princely families who claimed precedence above French dukes.

The King at prayer. From
one of the King's illuminated
Books of Hours (1688).

prove to be my opportunity. I consented to stay on condition that my wife was not required to collect, but since no such assurance could be given me, we went to Paris. The Maréchale de Coeuvres next refused, on the grounds that she was a grandee of Spain, and the Duchesse de Noailles sent her daughter as a substitute. On another feast-day Chamillart's two daughters,[1] both duchesses, were appointed and both refused although they were unable to leave Versailles. Then the rocket went up.

The King had been exasperated by all this intriguing. He ordered Monsieur le Grand [Louis de Lorraine] to make his daughter collect in church on the first day of the new year, 1704. Early next day I was warned by the Comtesse de Roucy, who had been told by Mme la Duchesse de Bourgogne, who was present at the time, that the King had gone to Mme de Maintenon looking very grave, saying that he was extremely vexed with the dukes because they showed less obedience than the princes, and that although none of the duchesses would collect, Monsieur le Grand had consented for his daughter as soon as he was asked. He added that there were two or three dukes, whose behaviour he

[1] The Duchesses de la Feuillade and de Quintin-Lorges; the latter was Saint-Simon's sister-in-law. He was very fond of her and used to call her 'ma grande biche' (my big sweetheart).

would never forget. Mme la Duchesse de Bourgogne would not name them out loud, but whispered them to Mme de Dangeau and a moment later begged her to warn me to be wary. This we heard at the Chancellor's house, he being a third party to the conversation, and neither of us had any doubt that I was one of the three dukes mentioned. I then told them what had happened and asked the chancellor for his advice, which was to do nothing whilst I was still in the dark.

Very early next day I went to see Chamillart. He told me that at Mme de Maintenon's apartment on the previous evening, even before he had had time to open his portfolio, the King had asked him angrily what he thought of dukes who were less dutiful than princes, and had added hastily that Mlle d'Armagnac had agreed to take the collection. Chamillart replied that such matters never reached his department and that he had only heard of the affair on the evening before. He knew, he said, that the dukes were distressed because the King blamed them for not guessing his wishes, and that the princes were delighted at receiving credit for what the dukes would gladly have done had the King spoken as frankly to them as he had done to Monsieur le Grand.

The King then muttered to himself and said that it was very strange, but since I had left his service I thought only of my rank and privileges and of picking quarrels with everybody; that I was the chief instigator of this pother, and that he had a good mind to send me so far that I should be prevented from annoying him for a long time to come. Chamillart answered that I concerned myself in such matters because I was abler and more intelligent than the rest, and that since the King himself had granted me my rank and precedence he should be pleased to see me striving to maintain them. Then, smiling a little, he had added soothingly that of course the King could send anyone where he pleased, but that it seemed scarcely worth while when a single word would have the desired effect. This did not mollify the King. He merely answered that what had annoyed him most of all was the refusal of Chamillart's daughters-in-law (especially the younger), through their husbands and apparently at my suggestion. To this Chamillart replied that one of his sons was absent and the other had merely made his wife conform. The King, however, still went on grumbling until at last they settled down to work. Chamillart advised me to speak to the King at the earliest possible opportunity about the dukes' point of view regarding the church collections, and then to say something on my own behalf.

After I left Chamillart, I went to consult the Chancellor. He too advised me to see the King without delay. He said that to wait would merely increase his irritation, and that in speaking to him I must be careful not to get angry. He bade me have faith in the outcome, ask for an interview in the study, and if the King stopped and wished to hear me then and there, to say that I could see he did not wish to grant me an audience then, that I hoped it might be for another time, and instantly retire. It was indeed no small matter for me, young and out of favour, as I was, to go and engage the King in conversation.

I usually did nothing without the advice of the Duc de Beauvilliers. Mme de

LEFT Trial of coquettes by ladies of virtue.

87

Saint-Simon, however, did not wish me to hear it now, for she was sure that he would tell me to write, which would have been less tactful and less effective than speaking; besides which, letters are never answered. She also thought that Beauvilliers' advice might embarrass me if it were contrary to that of the two ministers. I agreed, and went to wait for the King to pass on his way from dinner to his study, where I asked permission to follow him. Without answering, he made a sign for me to enter and walked over to one of the window-recesses.

Just as I was about to speak, I saw Fagon[1] and other members of the household crossing the room, so I waited until they had gone and I was alone with the King. Then I told him that I had heard he was vexed with me in the matter of the church collection, that I was deeply anxious to please him and could not bear to delay in entreating him to hear my side. At this he looked very stern and said nothing. 'Sire', I continued, 'it is true that after the princesses had refused to hand the bag, I avoided the duty for Mme de Saint-Simon in the hope that all the duchesses would abstain, and some of them, indeed, I restrained, thinking that would be Your Majesty's desire'. 'But', interrupted the King angrily, 'refusing the Duchesse de Bourgogne is failing in respect. It is refusing Us!' I answered that the manner in which the ladies were appointed gave us reason to believe that Mme la Duchesse de Bourgogne had no hand in the matter, and that the Duchesse du Lude or, more frequently, the first gentlewoman-in-waiting chose whom she pleased. 'But, Monsieur', the King again interrupted in the same haughty, angry tone, 'you have been speechifying, have you not?' 'No, Sire.' 'What? Are you saying that you have not talked? . . .' And he ran on in this furious manner until I, also, had the courage to interrupt in a voice louder than his own. 'No, Sire', I said, 'I have already explained, and had I said any such things I should have told Your Majesty, just as I have admitted avoiding the collection for my wife and restraining the other duchesses. I always believed, and with good reason, that since Your Majesty expressed no wishes in this matter, you were either ignorant of what was happening, or knowing, did not care. Let me entreat you most earnestly to believe that had any of the dukes, more especially myself, any reason to think that Your Majesty desired it in the very least, all the duchesses would have been eager to take the collection, and Mme de Saint-Simon with them, on all feast-days. If that were not enough to show my anxiety to please you, I would gladly have handed the bag myself, like any country churchwarden.

'How, Sire', I continued, 'could Your Majesty suppose that we should think any duty beneath us that was performed in your presence, especially one which the duchesses and princesses do every day in the Paris churches, as a matter of course? The truth is, Sire, that the princes are so quick to snatch special privileges that we are obliged to be on the watch, particularly in this matter of refusing to hand round the bag'. 'But they did not refuse', said the King, somewhat mollified, 'they were never asked'. 'Indeed, Sire', I answered

[1] The King's doctor.

88

Guy Crescent Fagon, Chief
Physician to the Royal
Family. By Fiquet after
Rigaud.

stoutly, 'they did refuse. Not the Lorraines, but others (by whom I meant
Mme de Montbazon). The Duchesse du Lude may so have informed you, or
she should have done, for that was what decided us to act. We know that Your
Majesty is plagued by discussion and decisions and we hoped that our evading
the collection would suffice to prevent the princes from taking an advantage. As
I have already said, Sire, we believed that Your Majesty neither knew nor cared
since you made no sign.' 'Oh! very well, Monsieur', said the King quietly. 'The
matter will not arise again because I have already told Monsieur le Grand that

I wish his daughter to collect on New Year's Day, and I am glad that she sets the example, for I love her father well.'

Then, looking straight at the King, I entreated him, for my own sake and that of the other dukes, to believe that he had no more dutiful subjects than ourselves. For we knew that all our dignities came from him and that all our lives were enriched by his bounty. He was our King and universal benefactor, the absolute master of our rank and privileges; it was for him alone to raise or lower them, to treat them as his own, in the hollow of his hand. Then, most graciously, with an air wholly kind and gentle, he said several times that that was a very proper way of thinking and speaking, and that he was well pleased with me. I seized the occasion to tell him how much it grieved me that no matter how hard I tried to please him, some people never failed to do me the worst of ill turns, which I confessed I could not forgive. I added that I could not help but suspect Monsieur le Grand, for he had not forgiven me since the affair of the Princesse d'Harcourt.[1] 'But', I said, 'Your Majesty saw then that I spoke the truth, whereas Monsieur le Grand did not. I think that Your Majesty remembers, so I shall not weary you by repetition.'

The King answered that he remembered perfectly, and I believe that he would have listened to me patiently had I repeated the story, for his manner was both kind and considerate, but I did not think it wise to detain him any longer. I therefore concluded by imploring him to be so gracious as to tell me if ever he heard ill spoken of me, for he would see that such a favour would be followed by a justification, or else by a confession and a plea for forgiveness. After I had finished speaking, he remained silent for a moment, as though waiting to see whether I wished to say more. Then he left me with a slight, but most gracious bow, saying that all was now well and that he was satisfied. I retired, bowing very low, feeling mightily relieved and at the same time most thankful that I had managed to put the whole matter before him, about the dukes, the princes, and especially about Monsieur le Grand. The fact that the King remembered the affair of the Princesse d'Harcourt and his silence over Monsieur le Grand convinced me that it was to the latter I owed what I had once again circumvented.

As I left the King's study looking well content, I encountered Monsieur le Duc and some other gentlemen waiting to attend at the King's *botter*.[1] They stared hard as I passed, for they were surprised by the length of my audience, which had lasted for half an hour. It was exceedingly rare for private persons to be granted any audience at all, and none lasted more than half the time of mine. I then went to my apartment and relieved Mme de Saint-Simon of her anxiety.

[1] An earlier quarrel about precedence between the Princesse d'Harcourt (a Lorrainer) and the Duchesse de Rohan, in which Mme de Saint-Simon had innocently become involved.

[1] The ceremony of putting on the King's boots.

'The Song-book' by
B. Picart, 1708.

1703

Madame de Charlus

The Marquise de Charlus, Mézières's sister, and mother of the Marquis de
Levis who has since been created duke and peer, died old and rich. She always
got herself up like an old-clothes woman and encountered many snubs because
people failed to recognize her, which she thought monstrously ill-bred. As a
relief from more serious matters, I propose to tell an anecdote about her of a
very different kind.

Mme de Charlus was greedy and a great gambler. She used to spend whole
nights wildly doubling against increasing odds, for at that time they played
lansquenet for high stakes, at the house of Mme la Princesse de Conti.[1] One
Friday night, Mme de Charlus was supping there with a large company. She
was ill-dressed as usual, but for once, most fashionably, wearing one of those
headdresses called commodes that were not fastened in any way to the ladies'
heads. They were vastly high constructions and were put on or removed just as
men put on and take off their wigs and nightcaps.

Mme de Charlus was sitting next to Le Tellier, the Archbishop of Rheims.
As she was removing the top of a boiled egg she leaned forward to take the salt
and accidentally stuck her head into the flame of a neighbouring candle. The
Archbishop, seeing her on fire, hurled himself at the headdress and flung it on
to the ground, whereupon Mme de Charlus, in amazement and fury at finding
herself thus dis-wigged for no apparent reason, threw her egg into the

[1] The Dowager Princesse de
Conti, daughter of the King
by Mlle de la Vallière.

91

Archbishop's face, and it ran down all over him. He did nothing but laugh, and the entire company was in fits at seeing the ancient grey, dirty head of Mme de Charlus, and the omelet she had made on the Archbishop. Especially comic was her rage, and abuse, for she imagined that she had been insulted and would hear no excuse, and then suddenly perceived that she had been left bald before all the world. By this time, the headdress had been burnt and Mme la Princesse de Conti had sent for another, but before it could be placed on her head there was plenty of time to contemplate her charms, and for her to continue with her furious protests.

Gambling was again forbidden, under threat of severe penalties.

RIGHT Bleeding, the remedy for every ill. 'Use as a precaution. There is no need to reproach oneself if one dies according to the rules.'

FAR RIGHT A surgeon and his instruments. Cartoon.

1704

Saint-Simon is Bled

About this time I met with an unfortunate accident and allowed myself to be bled because the blood was rushing to my head. The operation seemed to me vastly well done. During the night, however, I felt a pain in my arm which Ledran, the well-known surgeon, who had performed the blood-letting, assured me was due to a tight bandage. To make a long story short, in two days' time the arm had swollen bigger than my thigh and I was in great pain and feverish. They kept me for two days longer with applications over the wound to draw out the poison, following the advice of the most renowned Paris surgeons. M. de Lauzun, rightly thinking that I was very ill indeed, insisted upon my seeing Maréchal, the King's surgeon, and himself went to Versailles to ask the King's permission, for without it Maréchal could not come to Paris and rarely slept away from the King. He was allowed to come and to spend the night and even to remain with me, and as soon as he arrived, he opened the arm from end to end. It was high time, for the abscess had spread to the body and was manifesting itself by fits of shivering. Maréchal stayed for two days, then came to see me every day, and afterwards, every two days. The skill and speed with which he performed the operation and dressings, and the pains he took to make me comfortable, pass all description. He made this accident an excuse to speak to the King on my behalf, who overwhelmed me with kindness after my recovery. A short time before this happened, Chamillart had managed to mend matters somewhat between us and what Maréchal said finally healed the breach.

On the day that I was bled I had strained my arm slightly, to which I attributed my accident, and during the course of the operation I asked Ledran to bleed me again, so that I might not lose the use of it. Maréchal and Fagon

¹The Comte de Marsan,
Charles de Lorraine-
Armagnac.

thought that a tendon might have been damaged, but they put weights upon
my arm so that it remained its natural length and I felt no ill-effects. Every day
and night the best surgeons of Paris were by my bed, relieving one another by
turns. Tribouleau, surgeon to the French guards and a man with a high
reputation, said that he supposed M. de Marsan¹ must be a dear friend of mine,
for he had stopped him in the street to inquire after me and seemed greatly
concerned to hear every detail. The fact was that he was after my governorship
[of Blaye] and had actually applied for it; but the King asked him whether I
had no son, which silenced and embarrassed him. Chamillart, in case I should
not recover, had secured the post for my son without being asked, and lost no
time in doing so. I afterwards pretended to know nothing of M. de Marsan's
manoeuvre. In any case I had no truck with him, nor with any other of the
Lorraines.

The Embassy to Rome

For the past five years, Cardinal de Janson had been in the charge of the King's affairs in Rome. He had filled the post with dignity, although more as a good Frenchman than as a cardinal, which had pleased neither the Pope nor his Court. Indeed, he had not been on good terms with the Pope, and was thoroughly disapproved of by the Court which always expects obedience from everybody. Cardinal de Janson had been seriously ill for some time and had been asking for leave to return, which was finally granted him, but there being no suitable cardinal to replace him, the Abbé de la Trémoïlle was made chargé d'affaires after his departure, for want of a better man. Then came the question of sending an ambassador as soon as possible, for none had been appointed since the Duc de Chaulnes's sudden mission to attend the election of a new Pope, after the death of Innocent XI.

It was the Nuncio Gualterio who first broached the subject to me. He was a Frenchman at heart and it was of great importance to him to be able to rely upon the friendship of the French Ambassador. But I was only thirty years of age at that time, and the idea of my being appointed an ambassador seemed utterly fantastic in view of the King's known aversion to young men and his determination never to employ them. Callières, the King's secretary, also mentioned it, and I said the same to him, pointing out the difficulty of having any success in Rome without becoming a bankrupt in the process, and adding that in my situation the embassy was unlikely to bring further promotion.

On Tuesday, March 11th, just eight days after the nuncio had spoken, about one o'clock in the afternoon, he entered my room with arms outstretched. Beaming with pleasure and, hugging and kissing me, he begged me to lock the door and the door of the ante-room as well, lest anyone should notice his liveries. He then informed me that he was as glad as could be, because I was indeed about to be appointed ambassador to Rome. I made him repeat this twice, for I could not believe my ears, and I told him that his wish must be father to his thought, because the whole thing seemed to me impossible. He then joyfully and impatiently swore me to secrecy, saying that Torcy had just told him in confidence that the thing had been decided at that morning's council, but that the King had forbidden him to announce it until after the next meeting. If one of the portraits in my study had opened its lips to speak, I could not have been more surprised. Gualterio did all that he could to persuade me to consent; then, it being time for the dinner to which he was bidden, he left me and I went instantly to tell the news to Mme de Saint-Simon, who was as much amazed as myself.

I must admit to feeling flattered at being chosen so unexpectedly, at my age, and for so important a post, for no one had recommended me, and at that time I had no acquaintance, not even the slightest, with Torcy. M. de Beauvilliers was far too cautious to have proposed me without first ascertaining whether my circumstances would permit the expense, the Chancellor was out of range, and Chamillart would have done nothing without my consent, besides which, being on none too good terms with Torcy, he would never have risked interfering in his department.

After the King's death, Torcy and I became firm friends, so that I was able to ask him how I came to be chosen. He protested that he was ignorant of the matter, save that at the time of the Council the King had already decided to send someone, and was weary of aspirants for a dukedom which he did not intend to create. He had interrupted Torcy as soon as the latter had begun to read the dispatches from Rome, saying that the time had come to appoint an envoy, that he wanted a duke, and that all that remained to do was to read down the list until he came to a suitable name. He then took a small almanac and

Jean Baptiste Colbert, Marquis de Torcy. Postmaster General, member of the King's privy council 1691–1715. He censored private letters and showed the King any that seemed dangerous, or scandalous, or even a good joke. Engraving by M. Dossier, 1711.

began to read out the names. My seniority soon brought him to mine, whereat he paused and said, 'What about this one? He is young, but he is capable, etc.' Monseigneur wished for d'Antin and therefore said nothing, but M. le Duc de Bourgogne supported me, and so did the Chancellor and M. de Beauvilliers. Torcy commended their judgment, but suggested continuing down the list. Chamillart thought no one better could be found. The King thereupon closed the almanac, saying that there seemed little point in pursuing the matter further since he had already decided on me, and he ordered them to say nothing for the time being, until he should desire them to have me informed. That was all that happened. Torcy went on reading his dispatches, and there was no more argument. This was told me more than ten years later by that honest man, who had no possible reason for concealing anything.

Beauvilliers and Chamillart each separately examined my circumstances, debts and revenues as compared to the expenses and emoluments of an embassy. The former they learned from our account books, which Mme de Saint-Simon fetched and considered with them; the rest they computed by guesswork. Both gentlemen concluded that I should accept. The duke was satisfied that I could afford the post without being ruined and said further, that if I refused it, especially after having left the service, the King would never forgive me. He would henceforward regard me as an idler by preference, would be sure to make me feel his displeasure on every possible occasion, and would refuse me things that I might really need. All of which would be more harmful to my interests, present and future, than any failure in an embassy.

In the end they did so persuade me, and I accepted. That is to say, I resolved to accept, and with great pleasure, as I am bound to admit. As for Mme de Saint-Simon, wiser and more prudent than I, and sad at the idea of separation from her family, she also gave her consent, but less gladly. Here I cannot deny myself the pleasure of relating what these three ministers, each separately and of their own accord, said to me of that young woman of twenty-seven (as she then was), whom they had known well in Court and family affairs, for they had been our advisers at every step of our married lives. They all three most earnestly counselled me to have no secrets from her in all the embassy matters, to seat her at the end of my table when I read and wrote my dispatches, and to consult her judgment in everything. I have rarely listened to advice so gladly, and I hold it an equal merit in her that she both deserved their praises and lived ever afterwards as though she had not heard them. But hear them she did, from my lips, and afterwards from theirs.

As it happened, I had no chance of following their counsel in Rome, for I never went there, but I had practised it at home long before that time, and for the rest of our lives I continued to hide nothing from her. I cannot resist adding that I never found advice more wise, prudent, and useful than hers, and that she saved me from many disasters, both small and great. I took advantage of it in everything, without reserve, and it was of inestimable benefit to me in my personal conduct as well as in the part that I played in foreign affairs, which, during the last years of the King's life and throughout the Regency, was not insignificant. She provided a most rare and sweet contrast to those idle women who are forbidden to accompany ambassadors or to share their secrets, and whose chief occupation is to entertain prodigally and run up accounts. How different are the latter from those few able women who make their influence truly felt, but with perfect discretion, very quietly and gently, and who, far from being self-righteous, always seem unconscious of the justice of their opinions throughout a lifetime of modest amiability and virtue.

The Duchesse de Saint-Simon, wife of the Memoirist.

Notwithstanding the King's injunction, it gradually became known that the choice had fallen on me. Torcy, however, still said nothing, and I scarcely knew what to tell my friends as I was dragged from one meeting of the Council to another. We returned to Versailles; we went on another excursion to Marly; people ceased to be guarded; indeed, at one of the balls, M. de Monaco, the son of an earlier ambassador, offered to provide me with what remained in Rome of his father's furniture and carriages, and all the time that we were dancing, Mme de Saint-Simon and I heard people exclaim, 'There is the new ambassador', or 'the new ambassador's wife'. The situation became so embarrassing that I implored Torcy (through a friend) to put an end to the affair in one way or another. He felt the impropriety of the thing itself, and the awkwardness for me, but did not dare to hurry the King. The real reason for the delay was that some hope had arisen of persuading the Pope to accept the Abbé de la Trémoïlle, and to press on with the nominations for the nineteen empty hats,[1] a matter that was setting all Rome in a fever, and that could not long be postponed on account of the great number of the vacancies. Yet postponed it was, so that in spite of not having been announced, my own nomination gradually became public property both in Rome and Paris.

When we were at Marly, M. le Duc de Bourgogne secretly congratulated me, even although we were not then on familiar terms. He thought that there had been too long a delay, and when I answered modestly, he encouraged me, saying that I had better begin to train myself for foreign affairs and high offices. He added that he was very glad I had resolved to accept the post, especially as the King would never have forgiven me had I refused.

Whilst I was thus in the limelight, the Comtesse de la Marck died of the smallpox, in Paris. She was the daughter of the Duc de Rohan, and a very dear friend of Mme de Saint-Simon, for they had been school-fellows at the same convent. Her goodness made her deeply regretted and Mme de Saint-Simon wept bitterly for her; I myself was much moved. Five or six hours after learning of this death, we had to go a ball, although the eyes of Mme de Saint-Simon and her sister were red and swollen with weeping, and no excuses to offer. The King had little understanding of the laws of nature or the sentiments of the heart; his own were directed entirely towards affairs of state and the most trivial pleasures. He made the Duchesse de Duras dance at Marly in the first days of her widowhood, and we have already seen how, when Monsieur died, he showed little consideration or respect for the most honoured conventions.

To end this long-drawn-out story of my Roman embassy, matters dragged along in this fashion until the middle of April, when I at last learned how my fate had been decided. We were then at Marly, lodged in the same pavilion as Chamillart, whom I had begged, when he returned from the council, to come to my apartment before going up to his own, and to tell me privately what was to be done with me. He accordingly came to me in Mme de Saint-Simon's room, where we awaited him impatiently. 'You are going to be much relieved', he said, 'and I am very sorry, for the King is not now sending an ambassador to

[1] The nomination of nineteen Cardinals.

98

Plans for the interior and exterior of the Marly pavilions by Charles Le Brun.

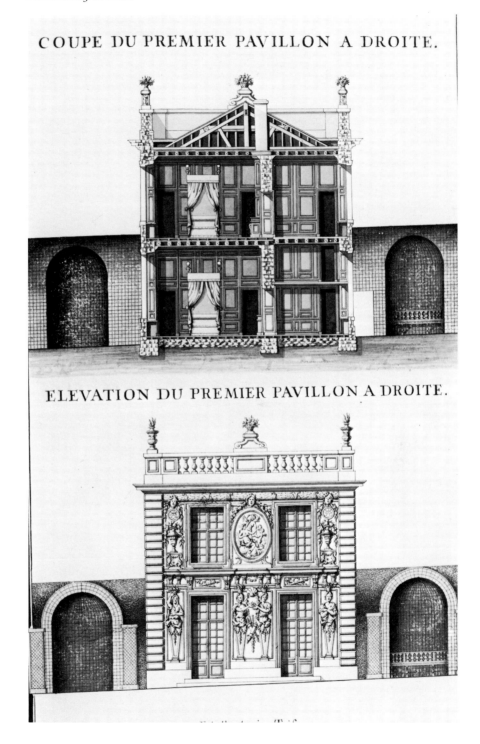

COUPE DU PREMIER PAVILLON A DROITE.

ELEVATION DU PREMIER PAVILLON A DROITE.

Rome. The Pope has at last consented to make the Abbé de la Trémoïlle a cardinal, and to proceed with the other nominations, which have been so long delayed by his refusal to include the Abbé. The new cardinal will have charge of the King's affairs, without any ambassador'. Mme de Saint-Simon was indeed delighted. It almost seems as though she foresaw the discredit into which the King's Italian affairs would fall, and all the subsequent financial embarrassments, as well as the grievous situation to which these misfortunes would have reduced us had we gone to Rome.

1706

The Duc de Vendôme

At that time, the Court and Paris witnessed the most extraordinary spectacle. M. de Vendôme had not left Italy since he had succeeded the Maréchal de Villeroy after the disastrous affair at Cremona.[1] His victories (such as they were), the fortresses he had taken, the power he had seized, his borrowed reputation, his unbelievable success with the King, his powerful friends, all made him anxious to return to the Court and assume a brilliant role which, in the event, surpassed anything that he had the right to expect. But before describing the arrival of one who was to cast so strange a spell and whom, until now, I have mentioned only in passing, it would be well to describe the man himself, and even to include some details of a shocking nature because they were characteristic of him.

He was of ordinary height, rather stout, but strong, hearty, and active. He appeared handsome and well-bred, had the grand manner, and was naturally graceful in speech and bearing. Born with an intellect that was never cultivated, quick of tongue, with an audacity that gradually turned to downright rudeness, he had a vast knowledge of the world, the Court and its various personalities, and, beneath an air of carelessness, hid a very keen eye to his own advantage. Above all he was a most polished courtier and managed to escape the consequences of his worst excesses because of the King's respect for his noble birth.[2] When it suited his convenience he was artfully courteous, but with measure and discrimination, and was insolent beyond all bounds when he could be so with impunity. With the common people he affected a hearty familiarity that fed his vanity and made him popular with the vulgar. At heart he was eaten up with a pride that governed all his actions. As he rose in rank and favour, his arrogance and self-will rose in proportion, to a point where he became impervious to advice of any kind, and refused to listen to any but a very small number of intimates and to his servants. Praise, flattery, and, finally, adoration were the only channels by which one might approach this demi-god,

[1] On February 1st, 1702, Villeroy had been surprised and taken prisoner by Prince Eugene at Cremona. Yet despite their commander's absence the French garrison succeeded in throwing back the Imperial army.

[2] Vendôme's father was a bastard of Henri IV.

Louis Joseph, Duc de Vendôme (1707). This drawing belonged to Horace Walpole, at Strawberry Hill.

who flaunted ridiculous opinions, with which no one dared to disagree, let alone to contradict.

Better than any man living he knew and took advantage of the servile instincts of the French, and gradually accustomed his junior officers and then the whole army to call him 'Monseigneur' and 'Votre Altesse'. As no one opposed him, this gangrene spread to lieutenant-generals and other distinguished persons, who followed one another's example like sheep. Not one of them dared to address him otherwise, so that after a time the improper title became a right and anyone who had ventured to do differently would have seemed deliberately insulting.

It is most extraordinary that the really filthy nature of his private life never seemed to disturb the King, who, although he himself had been free with women, was horrified at the idea of unnatural vice. Yet there is no doubt that he knew of Vendôme's perversions. Vendôme himself was quite frank about them, and behaved as though he were conducting trivial and normal love-affairs. His servants and junior officers pandered to his tastes and were known to do so, and many used them to curry favour, in the hope of gaining promotion. I have already described the blatant manner with which he twice retired to take the grand cure.[1] Indeed, he was the first man who ever dared to obtain leave for that express purpose, so that his condition was a general topic at the Court, for the King himself set the example by condoning conduct which he would never have tolerated in one of the Sons of France.

M. de Vendôme's idleness was inconceivable. More than once he was nearly captured by the enemy because he refused to leave headquarters that were comfortable, but isolated, and he often hazarded the success of an entire campaign because he would not move from a camp when once he had settled there. In the field he saw little for himself, relying for information on his staff, whom he more often than not disbelieved, indeed, his daily routine, which he would not alter, scarcely allowed him to be more active. He was excessively filthy in his habits and boasted of them; the fools around him said that he was a child of nature. His bed was full of his dogs and bitches, that sometimes pupped beside him, and he relieved the needs of nature wherever he happened to be. One of his favourite sayings was that everyone acted in the same way but had not the honesty to admit it, and he upheld this proposition one day to la Princesse de Conti, the daintiest and most fastidious person in the world.

When he was with the army, his custom was to rise rather late and at once to take his seat upon his chaise-percée, and in this curious position he wrote his dispatches and issued his orders for the day. Anyone who had business with him, even general officers and distinguished visitors, found this the best time to talk with him. He gradually accustomed the entire army to that indecent habit and, still sitting there, would consume an enormous breakfast with two or three boon companions, eating, talking, and issuing orders, with a large audience of bystanders. He evacuated copiously and the pot was carried away in front of the entire company. On the days when he shaved, the same pot was used. He called this a good honest custom, worthy of the Romans, and a fine contrast to the finical ways of some other army commanders. When he had finished, he would dress and play piquet or hombre for high stakes, then if it were really necessary to make a reconnaissance he would mount his horse, but once he had given the order to return, the day's work was over for him. He supped hugely with his intimates, for he was a great eater, no judge of good food, but with a monstrous fondness for fish, and he preferred the stale and often stinking to the fresh. His table conversation consisted in airing his opinions and quarrelling, while from all around came praises, flattery, and adulation, from morning to night, and from every quarter.

[1] The mercury cure for syphilis.

He never forgave criticism, wished to be considered the finest soldier of the age, and spoke slightingly and improperly of Prince Eugène and all the other commanders. It was an offence to contradict him. The common soldiers and lower officers adored him because he was familiar with them and allowed them to take liberties in order to win popularity; but he lost credit in other directions because of his unbearable arrogance towards anyone of rank or breeding. When he was in Italy he treated the distinguished men who came to treat with him in the same insolent manner.

That was how the celebrated Alberoni came to make his fortune. His master, the Duke of Parma, having matters to negotiate with M. de Vendôme, first sent the Bishop of Parma, who was shocked beyond measure at being received by the duke seated upon a chaise-percée, and was still more so when the latter stood up and turned round to wipe himself. He returned to Parma without further ado, declaring that nothing would induce him to have further dealings with such a monster. Alberoni was a gardener's son, who, being clever beyond the average, had taken minor orders so as to gain an entrée into circles where a peasant's smock would have been unacceptable. He was a clown, but he amused the Duke of Parma, who thought him sufficiently intelligent to be capable of employment. The sight of M. de Vendôme upon his chaise-percée was hardly likely to affect him unduly, and therefore the Duke of Parma decided to make him finish the work which the bishop had left undone.

Alberoni had no dignity to lose. He knew Vendôme for what he was and resolved to please him at any personal cost, in order to advance his master's affairs and himself into the bargain. He was received in the usual way by M. de Vendôme and leavened his arguments with much flattery and praise, and with several jokes that made the general laugh even louder than usual. Vendôme, behaving in exactly the same way as to the bishop, eventually rose and began to wipe himself without ceremony; but when Alberoni saw the exposed portions of the ducal posterior, he exclaimed, '*Oh! culo de angelo!*' and rushed to embrace them. Nothing could have served him better than this despicable action, for the Duke of Parma was constantly having to negotiate with the Duc de Vendôme, and when he saw how well Alberoni had begun, continued to employ him regularly as his envoy. Alberoni made himself pleasant to M. de Vendôme's household and managed to prolong his visits. He took the trouble to make cheese soups and other special dishes which the general enjoyed exceedingly, and was often asked to share the meal.

Gradually, he became so comfortable in that household that he began to imagine himself doing better there than at the Court of Parma, where his qualities, as he thought, were not fully appreciated. He accordingly acted so as to get himself dismissed and persuaded M. de Vendôme that he had sacrificed his whole future for the latter's sake. He thus changed masters and, shortly afterwards, without relinquishing his post as court jester and concoctor of exotic soups and stews, he began to pry into M. de Vendôme's correspondence with so much success that he became principal private secretary and confidant.

Drawings of the entrance to
the King's privy.

The rest of M. de Vendôme's staff were not pleased and at last jealousy rose to such a pitch that Magnani, one of the other secretaries, chased him with a stick for more than a hundred yards, before the whole army. M. de Vendôme was annoyed, but did nothing about the matter. Alberoni, however, was not the man to give up for so little in a good cause. He managed to turn the incident to good account with his master, who liked him all the more for it, made him a party to all his plans and treated him thenceforth as a trusted friend rather than a servant, so that even the intimate circle and the smartest officers had to reckon with him.

I have already described how artfully M. de Vendôme fed the King with exaggerated reports of his plans and actions in the field. Small skirmishes were blown up into battles, real, but indecisive battles were proclaimed as victories with an effrontery that defied contradiction. A continual succession of couriers brought news, and the King was pleased to be duped by them and believed all that Vendôme desired, for he was supported and praised by the inner council, opposed by no one, and protected, as I have said, by that constant stream of couriers from Italy. Nothing was heard of him, except the acclamations which his rank and influence evoked from the army. In such favourable circumstances, he decided that, since Prince Eugene was in Vienna, the time had come for him to return and harvest the fruits of his labour, and he received permission to visit the Court.

Vendôme came straight to Marly, where we also were, on February 12th. There was an appalling racket when he arrived, postillions, chair-carriers, and all the court footmen left their posts to surround his coach. He had hardly reached his rooms before the entire Court came flocking to welcome him. The Princes of the Blood were the first to arrive, they who had been so piqued by his promotion above them in the service and by many other things. I leave you to imagine whether the bastards kept him waiting. Ministers rushed to attend on him, and so many of the courtiers that only ladies remained in the salon. M. de Beauvilliers was away at Vaucresson; as for me, I was content to observe events and did not go to adore the idol.

The King and Monseigneur sent for him, and when he had been allowed to change his coat he was almost borne upon the shoulders of the crowd to the salon, where Monseigneur had the music stopped in order to greet him. The King was with Mme de Maintenon, working with Chamillart. He summoned Vendôme again, and came out of the little inner room into the large study, embraced him many times, spent several minutes talking to him, and said that he would see him at leisure on the following day. Indeed, he did then converse with him for more than two hours in Mme de Maintenon's apartment.

Chamillart carried him off to L'Etang on the pretext of working with him in more peaceful surroundings, and gave a most magnificent fête that lasted for two whole days. Following this example, Pontchartrain, Torcy, and many of the greatest nobles thought fit to treat him in the same way, and outrivalled one another in entertainment. People schemed to secure him; they intrigued to be

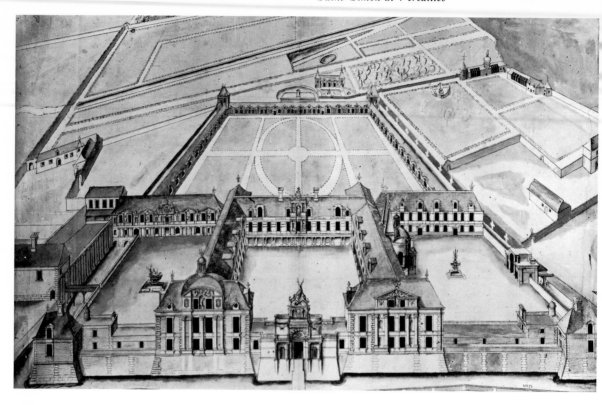

invited where he was asked. No triumph ever equalled his, and he made fresh conquests every day. It is not too much to say that everyone else seemed to pale beside him; Princes of the Blood, ministers, the high nobility, served only to set off his brilliance. Even the King himself appeared to rule for the sole purpose of raising him still higher. They flocked after him to Versailles and to Paris, when he went, ostensibly to the opera, but really to bask in his incredible popularity. He was mobbed in the streets. His presence was advertised in advance, the entire house was sold out, packed so that it was stiflingly hot, and the price of the seats was doubled as for a first performance.

Vendôme received these tributes with apparent calm, but inwardly he was astonished at the enthusiasm. He had never intended to stay long at the Court, but fearing lest his popularity fade, and in order to make himself precious, he asked for permission to go to Anet between two Marly excursions. He therefore spent only two days at Versailles, broken by a night's visit to Meudon, in order to please Monseigneur. No sooner was he established at Anet with a few boon companions, than Versailles became a desert and the village of Anet crammed to the very attics. Monseigneur went there to hunt, as did the Princes of the Blood and the ministers. Anet became the height of fashion and everyone made it a point of honour to go there. Vendôme's pride was swollen by so much adulation; he behaved towards the company as though they were his courtiers, and they

The Château of Anet, home of the Duc de Vendôme. Watercolour.

106

were base enough to accept this treatment without complaint, saying it was country manners. Even the King, who usually took offence if he were neglected for any reason whatsoever, delighted at Versailles' being abandoned for Anet, and continually inquired whether people had been there, or intended to go.

Everything points to the fact that Vendôme was quite deliberately made into a hero, that he realized what was happening and took advantage of his situation, for he seized on that moment to renew his demand to rank as commander-in-chief over all the marshals of France. He had been set up as the god of war; how could he be refused command over the marshals? A warrant as marshal-general was granted to him secretly, drawn up in the same terms as that which was given to M. de Turenne, since whom none had claimed such rank. It was not a suitable position for M. de Vendôme, nor even for M. du Maine, and was only offered in order to avoid something which the King never intended to grant. It was a temporary expedient to provide some distinction for a man with royal blood in his veins. Vendôme, however, insisted that his original claim to superiority over the marshals should be written into the letters patent, as granted to M. de Turenne. I do not know how the Maréchal de Villeroy got wind of this proposal, but he certainly heard of it in time to remonstrate with the King who, by then, was ready to listen to reason. The Maréchal was in favour, he won his point, and M. de Vendôme was informed that nothing new would be added to the warrant, which would in every way correspond with that granted to M. de Turenne. He then took umbrage and refused it, a most rash action, but M. de Vendôme well knew with whom he had to deal and the power of his friends. He had been categorically refused the authority to command the marshals who were appointed after he had taken over the armies in Italy, but he disobeyed the King's repeated orders and avoided the consequences with remarkable dexterity. It now seemed to him that it had been a longer step to this appointment as marshal-general than it would be to the granting of his original demand. Indeed, events proved him right, during that very same year.

His brother, Philippe de Vendôme, the Grand Prieur,[1] was out of favour and went to Anet to seek M. de Vendôme's help, although they had not been on good terms. Vendôme offered to present him to the King and to obtain for him a pension of ten thousand écus, but the impudent fellow would not be satisfied with anything less than a return to Italy and command of an army. He left Anet in a vile temper, and when Vendôme went back to the Court, he returned to rage and fume at his château at Clichy.

This Philippe de Vendôme had all his brother's vices. In debauch he was even worse, since all was fair game to him. Moreover he had the advantage in that for the past thirty years he had never been to bed at night without being carried there dead drunk, a custom to which he adhered faithfully for the rest of his life. He had none of the qualities of a good general, for his known cowardice was accompanied by a most sickening rashness. More conceited even than M. de Vendôme, his manner verged on insolence, and for that very reason he saw none but underlings. Liar, swindler, rogue, thief (as he demonstrated by his

[1] Le Grand Prieur de France. The highest national rank conferred by the Order of Malta.

management of his brother's affairs), dishonest to the very marrow of his bones, a perfect coxcomb, and extraordinarily servile and flattering to those whose help he needed, ready to do and put up with anything for the sake of money, withal the most dissolute, and the greatest waster in the world. He had much wit and, in his youth, a fine figure with a singularly handsome countenance. In short, he was the vilest, the most contemptible, and at the same time, the most dangerous creature imaginable.

1706

My Relationship with M. le Duc d'Orléans

Although the time has not yet come to speak of the character of M. le Duc d'Orléans, I can no longer refrain from describing the terms on which I stood with him after our reconciliation, which I have mentioned elsewhere. His friendship and his trust in me were great, and I always held him in sincere affection. I saw him alone in his study almost every afternoon at Versailles. He would reproach me if I were unable to visit him regularly, and he always allowed me to speak freely. No subjects were barred. He discussed everything with me and liked me to conceal nothing about himself. I saw him only at Versailles and Marly, that is to say at the Court, I never called on him in Paris. For one thing, I seldom went there, and when I did go for one, or, very occasionally, for two nights, I had duties or business to transact. His pleasures, the company that he kept, and the life which he led in the city, did not attract me, and I had settled from the very beginning to have nothing to do with anyone from the Palais Royal, nor with his friends or mistresses. Neither did I desire any greater intimacy with Mme la Duchesse d'Orléans, whom I saw only on state occasions, or when I called formally upon her at long intervals, staying only for a moment; and I never in any way meddled with what went on in their houses. I always believed that to act in any other manner would be extremely vexatious and lead only to mischief-making, and thus I would never listen to gossip about them.

On that evening, when he was appointed general for Italy,[1] I followed him out of the salon into his own room, where we had a long talk together. He told me that orders had been sent to the Maréchal de Marsin, who was still in Flanders with reinforcements for the Maréchal de Villeroy (who had not waited for them to arrive before attacking), to proceed at once to take personal command of the armies on the Rhine. Other orders had gone to bid Villars leave that army and go by way of Switzerland to Italy, where he was to command under M. le Duc d'Orléans. M. de Vendôme was not to leave until

[1] The King gave him this first command on 26 June, 1706. His mother said he grew three fingers taller overnight.

The Palais Royal, Paris home
of the Ducs d'Orléans.
Engraving.

both had arrived and had conferred with him. M. le Duc d'Orléans said further
that he had been appointed general only on condition that he did nothing
without the Maréchal de Marsin's advice, no matter how much he might
disagree, and the King had extracted from him a promise to that effect. But he
said that he minded the restraint less than he felt the pleasure of attaining his
lifelong wish, without asking, and at a time when he had ceased to hope or even
to dream of it. M. le Prince de Conti held himself under firm control and
behaved very well all that evening in the salon, but Madame la Duchesse, who
was playing cards when the appointment was announced, did not trouble to
leave the table or go up to M. le Duc d'Orléans. She merely called out as he was
passing that she congratulated him, and looked hurt while doing so. He did not
answer her. Monsieur le Duc had not yet returned from Burgundy.

In the days that followed he was anxious to discuss all manner of things with
me and listened in a friendly, pleasant way to everything that I said. He
explained his orders at great length, and the advice which he had received,
asking me to write often and freely offer my suggestions.

He had been in love for a long time with Mlle de Séry, a young lady, well-

109

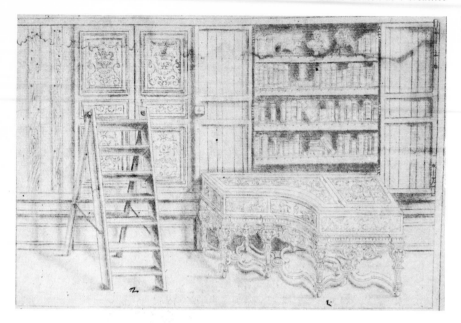

The Duc D'Orléans's small
library at the Palais Royal.

born but without property, a pretty, lively, unruly, impulsive girl, with a
roguish look that gave as good as it promised. Mme de Ventadour, her cousin,
found a place for her as one of Madame's ladies, and it was while she was in that
household that she became pregnant and bore a son[1] to M. le Duc d'Orléans.
This caused her dismissal, but M. le Duc d'Orléans became increasingly
attached to her. She was overbearing and let him know it, but he only loved her
the more. Many things at the Palais Royal were ordered by her, she gathered a
small court about her, and made many friends. Mme de Ventadour, for
instance, in spite of her cult of repentance and moral views, continued to be a
close friend and did not attempt to conceal their intimacy. Mlle de Séry
apparently had good advisers, for she took this opportunity when M. le Duc
d'Orléans was radiant with success to make him acknowledge and legitimize
her son, and not content with that, she avowed that it was unseemly to be
acclaimed publicly as a mother and addressed as Mademoiselle. There was no
precedent for calling her anything else, for Madame is an honour reserved for
Daughters of France and daughters of duchesses in their own right, but that
did not deter either the mistress or her lover. He presented her with the lands
and estate of Argenton, and took advantage of the King's favour, albeit with
much hard work, to have her granted letters patent with permission to bear the
title of Madame, and Comtesse d'Argenton. The thing was unheard of. It was
feared that there might be difficulties over the registration by the Parlement,
but M. le Duc d'Orléans, although he was on the eve of departure and
overwhelmed with affairs of state, went himself to the Premier Président and
the Procureur Général and the registration was effected. His appointment to
Italy had been received with general applause in Paris and at the Court; this

[1] Jean Philippe, le Chevalier
d'Orléans, made Grand
Prieur de France, 1719.

news somewhat abated the rejoicings and caused a good deal of grumbling, but a man when he is much in love thinks only of contenting his mistress and gladly sacrifices all for her sake.

Everything regarding this matter was set, sealed, and delivered without a word of it passing between us. I was angry about the act in itself, and angry that he should have spoiled the brilliance of his departure by so public and improper a breach. But that was all. I remained firm to the decision I had taken when I first resumed our friendship, never to speak to him of his household or his mistresses. He knew very well that I disapproved of what he had been doing for this one, and was exceedingly careful to keep his mouth shut.

This much, however, he did tell me in the salon at Marly, one day when he had just returned from Paris and was about to start for Italy. The very strangeness of his story, and the fact that it was verified by future events which he could not have foreseen, forbid that I should omit it. M. le Duc d'Orléans was interested in all kinds of arts and sciences and, despite his superior intellect, had suffered all his life from that failing which is so common among the descendants of Henri II, and which was brought from Italy with other evils by Catherine de Médicis. He had tried his best to call up the devil on several occasions but, as he told me himself, had never succeeded. He was curious about the supernatural and keenly desired to know the future.

La Séry had a little girl of eight or nine years old living in her house, who was born there and had never been away, and who had all the ignorance and innocence of children of that age and upbringing. One of the many rascally dealers in mystery whom M. le Duc d'Orléans had encountered during his life was a certain man who professed to be able to make events visible in a glass of water. This man, having been produced at Mme de Séry's apartment, asked for some young and innocent person to look into the glass and the little girl was accordingly sent for. The company then diverted themselves by asking what was happening in distant lands, and the child looked and reported whatever she saw.

M. le Duc d'Orléans had so often been tricked by similar experiments that he determined to check this one. He quietly whispered to one of his servants to go to Mme de Nancré's apartment next door, to see who was there, notice the position of the furniture and the nature of it, and all that was happening, and then, without losing a moment or speaking to anyone, to return and report into his ear. All of which he did unobserved upon the instant and whilst the little girl still remained in the room. Then M. le Duc d'Orléans asked the child to see who was in Mme de Nancré's apartment, and to tell him what they were doing, and she related word for word what the messenger had seen, even to describing the faces, figures, and dress of all the people there, their positions in the room, those who were playing cards at two different tables, the onlookers, whether they were standing or sitting, the arrangement of the furniture, in short, everything. That instant, M. le Duc d'Orléans sent Nancré, who came back with word that everything was exactly as the little girl had described and just as the servant had whispered into M. le Duc d'Orléans' ear.

M. le Duc d'Orléans never ordinarily spoke to me of such experiences, because I took the liberty of making him feel ashamed of them. I tried to do so now, crying down the story and saying all that I could to prevent his believing in, or diverting himself with such delusions, especially at a time when his mind should have been filled with much greater matters. 'That was not the whole of it', he said. 'I have only told you that much as a prelude to what followed.' He then related how the child's success had inspired him to inquire after matters more important for him, namely, the state of affairs after the King's death, but without asking to know the date, which could not be seen in the glass. Now the little girl had never heard of Versailles and knew no one at the Court, but she looked into the glass and gave them a long description of all that she saw. She depicted the King's bedroom at Versailles exactly, with all the furniture arranged as it was when he later came to die. She saw the King, lying upon his bed, and the people standing by his side or elsewhere in the room, for example, a little boy wearing the Order and holding the hand of Mme de Ventadour, at whom she exclaimed, because she had seen her with Mme de Séry. From what she said they were able to recognize Mme de Maintenon, the arresting figure of Fagon, Madame, Mme la Duchesse d'Orléans, Madame la Duchesse, and Mme la Princesse de Conti. She exclaimed again when she saw M. le Duc d'Orléans. In a word, she made known to them everyone she could see, princes, servants, gentlemen and valets. When she had quite finished, M. le Duc d'Orléans, who was astonished at her not describing Monseigneur, Mgr le Duc de Bourgogne, Mme la Duchesse de Bourgogne, or M. le Duc de Berry, asked whether she could not see other persons who looked in such and such a way, but she persisted in saying that she did not, and repeated her descriptions of the rest. This, M. le Duc d'Orléans had failed to understand; he expressed his astonishment to me and tried vainly to discover the reason, which subsequently was made plain. The year was 1706, and the four persons he had mentioned were then alive and well. In 1715, when the King died, they were already dead. The same was true of Monsieur le Prince, Monsieur le Duc, and M. le Prince de Conti whom she did not see, although she described the children of the two latter, also M. du Maine and his family, and M. le Comte de Toulouse. But nothing of all this was understood until after the King's death.

This inquiry having been answered, M. le Duc d'Orléans wished to know his own future, but that could not be seen in the glass. The man offered to show it him like a painting on the wall, provided that he did not fear to see himself, and after a quarter of an hour of gesticulating and grimacing, the figure of M. le Duc d'Orléans suddenly appeared before them all, dressed as he then was, life-size, and with a closed-in crown upon his head. It was not the crown of France, nor of Spain, nor of England, nor yet the Imperial crown. M. le Duc d'Orléans stared at it with the eyes starting out of his head, but could not imagine what it was, for he had never seen anything to resemble it. There were only four hoops and nothing at the top. The thought of this crown preyed upon his mind.

Louis XV and his governess, the Duchesse de Ventadour. Detail from the painting by N. de Largillière.

Arguing from this and the previous conundrum, I took occasion to point out the vanity of such idle curiosity, a temptation of the devil which God permits in order to punish those who search for forbidden knowledge. I also drew attention to the dissatisfaction and obscurity that had resulted, instead of the light and certainty for which he sought. At that time, he was very far from being Regent of France or from thinking such a thing possible.

All this occurred in Paris, at the house of his mistress and in the presence of their most intimate circle. He told me of it that same evening, and I thought the story so singular that I give it here, not because I approve of it, but merely to put it upon record.

The 'Parvulo' at Meudon

Before proceeding to other and more important matters, I observe that I have said nothing of what the Court used to call the 'Parvulo' of Meudon. I must, however, try to explain this code-word in the secret language of the Court if you are to have any understanding of the things which I am about to relate. I have told elsewhere about the actions of Mme la Princesse de Conti, why and how she came to dismiss Mlle Choin,[1] who the latter was, who her friends, and the partiality which Monseigneur felt for her. His fondness was only increased by the difficulty of meeting her after she was dismissed. Almost the only people who knew of the attachment in its early stages were Mme de Lillebonne and her daughters,[2] and in spite of all that they owed to Mme la Princesse de Conti, they fostered it because it made them parties to an intrigue from which they hoped to reap much benefit.

After her dismissal, Mlle Choin retired to the house of her kinsman La Croix, near the Petit Saint-Antoine convent, in Paris, where she lived in complete seclusion. Every time that Monseigneur went to Meudon for the day only, in order to inspect his new buildings and plantations, she was warned beforehand. She would go there in a hired carriage on the previous evening, passing through the courtyards on foot, poorly dressed, like any common woman going to visit one of the servants, and entering Monseigneur's apartments on the entresol by the back way. When he came on the following day, he would spend a few hours in her company. For a long time she continued in this fashion, but later she began to take a maid with a bundle in her pocket, and always stayed from the evening before until the following night, on the occasions when Monseigneur slept at Meudon. Whilst she was there, she remained shut up with her maid, seeing no one but him and never leaving the entresol of the château. One of the pages, the only one whom Monseigneur trusted, brought her meals.

Not long afterwards, Dumont, Monseigneur's equerry and governor of Meudon, was given permission to see her, then the daughters of Mme de Lillebonne came when there were ladies staying at Meudon. Gradually the numbers increased as some of the more intimate circle were included—Sainte-Maure, the Comte de Roucy, then Biron, later, one or two others, a few of the ladies, and M. le Prince de Conti, shortly before he died. Next, Mgr le Duc de Bourgogne and M. le Duc de Berry, and very soon afterwards, Mme la Duchesse de Bourgogne, were admitted to the apartment on the entresol, so that the secret soon became known. The Duc de Noailles and his sisters were occasionally invited. Monseigneur took to dining there with Mme de Lillebonne's daughters, and sometimes with them and Madame la Duchesse,

[1] Mlle Choin, the Princesse de Conti's maid of honour, had been dismissed twelve years earlier for an affair with a lover of her mistress. The scandal was complicated because Monseigneur also loved her. He remained faithful to her and later is supposed to have married her.

[2] Anne de Lorraine, Princesse de Lillebonne, Mlle de Lillebonne, and Mme d'Espinoy.

Meudon, the seat of the Dauphin, near Paris. By Pierre Denis Martin.

or with a few specially privileged friends. But there it stopped. The same air of mystery always surrounded these parties that were held pretty often. And it was those gatherings that came to be known as the 'parvulo'.

At this time, Mlle Choin was no longer kept on the entresol solely for Monseigneur's convenience. She now slept in the great bed in the state apartment which Mme la Duchesse de Bourgogne usually occupied when the King came to Meudon, and she always took an armchair in Monseigneur's presence, whereas Mme la Duchesse de Bourgogne had only a tabouret. Mlle Choin never stood up to receive her. When speaking of her, even in the presence of Monseigneur and the whole company, she referred to her simply as 'the duchess', and treated her exactly as Mme de Maintenon did, except that she did not say 'my dear child'. Mme la Duchesse de Bourgogne would never call her 'Aunt', nor was she so familiar and easy with her as with the King and Mme de Maintenon. When Mgr le Duc de Bourgogne visited the entresol, he was exceedingly stiff; his manners and morals did not easily adapt themselves to that kind of society. M. le Duc de Berry, on the other hand, was not so straitlaced and seemed perfectly comfortable. Madame la Duchesse usually monopolized the conversation and occasionally invited some of her cronies, but none the less Mlle Choin never appeared in public. She went to hear mass at six o'clock in the morning on Saints' days, sitting in a quiet corner of the little chapel, alone, well muffled up in hoods and veils. She ate by herself when Monseigneur did not come up to sup with her, which he never did when he stayed at Meudon, except on the first night, and she never set foot beyond his apartments and the entresol. On the way between, the corridor was carefully watched and barricaded so that no one should meet her.

People gradually came to accept her as being to Monseigneur what Mme de Maintenon was to the King, and every courtier had his batteries trained upon her for future advantage. They intrigued to be allowed to visit her in Paris, and flattered and fawned upon her older friends and acquaintances. Mgr le Duc and Mme la Duchesse de Bourgogne did their utmost to make themselves agreeable by showing her respect and being especially attentive to her friends, but even they were not always successful. She treated Mgr le Duc de Bourgogne as familiarly as a step-mother, which she was not, but her manner was curt and unsympathetic, and it sometimes happened that she took a hectoring, tactless tone with Mme la Duchesse de Bourgogne, which made her cry.

Mlle Choin remained devoted to the daughters of Mme de Lillebonne, for she never forgot that although these ladies owed everything, their livelihood, their friendship with Monseigneur, their position in society, to Mme la Princesse de Conti, they had not hesitated to desert their benefactress for her sake. Moreover it was not from any sense of grievance that they forsook her, but solely because they knew of Monseigneur's fond passion and realized the advantages of enjoying his confidence after Mlle Choin's dismissal. She herself had witnessed Monseigneur's friendship for the two sisters long enough to refrain from annoying them in any way. Thus she remained on cordial terms with them and also with Madame la Duchesse whose gaiety, good humour and perfect health were a welcome refuge to Monseigneur from the constant nagging of Mme la Princesse de Conti.

The four women therefore came to a perfect understanding with regard to Monseigneur and in certain other matters. They never quarrelled but supported one another continually, yet each held herself free at the King's death, should Monseigneur survive him, to supplant the three others and become sole and independent mistress. In the meanwhile, they were united in this common bond and tyrannized over the few men who lived in hopes of the future because of Monseigneur's liking for them, or their own persistent flattery.

As for the King and Mme de Maintenon, they fully realized what was going on, but said nothing, and the Court spoke of it only in whispers. This outline will serve for the present. It will give a clue to many future events. M. de Vendôme and d'Antin were the people best informed.

The Duc du Maine and the
Comte de Toulouse

M. du Maine realized that Monseigneur detested him. Consequently, the best way of approaching him was through these female confidantes. Vendôme alone did not suffice. The King was advancing in age and Monseigneur towards the throne. M. du Maine trembled at the thought, I might say, less like an angel than like the devil whom he so closely resembled in malice, in perversity, in unkindness to all and good to none, in sinister plotting, in sublime vaingloriousness and most subtle falseness, in conceits without number and endless dissembling; yet with much seeming amiability, especially in the arts of pleasing and entertainment, for when he wished he could charm. Being the most arrant coward in heart and mind, he was also most dangerous, for, provided he could manage it unseen, he was ready to go to dreadful lengths in order to escape what he feared, and would lend himself to the meanest and most despicable actions, by which the devil lost nothing.

He was egged on by a wife of the same kidney, whose intelligence, and she too had much, had been spoilt and corrupted by the reading of plays and romances, to which passion she so entirely abandoned herself that for years on end she learned them by heart and acted them in public. This woman was courageous beyond measure, intriguing, bold, quarrelsome, recognizing only her present inclinations and setting them above all else, and despising her husband's subterfuges and precautions, which she called a lamentable want of spirit. She was always taunting him with having married above his station and kept him low and submissive by treating him like a slave. She snubbed him unmercifully and he never dared to protest, for he bore everything from her in terror lest she should go out of her mind. He did manage to conceal a certain amount from her, but her ascendancy over him was beyond belief and she drove him with blows to go her way.

They had no intercourse with the Comte de Toulouse, a man of few words, but the soul of honour, virtue, truth, and honesty, with a manner as gracious as his naturally cold, even icy, disposition would allow. He did his best to make something of himself but used only good means to that end, for he had a sense of justice in everyday affairs, which made up for any want of intellect. Thus, in his rank of Admiral of France, he had been most diligent in learning the affairs of the navy and merchant service, and he understood them very well. A man of this nature was not likely to live on familiar terms with such a brother and sister-in-law, for M. du Maine saw him loved and respected, as he deserved, and was jealous. The Comte de Toulouse, being wise, taciturn, and prudent, realized this fact but appeared not to, although he could not endure the follies of his sister-in-law, as she plainly saw. This made her furious; she, in turn, detested him, and thus further alienated the two brothers.

With Monseigneur, the Comte de Toulouse had always been on excellent terms, as well as with M. and Mme la Duchesse de Bourgogne, who treated him with respect and affection. He was nervous with the King, who far preferred the company of M. du Maine, the spoiled darling of Mme de Maintenon, his one-time governess to whom he had sacrificed his mother Mme de Montespan, a fact which neither lady could forget.[1] Du Maine was cunning enough to persuade the King that although extremely intelligent, which no one could deny, he had no opinions, no ambition, but was in fact a fool and an idler with a taste for solitude. He spent his time shut up in his study, eating alone,

[1] According to Saint-Simon, the King, though he had ceased to love Mme de Montespan, could not bring himself to send her away. It was du Maine, in conjunction with Bossuet, who turned the scale, thereby winning Mme de Maintenon's eternal gratitude.

The Duchesse du Maine by Pierre Gobert. Anne Louise Bénédicte de Bourbon-Condé, wife of the King's elder son by Mme de Montespan.

avoiding society, and hunting alone, and he managed to make this uncivilized life seem meritorious to the King, whom he saw every day at his private times. In short he was a consummate hypocrite, going ostentatiously to mass, and to vespers as well as communion on all Saints' days. He was the life and soul, and also the oracle, of Mme de Maintenon, whom he could twist round his little finger, and who thought only of giving him pleasure and advantaging him, no matter at whose expense.

This is a long digression, but in the end you will see how necessary it is for a full understanding of what I have to tell. These persons stirred up many matters which would make no sense without this clue. I give it here because the need arises and opportunity serves.

The Comte de Toulouse, younger legitimated son of the King and Mme de Montespan. Engraving by Drevet, after Rigaud.

Mishap to Mme la Duchesse de Bourgogne

Mme la Duchesse de Bourgogne was pregnant; she felt extremely unwell. Contrary to his usual custom, the King wished to go to Fontainebleau at the beginning of the summer and announced his intention. In the meantime, he wanted to make the usual Marly excursions. His granddaughter amused him, he would not go without her, but travelling was bad for her condition. Mme de Maintenon grew anxious. Fagon put in a discreet word. This merely irritated the King, who was not used to being crossed and had been spoiled by his mistresses, who had always accompanied him on journeys, even when pregnant or just risen from child-bed, and had always worn full court-dress. Objections to the Marly visits irritated him but did not prevent them. The most that he would concede was to defer twice the one arranged for Low Monday, and he insisted on going on the Wednesday of the following week despite all that could be said or done to stop him, or to gain permission for Mme la Duchesse de Bourgogne to remain at Versailles.

At Marly, on the Saturday, the King went out into the gardens after mass, and was diverting himself with the carp in the ornamental basin between the Château and the long vista when the Duchesse du Lude appeared, walking towards us, although there were no ladies with the King at that time—there seldom were in the morning. He realized that she must have something important to say and went to meet her, and as they approached one another we stopped and left him to join her alone. The conversation was short. The Duchesse returned to the Château, and the King to us and on towards the carp, without uttering a word. Everyone could see what had happened, but no one dared to comment. Eventually, when the King was quite near the basin, he turned to the chief persons present and said crossly, addressing no one in particular, 'The Duchesse de Bourgogne has miscarried!' nothing more. Thereupon M. de La Rochefoucauld actually exclaimed; M. de Bouillon, the Duc de Tresmes and the Maréchal de Boufflers echoed his words in an undertone, and M. de La Rochefoucauld protested out loud that it was a thousand pities, since she had miscarried before and might well have no other children. 'And if that should happen', interrupted the King furiously, 'what do I care? She has one son already, has she not? And if he dies, is not the Duc de Berry of age to marry and have children? Why should I mind who succeeds me; are they not all grandchildren of mine?' Then with a sudden rush of impatience, 'Thank God that she has miscarried, since it was bound to happen! Now, perhaps, I shall not be thwarted in my excursions and everything else that I want to do, by doctors' orders and midwives' argufying. At last, I can come and go as I please and they will leave me in peace.' A silence during which you might have heard an ant walking succeeded this outburst. All eyes were lowered, people scarcely dared to breathe. Stupefaction reigned. Even the gardeners and the craftsmen working on the buildings stood still. The silence lasted for fully a quarter of an hour.

It was the King himself who broke it by leaning over the balustrade and speaking of a carp. No one answered him. Thereafter, he addressed his remarks about carp to the gardeners, who were not usually included in his conversation, and then he spoke to them only of the carp. It was all vastly dull and the King went away soon afterwards. As soon as he was out of sight and we dared to look at one another, our eyes met and spoke volumes. For a moment all those present became intimate. They marvelled, were sorry, and finally shrugged their shoulders. Although this scene happened so long ago it is as vivid as yesterday to me. M. de La Rochefoucauld was furious and, on this occasion, rightly so. Beringhen, the first equerry, was almost swooning with fright. As for me, I was all eyes and ears as I noted these people, and I congratulated myself for having long ago discovered that the King only loved and considered himself, and was his own prime object. His dreadful speech had repercussions far beyond Marly.

1708

Samuel Bernard the Banker

I must not omit a trivial affair which I witnessed on this same excursion, when the King was showing his gardens at Marly. It was about five in the afternoon when he came out walking; he proceeded past all the pavilions on the Marly side, and stopped at the one in which Desmarets, then controller-general of finance, was lodging. Thereupon Desmarets came out accompanied by the famous banker Samuel Bernard, whom he had invited to dine and consult with him. The latter was then the richest man in Europe and the owner of the greatest and safest banking business. He was one who knew his own power and required to be treated with respect, so that the controllers-general, who usually had far greater need of him than he of them, were always most deferential in their manner towards him.

The King spoke to Desmarets, saying that he was glad to see M. Bernard, then turning to the latter, said, 'You are a nice one never to have seen Marly. Come with me now, and I will show you the gardens and afterwards hand you back to Desmarets.' Bernard accordingly followed him and during the entire walk the King spoke only to him, took him everywhere and showed him everything, with the charm which he knew so well how to assume when he had some object in view. I marvelled, and not I alone, that the King, who was

Cartoon for a tapestry of children gardening. Louis XIV was genuinely fond of children and had them represented in very many fountains and tapestries.

usually miserly with words, should so prostitute himself, as it seemed, to a man of Bernard's quality. It was not long, however, before I understood the reason, and then I marvelled at the straits to which the greatest kings sometimes find themselves reduced.

Desmarets had been at his wits' end to find money, which was needed for everything, every fund having been exhausted. He had been to Paris hat in hand to every banker, but so often and so flagrantly had all manner of contracts been dishonoured and firm promises broken that he had met with nothing but apologies and closed doors. Bernard, like the rest, would not lend, indeed there was already much owing to him. In vain Desmarets had urged the pressing need and the enormous profits which he had at times made in the King's business. Bernard was not to be moved. So there were the King and Desmarets sorely perplexed. Finally, the latter told His Majesty that all things being considered, Bernard was the only man capable of extricating him because, as was well known, he had enormous sums at his command. The difficulty would be to persuade him to change his mind and to overcome his stubbornness that verged on insolence. Desmarets added that Bernard was eaten up with vanity and might be more ready to open his purse if the King were to condescend to flatter him. In the critical state to which his affairs had come, His Majesty consented, and Desmarets proposed the expedient which I have already described, so as to give the affair a cloak of seeming respectability and avoid a refusal. Bernard fell for the bait. He returned to Desmarets after his walk with the King so delighted that, of his own accord, he said that he would prefer ruin rather than leave in difficulties a prince who had shown him so much honour, and he proceeded to praise him to the skies. Desmarets took instant advantage of the situation and extracted far more than ever he had intended.

Samuel Bernard, the
millionaire banker.

Death of Mansard

Mansard died very suddenly during that Marly excursion. He was the surveyor of the works, and a character on whom we may well pause for a moment. A tall, well-built man, of very humble origin, he had a pleasant face and exceedingly sharp wits, which he cleverly used to ingratiate himself with his betters, although he never wholly shook off the vulgarity belonging to his earlier condition. First a drummer-boy, then a stone-cutter, then a mason's apprentice, later a groom, he managed to endear himself to the great François Mansard, who left so fine a name in French architecture, and who used him on the King's buildings in an endeavour to train and make something out of him. People used to say that he was Mansard's bastard, but he gave it out that he was a nephew of the great man, and took his name after his death in 1666, by which means he hoped to become better known, and he succeeded. Finally, he attracted the King's notice. Thereafter, he proceeded to put his acquaintance with the gentlemen, valets, and masons to such good purpose that His Majesty, who already admired in him the virtues of obscurity and unattachment, endowed him with his uncle's genius, and, hurriedly dismissing Villacerf, the then surveyor, put Mansard into his place. None the less, Mansard did not know his work, and De Coste, his brother-in-law, whom he made his head architect, was as ignorant as he. They took all their plans, drawings, and ideas from another architect nicknamed L'Assurance, whom as far as possible they kept firmly under lock and key.

Mansard cunningly enticed the King from small beginnings to embark on long and costly enterprises. He showed him unfinished sketches, especially for gardens, which fired his imagination so that he made suggestions. Then Mansard, exclaiming that he would never have thought of such a thing, would go into raptures, declaring that compared with His Majesty he was no better than a student, so that the King quite innocently fell into the trap. Drawings in hand, he insinuated himself into the semi-private apartments and then gradually into all of them and at all hours, then often without any plans or business to discuss. Later, he took to sharing in the conversation and accustomed the King to discuss the news and other matters with him. Sometimes, he went so far as to ask questions, but he knew how to choose his moments, for he understood the King to perfection and never mistook the times for being familiar or formal. He liked to show off his privileges during the King's walks and to see people marvelling at the lengths to which he dared to go. Yet he never used his influence to harm anyone, although it might have been dangerous to attack him. In this way he acquired status and induced not only the nobles and Princes of the Blood, but even the bastards and ministers to

The goldfish pond in the gardens of Marly.

serve his interests. They and the upper servants were very careful to remain on good terms with him.

The King had precisely the same kind of partiality for Mansard as he had for Fagon. Just as he was greatly vexed when courtiers did not consult the latter when they were ill, and obey his orders, so it was thought most rash for anyone to consider building a house or making a garden without employing Mansard. As a matter of fact, Mansard thought the same himself, but he was not capable. He built the bridge at Moulins, called it a masterpiece of stability, and boasted of it in a monstrously complacent way. Four or five months after it was finished, however, Charlus, the father of the Duc de Levis, happened to attend the King's *lever* on returning from his estates near Moulins. Mansard was present at the time and, hoping to hear praise of his bridge, after a while asked the King to inquire about it. But Charlus was a clever man, although disappointed and inclined to be cynical, and he made no reply, which the King noticed and asked him again. 'Sire', said Charlus then, 'I have heard nothing of it since it went away, but I believe that at present it must be somewhere near Nantes'. 'What are you talking about?' said the King. 'I mean the bridge at Moulins.' 'Precisely, Sire', replied Charlus soberly, 'the bridge at Moulins. It came adrift the night before I left, and went floating off down the river'. The King and Mansard looked astounded, and the courtiers laughed behind their hands. This was indeed exactly what had happened; and the bridge at Blois, which Mansard built shortly before, played him the same trick.

125

He made an enormous deal of money out of his buildings, contracts, and all other aspects of his work. He was autocratic in the extreme. No craftsman nor contractor, nor any other person concerned with his buildings ever dared to argue with him or make the slightest protest. Since neither he nor the King had any taste, he never created a thing of beauty, nor even anything convenient for its purpose, to justify the vast expenses which he incurred. Monseigneur ceased to employ him at Meudon after others had convinced him that Mansard merely led him into extravagances, but the King, instead of being grateful to Monseigneur and angry with Mansard, did his best to reconcile them and even offered to defray some of the costs. None the less, Monseigneur was annoyed at being taken for a fool; he refused the offer, and remained vexed about the whole affair. Du Mont told me this as a fact.

The fine chapel at Versailles, for fine it is, so far as craftsmanship and ornamentation are concerned—that chapel that took so many years to build and cost such millions of francs—is so badly proportioned that it seems to overpower the palace. It was designed in that way for a special purpose. Mansard indeed calculated the proportions solely from the viewpoint of the royal pew, because he knew that the King was most unlikely to enter the chapel

Interior of the Royal Chapel at Versailles.

from below. He then deliberately made that hideous excrescence above the roof of the palace so as to force the King to raise the whole building one storey in order to hide it. Had not war broken out at the critical moment, the work would have been carried out. In the meanwhile, however, Mansard died.

Effects of the terrible winter of 1709.

1709

The Fearful Winter of 1709

It was a terrible winter, worse than any within living memory. A bitter frost continued without respite for two months, freezing the rivers down to their very mouths and making the edge of the sea so hard that heavily laden wagons were driven over it. A false thaw then set in, melting the snow that had covered the land, and this was followed by a sudden renewal of the same hard frost that lasted for another three weeks. It was so cold that bottles of Queen-of-Hungary-water, the strongest elixirs, and the most spirituous liquors burst in the cupboards of rooms in the palace of Versailles, rooms that were heated with

127

fires and surrounded by chimney-flues. I saw this happen with my own eyes, several times. Once, indeed, when I was supping with the Duc de Villeroy in his small bedroom, pieces of ice fell into our glasses from bottles that had been standing on the chimneypiece after being brought from his tiny kitchen where a great fire was burning, and which was on the same level as his bedroom, with only a little ante-chamber between the two. That apartment is the one now occupied by his son.

It was the second frost that proved disastrous. The fruit trees were all killed; no walnuts, olives, apples, nor vines survived, or none worth mentioning. Other kinds of trees perished in great numbers, the gardens were ruined, and the seeds died in the ground. You can form no idea of the destruction caused by this national calamity. Everyone began to hoard their old grain and the price of bread rose, as hopes of a harvest receded. The wisest resowed their wheat fields with barley; others followed suit, and they were the fortunate ones, for it proved to be their salvation. However, the police took it into their heads to forbid it, and then repented too late. Several government decrees were issued about wheat, searches were instituted for hidden stocks of grain, and commissaries were sent into the various provinces three months later than was advertised. Yet all that this policy achieved was to bring poverty and prices to a fatal height at a time when the computations showed that there was enough wheat stored in France to feed the entire nation for two years, independently of the harvest.

Many people began to think that the gentlemen of the finance department were using the opportunity to lay hands on the wheat by sending their agents to buy in all the markets of the kingdom, and then selling to the King's profit, not forgetting their own. It then happened that a very great number of bargeloads of corn purchased by the King went rotten and had to be thrown into the Loire, and this gave weight to suspicion, for they could not hide the circumstances. It is very certain, at any rate, that wheat was sold at the same price in all provincial markets, whereas in Paris, the commissaries kept prices at a higher level and often obliged vendors to raise them against their will. When the people cried out to know how long this dearness would last, some commissaries—and this in a market not two paces from my own house in Saint-Germain-des-Prés—were moved by pity to let slip the revealing answer, 'As long as you choose.' They meant by this, so long as the people suffered no wheat to enter Paris without a permit from d'Argenson, the police-lieutenant, for none was allowed to enter otherwise, and this prohibition was enforced with the utmost severity especially as regards the bakers. What I have been describing soon became the general practice all over France, for the administrators everywhere did what d'Argenson was doing in Paris. Moreover, in all provincial markets, wheat that remained unsold at closing time at the prices they had fixed was forcibly removed, and any dealer with sufficient compassion to sell lower was severely punished.

Maréchal, the chief surgeon, of whom I have spoken more than once, had the courage to tell the King of all this, and to warn him of the dreadful conclusions to which the people were driven, even the more dependable among them and those of better condition. The King seemed moved and was not vexed with Maréchal for speaking, but he would do nothing.

Vast stocks of wheat were stored in many different places and with the greatest possible secrecy, although nothing was more expressly forbidden in the edicts. The people were even enjoined to denounce hoarders, but one unfortunate man who tried to lay information with Desmarets was very roughly handled by the mob. The houses of the Parlement assembled separately on account of the unrest, and then held a meeting of deputies in the great chamber. A resolution was passed that the King should be advised to send counsellors throughout the provinces, at their own expense, to inspect the wheat stocks, instruct the police, and punish those who disobeyed the edicts, and a list was added of counsellors willing to make such tours through the different départements. When the King was informed of this by the president, he became amazingly angry and wished to send back a severe reprimand, bidding them mind their own business and concern themselves solely with adjudicating in lawsuits. The Chancellor dared not remind him that what the Parlement proposed was perfectly correct and well within its province, but he emphasized the love and respect with which the advice had been proffered and

After the terrible winter of 1709, it was the appalling frosts and storms at harvest-time that destroyed the fruit and corn and vines of France.

CERÉS AFFLIGÉE
DE VOIR LA TERRE STERILE.

the ministers' full realization that he was master, to accept or reject it. After some argument the King was sufficiently pacified to refrain from sending the reprimand, but he absolutely insisted on the Parlement being informed that he forbade it to concern itself with wheat. This message was given in open council, when only the Chancellor spoke. All the other ministers preserved absolute silence. It was very obvious what they were thinking, but they were careful to say nothing in a matter that touched the Chancellor's own department. Indeed, although like other public bodies the Parlement was well used to snubs, it felt this one deeply and obeyed with great reluctance.

The public, as a whole, were equally distressed. Not a man but believed that had the finance department been forced to give up these cruel practices the resolution might have pleased the King, and served him by interposing the Parlement between him and his people. It would have demonstrated that no chicanery was intended, without diminishing by anything, either real or apparent, that absolute, boundless authority of which he was so acutely jealous.

Without probing into the question of who devised or most profited from the transactions, it may be said that scarcely another age can show a plot more sinister, more brazen, or better organized or a tyranny more lasting, sure, and cruel. The fortunes it made were countless,[1] and countless were the people who died literally of starvation, or perished afterwards from illnesses caused by extremes of poverty. Infinite numbers of families were ruined and cascades of misfortunes of all kinds followed thereafter.

In the meanwhile, the most sacred trusts began to cease payment; returns from customs duties and the various mortgage and lending establishments, even the hitherto inviolable *rentes* of the Hôtel de Ville were all suspended. The repayment of the *rentes* was only delayed, but because of the delays and subsequent reductions, most families in Paris and many other large towns were distressed. At this time, taxes were raised and multiplied, and applied with a rigour that completed the ruin of France. Prices reached fantastic heights so that no money was left to buy in even the cheapest market; yet, although through the poverty of their owners cattle were dying for lack of food, still another tax was levied upon them. Very many people who had assisted the poor in previous years found themselves reduced to a bare subsistence and many of these were even driven to receive alms in secret. No one can tell how many others tried to gain admission into almshouses that had been the dread and shame of the poor, nor how many ruined almshouses vomited back their poor upon the public charge (which meant certain death by starvation), nor yet how many worthy families died of want in their empty granaries.

Again, it can hardly be told how the sight of such misery awakened the zeal for charity, nor how immense were the alms given. Yet at this very time when poverty was increasing day by day, some meddlesome, autocratic philanthropist conceived the idea of new taxes and a levy for the benefit of the poor. These were applied with so little discretion in addition to the other taxes that vast numbers of people were placed in even greater need and some were

[1] Madame said that while Mme de Maintenon ostentatiously ate black bread in public, she was privately making a fortune speculating in wheat.

A voluntary levy, 'willingly accepted' by the King's subjects, who thought it a small price to pay in return for peace.

provoked to curtailing their voluntary alms-giving. Thus apart from the cost of collecting these ill-distributed taxes, the poor were left in a worse state than before. What, however, has proved far more disturbing is that these taxes, which were levied to succour the needy, have been appropriated by the King, in a modified but perpetual form. Officials of the finance department collect them openly even today as a branch of the royal revenues and have not even troubled to change their names.

The same is true of the tax levied in each division annually for the maintenance of the highroads. That, too, has been appropriated by the finance department in the same flagrant manner and without changing the name. Most bridges in the kingdom are broken and main roads have become impassable. Trade has suffered immense damage, but the merchants are now alive to what has been happening. In Champagne, Lescalopier, the administrator, devised a scheme for repairing the roads by forced labour, and did not pay even with bread. Other regions copied him and he has been rewarded by being made counsellor of state. Officials employed on these works were enriched by a government monopoly, but the labourers died in gangs. In the end the whole system became impossible and was abandoned, like the roads themselves. None the less, the tax for constructing and maintaining the roads was in existence during the whole time of the forced labour gangs, has continued ever since, and is still collected as part of the royal revenues.

Let us, however, return to the year 1709. At that time, people were constantly wondering what had become of all the money in France, for no one could pay because no one was paid. In the country, people were insolvent on account of extortions and bad debts, commerce brought in no returns, good faith and confidence were shattered. Thus the King was left with no resource beyond terror and the exercise of supreme power, but boundless though that was, it often failed for want of anything to act upon. The circulation of money stopped and there was no means of restarting it. The King ceased even to pay his troops, and no one could imagine what became of the vast millions that were entering his coffers.

Such was the dreadful state of affairs when Rouillé, and after him, Torcy, were sent into Holland to negotiate a peace. The description which I have given is exact, faithful, and not exaggerated. For, indeed, I must be accurate if you are to have any understanding of the desperate straits to which we were reduced, the enormous sacrifices which the King was compelled to make in order to obtain a peace, and the evident miracle performed by Him who encompasses the sea with bounds and calls to that which is not and to that which is; by Whom France was delivered from the clutches of a Europe ready and willing to destroy her. In truth, the country was saved with many advantages, considering her condition and the little hope of salvation which she had possessed.

In the meanwhile, the reminting of the currency and its revaluation at a third above its intrinsic value brought the King some profit, but at the same time private persons were ruined and trade was thrown into such confusion that it nearly came to a standstill.

Lyons was destroyed by the unexpected, stupendous bankruptcy of Samuel Bernard and its terrible after-effects, although Desmarets supported him as far as he was able. Paper-money and its depreciation were the cause of it. The famous banker had issued notes to the equivalent of twenty millions and owed for almost as much at Lyons. He was given fourteen millions in good assignations in the hopes that with that, added to what he could scrape together from his bank-notes, he would be saved. It has since been suggested that he managed to make a good thing out of his bankruptcy. In fact, whilst no single person of his rank has ever spent or left so much, or possessed anything approaching his credit throughout the whole of Europe until his death thirty years later, he was never able to re-establish himself in Lyons nor the part of Italy adjacent.

1709

Fall of the Duc de Vendôme

On his return from Flanders, Vendôme had audience of the King, but only one, and that a short one. Nevertheless, he did not forget Puységur,[1] and complained of him most bitterly, saying everything bad to which he could lay his tongue, on his usual assumption that his bare word was enough. Puységur, of whom I have spoken more than once, was well known to the King and had a privileged kind of relationship with him, because he reported constantly on the Royal Regiment of Infantry, which the King actually believed himself to command. Puységur had spent most of his life in that regiment, either as major or lieutenant-colonel, and he possessed the King's full confidence.

Puységur was thus quite accustomed to private audiences, and knew that after such an awkward campaign[2] he would be questioned very closely if he arrived hot on the news. He therefore prudently lay low for a couple of months at his house in Soissonnais, before appearing at Paris or Versailles. By that time interest had begun to cool and he had learned of the Duc de Vendôme's unflattering remarks. He did not care to give the impression that he feared to show himself and thus at last came to Court.

The King, who had always liked him and who had been grieved by M. de Vendôme's aspersions, called him alone into his study a few days later, and asked him, in a kindly way, to explain the many foolish actions of which he had been accused. Whereupon, Puységur enlightened him so vividly that the King was surprised into admitting that M. de Vendôme was his informant. At that name, Puységur was stung into seizing his opportunity. He told the King first, what had kept him so long from the Court, and then described simply and courageously the faults, follies, mulishness, and arrogance of M. de Vendôme, all with so much detail and clarity that the King listened attentively, asking many questions and demanding ever more information.

Puységur answered all that he was asked; then, seeing the King receptive, silent, and at every point convinced, he pressed on to say that since Vendôme had spared him so little, in spite of all his restraint and consideration, he felt it to be both permissible and his bounden duty as a soldier to make him known to the King, once and for all. Thereupon, he gave a complete picture of the Duc

[1] The Marquis de Puységur, an able general and a brave and upright man. He had incurred the hatred of the great Duc de Vendôme by openly protesting against his unjustified claims of victories won, his laziness, and his disgusting personal habits.

[2] The Flanders campaign of 1708, which included the French defeat at Oudenarde and the loss of Lille.

133

de Vendôme, his personal life with the army, his bodily unseemliness, his unsound judgment, his warped mind, the falseness and danger of his military principles, and his total ignorance of proper conduct in wartime. Then reverting to all his Italian campaigns and the two last seasons in Flanders, he exposed him utterly, proving to the King beyond all possible doubt that only by a series of miracles had France not been lost a hundred times under his command.

The conversation lasted for more than two hours. The King, who knew and had proved by long experience not only Puységur's ability but his honesty and exactness, had his eyes suddenly opened to the true character of that man who had so artfully been represented as the hero and guardian angel of France. He was mortified and ashamed of his gullibility. From that instant Vendôme was as one dead to his mind and permanently excluded from holding any command — an exclusion that was not slow in becoming known.

Puységur, a naturally humble, modest gentleman, was none the less firm and courageous when roused. He had nothing more to lose with M. de Vendôme, after what the latter had said of him in public and to the King, and moreover he was well content with his audience. He at once repeated everything, word for word, in the great gallery, and nobly braved Vendôme's anger and that of his cabal, of whose existence he was fully aware.

The cabal raged. Vendôme was still more furious. But they could produce only wretchedly unsound counter-arguments that deceived no one. Those most knowledgeable now considered them to be almost out of favour. The rival, and hitherto downtrodden, party welcomed Puységur with open arms, and Mme de Maintenon, Mme la Duchesse de Bourgogne and, especially, the Duc de Beauvilliers, finally drove home to the King the truth of what he had first learned from Puységur alone.

The end came swiftly. Vendôme, thrown out of the service, sold his military equipment, dismissed his household, and retired to Anet, where the grass had already begun to grow.[1]

[1] The grass was growing again because courtiers, who had heard rumours of his coming disgrace, had ceased to tread it down.

1709

The Silver is taken to the Mint

In the meantime, especially in Flanders, the armies were lacking in everything. All possible efforts were made during the early part of June to send money and transport wheat by sea from Brittany and by road from Picardy. Nevertheless the money and bread arrived only in small quantities, and for long periods the army was left to forage for itself on a much narrowed frontier.

I have already said that I would not give an account of the peace negotiations, nor of the journeys which Rouillé and Torcy made to Holland. I will merely say that Torcy returned to Versailles on Saturday, June 1st, after being absent for a month. He had nothing good to report and was very coolly received by the King and Mme de Maintenon. The latter, especially, was exceedingly critical, partly because she did not care for him personally, and partly because she had not been informed of his mission in advance.

At this time, when Mme de Maintenon's influence was being so disastrous in great affairs, that nasty woman whom the Duc de Gramont[1] had married was being equally obnoxious in lesser matters, for such is the way of these unpleasant creatures. The King had compelled her to return from Bayonne, where her habits of looting by trickery and force had become too notorious, but

[1] She was English and her name had been Hamilton. The Duc de Gramont had married her in England, according to the *Mémoires du Duc de Gramont par lui-même*. But these were actually written by his brother-in-law Anthony Hamilton.

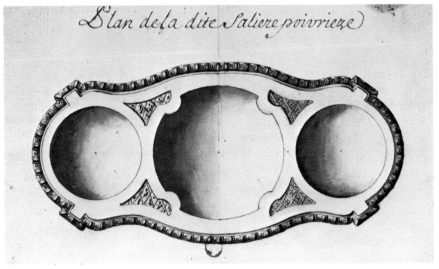

Design for a salt and pepper dish approved by Louis XIV. Drawing by Nicolas de Launay.

she managed to filch the dowager Queen of Spain's[1] pearls and had shown her want of propriety in every way imaginable. Now that she was back in Paris, she was driven to desperation at being deprived of the honours and privileges which should have been hers on marriage.

While the Court waited for the return of Rouillé, who had been recalled by the King, it was decided to arouse the loyalty of every class in the kingdom by publishing the enemy's monstrous conditions, or rather demands, for a peace settlement. A printed letter was accordingly dispatched to all provincial governors, with orders to spread the facts abroad and make it known to what lengths the King had gone in his efforts to secure a peace, and how unsuccessful those efforts had proved. The results fully came up to expectations. There was an immediate outburst of indignation, a clamour for vengeance, and offers from all manner of people to sacrifice all their possessions so as to continue the war, with many other such extravagant proposals to prove their zeal.

It was in these circumstances that the Gramont woman saw an opportunity of obtaining all that had been denied her and which she so passionately desired. She persuaded her husband to go to the King and offer to give his service of silver plate. She hoped that his example would be followed and that she would gain credit and rewards for procuring so swift, convenient and acceptable a relief. Alas! for her plan. The Duc de Gramont told his son-in-law, the

[1] Mariana of Neuburg, widow of Charles II, King of Spain.

Maréchal de Boufflers, who was so much delighted with the idea that he hastened to offer his own plate, of which he had a great deal and very beautiful. Altogether he made so much noise and fuss in urging others to follow his example, that he was taken for having originated the scheme and no mention was made of the old Gramont, nor even of her husband. They thus became their own dupes, which made her more furious than ever.

All this talk about silver made a great stir. No one dared not to offer, yet everyone greatly disliked the thought. Some people were clinging to their silver plate as a last resource and dreaded parting with it, others feared the uncleanliness of pewter and earthenware, while others again saw how thankless it would be to follow where only the first would be given credit. At the meeting of the Conseil de Finances on the very next day, the King showed a strong inclination to accept plate from everybody.

This same plan had already been proposed and rejected when Pontchartrain was contrôleur-général. Now that he was Chancellor, he spoke most emphatically against it, pointing out the smallness of the profit compared with the great sacrifice to the individuals concerned. He also stressed the shoddiness of the whole proceeding, for it would mean that the Court and nobility ate off earthenware, while in the provinces private gentlemen kept their silver plate, and if that were to be made illegal, the general discontent and concealment that would result. He represented the loss of prestige to the government, who might appear to be using this shift as a last resource, the rumours to which it would give rise in foreign countries, the contempt of our enemies, and the encouragement it would be to them. Finally, he recalled the jests made during the war of 1688, when the precious silver furniture in the gallery and the great and little apartments at Versailles, even including the silver throne, were sent to the Mint. Very little, he said, was gained from that transaction and, more precious than the metal itself, the loss of that magnificent craftsmanship which was then devoted to the designing of silver plate, had proved irreparable.

Notwithstanding such cogent arguments, the King persisted in wishing, without using any kind of compulsion, to accept freewill offerings of all the silver plate which people might choose to present. This was announced verbally, and patriots were offered two alternatives. They might give their silver outright by sending it to Launay, the King's goldsmith, who kept a list of names and of the number of ounces received. For a few days, at least, the King read the list with care, and promised, again verbally and in general terms, to return an equal weight to the donors when his affairs permitted (which no one believed) and to remit stamp duty from any new plate which they might purchase in the future. Those who desired repayment might send their silver for conversion to the Mint, where it would be weighed on arrival, the names, dates, and ounces written down, and the owners reimbursed as soon as money became available. Many were not sorry to be able to sell their plate without shame, and thus to find some relief in their present need for ready money. Inestimable damage was done, however, for much beautiful work was lost with

LEFT Drawing for silver table, like those in Louis XIV's beautiful collection, at Versailles.

the moulded, engraved, embossed or carved ornamentations, that had once adorned the silver plate of wealthy and tasteful persons.

When the final reckoning was made, there turned out to be fewer than a hundred names on Launay's list and the entire proceeds from the gifts and conversions amounted to less than three millions. The Court, Paris society, and some of the notables had not dared to refuse; a few others, who hoped to gain some immediate relief had followed in their wake, but almost no one else either in Paris or the provinces.

I must admit to having been one of the last to offer, for I was becoming monstrously weary of taxes and felt little inclined to submit to a voluntary levy. When I found myself to be almost the only man of my condition still eating off silver, I sent a thousand pistoles' worth to the Mint and locked away the remainder. I had had a little of my father's old silver, which was unornamented, so I regretted its loss less than the inconvenience and dirt. M.

Drawing for a porcelain plate, such as was used by the nobility, after they had sent their silver to be melted down.

de Lauzun, who had much plate, and all of it very fine, found that his reluctance overcame his loyalty and he did not send. I and several others were present when the Duc de Villeroy questioned him about it. He answered in his low voice, 'Not as yet, I do not know who would favour me by taking it, and besides, how can I be sure that it does not go up the Duchesse de Gramont's petticoat?' I thought that we should die of laughing as he turned sharp about, and left us.

All the nobility had put themselves on porcelain within a week, so that the china shops were emptied and the trade boomed; but the middle classes still continued to use their silver. Even the King began to talk of going onto porcelain. He sent his gold plate to the Mint and M. le Duc d'Orléans sent what little he possessed. The rest of the royal family began to use silver-gilt or silver services, and the Princes and Princesses of the Blood took to porcelain. However, the King soon discovered that most people were cheating, whereupon he expressed himself with a tartness that was unusual with him but had no effect. He would have done better to speak to the Duc de Gramont and his unpleasant old wife, who had caused this shameful, useless sacrifice. They were not duped, for they had locked up their good silver and she, herself, had taken their old plate to the Mint and had seen that she was given good value.

None of the donors enjoyed for long the sensation of having pleased the King. After three months, His Majesty at last realized the futility of this monstrous idea and said that he was sorry he had ever consented to it. That was how they managed things in the Court and kingdom.

1709

Why Saint-Simon wished to Retire from the Court

For a long time I had been realizing the truth in the Bishop of Chartres's warning that someone had spoken ill of me to the King and had made an impression. The change in his manner was most marked and although I still went on all the Marly excursions, I was forced to conclude that I was not being invited for my own sake. This vexed me much because chimney-pots seemed to be falling about my ears and I could not discover the cause nor, consequently, the remedy, and I was weary of the animosity of bitter and powerful enemies whom I had done nothing to provoke, for instance, Monsieur le Duc, Madame la Duchesse, the Vendôme clique, and other jealous, spiteful people such as usually inhabit courts. I had none to set against such enemies but friends like Chamillart, the Chancellor, the Maréchal de Boufflers, and the Ducs de Beauvilliers and Chevreuse, who were all without influence or out of favour, and thus, in spite of their good will, unable to help me. In short, my dissatisfaction grew to such a pitch that I seriously desired to leave the Court and abandon all my hopes.

Mme de Saint-Simon, always more prudent than I, argued the sudden changes that continually occur in Court life, those which time might bring, our total dependence on the King, not only for our condition but for my patrimony as well, and many other reasons for delay. Eventually we came to an agreement to go for two years into Guyenne, on the pretext of inspecting a large estate which we owned there but had never visited. In this way we hoped to absent ourselves for a long time without vexing the King and afterwards to proceed as circumstances might direct.

Pontchartrain and Chamillart kiss hands on their appointments, 1699.

M. de Beauvilliers had asked to be included in our consultations with M. de Chevreuse. He, and the Chancellor, to whom we spoke later, approved our plan, since they could not persuade me to remain at Court, but they strongly advised us to speak of the journey well in advance, so as to avoid an appearance of chagrin, and scotch any rumours that I had received a gentle hint to depart.

For so long an absence in a distant place it was necessary to obtain the King's permission, but as in the circumstances I did not care to approach him directly, my good friend La Vrillière, whose département included Guyenne, spoke for me and the King consented. However, for various reasons we were prevented from going to Blaye at that time and therefore decided to stay at La Ferté instead, resolving to spend a year or more at that place, only occasionally returning to the Court, and not always every year, if that were possible without failing in the absolute letter of my duty.

My continued attachment to Chamillart after his downfall had already given offence. I therefore waited to leave the Court until about a month after he had gone into the country in search of some estate where he might live away from Paris. His daughters travelled with us and remained at La Ferté, and he also came there between his excursions, so that I was able to welcome him with the entertainments and pleasure-parties which I could not give for him when he was in favour and office. Now that there was no obligation to court him and nothing to be gained I had no scruples, and he was clearly touched by my attentions. He stayed with us for a considerable time, and left his daughters with us when he went to Paris to conclude his affairs and the purchase of a property at Courcelles in Maine. In the meantime I remained in my own home, as I had intended, but made sure of being fully acquainted with all that happened at the Court.

Let us now return to the situation there both before and after my departure, which was much delayed although I continued to desire it keenly. Here I find myself without a word to express what I wish to explain, for the Court had become more than ever divided since the downfalls of Vendôme and Chamillart. To speak of cabals is perhaps too strong a word, but without endless circumlocution no better can be found and I shall therefore use it, adding that although it goes beyond my exact meaning, the sense can be rendered by no other single term. Thus I shall say that the Court was split into three different cabals that included all the principal personalities, very few of whom allowed their minds to be fully known, while others kept certain corners secret and had many reservations. Very few indeed had the country's good solely at heart, although all professed that its precarious state was their chief concern. By far the greater number thought only of themselves, each man following his own somewhat indefinite aims to secure fame, influence and, for the future, power. Some strove for wealth and office. Others, more cunning or less well placed, adhered to one or other of the three cabals, forming subordinate cliques that sometimes gave an impetus to affairs, and ever stimulated the civil war of tongues.

[*This is how Madame described the situation in a letter to the Duchess of Hanover. 'The entire Court is in a ferment of intrigue. Some try to win the favour of the all-powerful lady [Mme de Maintenon], others that of Monsieur le Dauphin, others, again, that of the Duc de Bourgogne. He and his father have no love for one another; the son despises the father, has ambitions and would like to rule. The Dauphin is completely dominated by his bastard-sister, Madame la Duchesse. The Princesse de Conti has become the latter's ally, so as not to lose all her influence with him. All of them are against my son [the Duc d'Orléans], for they fear that the King may look kindly on him and arrange a match between his daughter and the Duc du Berry. Madame la Duchesse would much like that marriage for her own daughter and that is why she monopolises the Duc de Berry. The Duchesse de Bourgogne, who wants to rule the Dauphin as well as the King, is jealous of Madame la Duchesse*] *and has accordingly made a pact of friendship with the Duchesse d'Orléans so as to thwart her. It all provides a vastly pretty comedy of intrigue and counter-intrigue, and, I might say, in the words of the song, "If we do not die of hunger we shall laugh ourselves to death." In the meanwhile, the Old Lady sets them all one against the other so that she may rule all the better.*[1]]

[1]Mme de Maintenon.

To make matters plain, let us now call these parties by their proper names and speak of the Cabal of the Nobles, as it was known at that time, the Cabal of the Ministers, and the Cabal of Meudon. The first sheltered beneath the wing of Mme de Maintenon, was on good terms with Monseigneur, alternately used and was used by Mme la Duchesse de Bourgogne, and basked in the reflected glory of Boufflers' fame and high reputation. The guiding hand was Harcourt's,[2] even from the Rhine, and in the second rank was Pontchartrain the Chancellor, in spite of his exasperation at Mme de Maintenon's aversion to him and his consequent lack of favour with the King. The second cabal was united by hopes that sprang from the birth, virtue, and capabilities of Mgr le Duc de Bourgogne. It included, bound together by a strong affection, the Duc de Beauvilliers, the most forthright of them all, the Duc de Chevreuse, the centre and strategist of the party, and the Archbishop of Cambrai,[3] who directed it from the depths of his exile and disgrace. In the subordinate clique were Torcy and Desmarets, Père Le Tellier, the Jesuits, and Saint-Sulpice. The third cabal, that of Meudon, I have already explained.[4]

[2]The Duc D'Harcourt, Marshal of France, not to be confused with the Lorraine d'Harcourts.

[3] Fénelon, who had been banished from the Court in 1698, for his unorthodox religious publications. It was widely believed that his real crime was not against religion, but a desire to reform the government of France.

The two first held each other at a respectful distance, the second pursued its course quietly, the first, noisily, using every opportunity to injure its rivals. The most fashionable people of the Court and army all belonged to the Cabal of the Nobles; others joined it out of disgust with the government, and wiser heads were attracted by Boufflers' honesty and the intelligence of Harcourt.

[4] The Parvulo at Meudon. See p. 114.

What the world calls chance, which, like everything else, is really an instrument of Providence, has caused me all through my life, in the strangest manner, to become attached to the most opposing personalities. It now played me the same trick with regard to the Cabals of the Nobles and the Ministers. I was in close friendship with the Ducs de Beauvilliers and Chevreuse and with nearly all their families; I was intimate with Chamillart even after his downfall; I stood well with the Jesuits and with Mgr le Duc de Bourgogne, and also with the Archbishop of Cambrai, although I did not know him personally. My real place, therefore, was with this cabal that counted Mgr le Duc de Bourgogne as one of themselves against the whole world.

On the other hand, I was the confidant of the Chancellor and his family in almost all their affairs both public and private; I was on friendly terms with the Duc and Duchesse de Villeroy and through them with the Duc de La Rocheguyon. I also had the confidence of Beringhen, and of Du Mont and Bignon who, with his wife, was a friend of Mlle Choin. The latter belonged to the Meudon Cabal, which was still so much alive that I could wish neither of the other two to succumb.

I dare say that the good opinion of these important people and the friendship which many of them felt for me allowed them to speak freely and confidentially of the most secret and serious matters. And although it sometimes happened that they let slip something concerning my friends on the other side, they were not unduly perturbed. It was through the Chancellor and the Maréchal de Boufflers that I learned most of what went on, for the Ducs de Beauvilliers and Chevreuse were less observant and often ill-informed.

Besides these reliable sources, I had access to one of the inmost circles of the Court through some of the most intelligent ladies, especially those in the entourage of Mme la Duchesse de Bourgogne. Old and young, and of various characters, they perceived many things from their own observation and learned the rest from the princess. Thus, day by day, I received confidential news of the inner workings of that fascinating sphere, and by the same channels I often learned the secret intrigues of Mme de Maintenon's sanctum.

I had still other sources of information regarding a circle no less private. I refer to the confidential valets who, day and night, were in attendance in the King's apartments and by no means kept their eyes and ears tightly shut.

By such means I was regularly informed of all that went on, both grave and trivial, through honest, direct, and sure channels. Thus, apart from my other concerns, my curiosity was satisfied, and, you must admit, whether you be somebody or nobody, that that is the only nourishment to be found at Courts, and that without it you would die of boredom.

1711

Death of Monseigneur

In that year, Easter Sunday fell on 5 April. On the following Wednesday, after the meeting of the council Monseigneur dined *in parvulo* at Meudon, taking Mme la Duchesse de Bourgogne tête-à-tête in his coach. What the *parvulos* were, I have already explained. The Court had asked for this Meudon visit, which was due to last one week, until the Marly excursion announced for the next Wednesday. I myself had been absent since the Monday in Holy Week and intended to go to Marly on the same day as the King. The Meudon parties were now intensely embarrassing to me, feeling, as I did, that the whole place was infested with devils. Mme la Duchesse had returned to queen it there and had brought her daughters. Mlle de Lillebonne and Mme d'Espinoy openly ruled the roost; d'Antin gave the orders, and between them they controlled Monseigneur. They were all my personal enemies and therefore I avoided the visits to Meudon, for although this made me feel ill at ease with Monseigneur and his circle, I might have felt far worse had I risked going there.

Although the present situation disquieted me, other thoughts were still more troubling. Every day, the prospect grew clearer of the future time when Monseigneur would sit upon the throne, and, when the quarrelling of those who now influenced him and aimed at ruling him exclusively had abated, would have raised beside him one or other of the enemies who above all things desired to ruin me. They would only have to express their wish. Failing all other comfort, I lived on my courage, telling myself that one never experiences all the good or all the ill which one has most reason to expect. In this way, hoping against hope, I put my trust in the uncertainty of all earthly things and wiled away my time, calm enough as regards the future, but in the utmost embarrassment where the present and Meudon were concerned.

That was why I had gone to spend the Easter fortnight resting and meditating far from the Court, where at that time, every prospect, with the exception of Monseigneur and some others, was pleasing to me. That sting seemed past all remedy and it plagued me cruelly until suddenly, at the most unexpected moment, it pleased God to deliver me. No one was staying with me at La Ferté, except M. de Saint-Louis, a retired cavalry officer who for the past thirty years had been living at the Abbaye de La Trappe, and a gentleman of Normandy, a former captain in my regiment, who was much attached to me. I had been walking with them in the garden on the morning of Saturday 11th, and was alone in my study shortly before dinner, when a courier brought me a letter from Mme de Saint-Simon to say that Monseigneur had been taken ill.

That prince, as I have already said, going to Meudon on the day after the Easter festival, was passing through Chaville when he saw a priest bearing Our Lord to a dying man, and got down from his coach with Mme la Duchesse de Bourgogne to kneel and worship. He asked to whom they were taking the Sacrament and heard that it was to a man dying of the smallpox, which was very prevalent at that time. Monseigneur had had the disease in early childhood, but very slightly, and was mortally afraid of it. He was much alarmed, and said to Boudin,[1] his chief physician, that it would not surprise him if he had taken it. None the less, the rest of that day passed without incident.

On the following day, Thursday 9th, Monseigneur had intended to hunt, but weakness overcame him as he was dressing and he fell over in his chair. Boudin had him put back to bed, but Fagon mentioned the matter so casually to the King that he thought nothing of it and drove out to Marly after his dinner. There he received reports several times from Meudon, where Mgr and Mme la Duchesse de Bourgogne stayed to dine, for they would not leave Monseigneur even for an instant. The princess, so naturally kind, did more than her duty as his daughter-in-law and fed him with her own hands. She cannot have grieved over what her mind told her to think probable, but she never failed in her devoted care and behaved without any affectation or pretence. Mgr le Duc de Bourgogne, so simple, so saintly, always so eager to pay his respects to his father, re-doubled his attentions. He had not had the

[1] Jean Boudin, the King's apothecary, a pupil of Fagon.

smallpox, which was already strongly suspected, yet neither he nor the Duchesse would desert Monseigneur until they had to leave him to go to sup with the King.

When the latter had heard their news, he sent such definite instructions to Meudon that he learned of Monseigneur's danger as soon as he woke on the following morning. He had already said that he intended to go to Meudon the next morning and to stay there throughout the whole of the illness, no matter what that might be, and he set off immediately after his mass. Just as he was leaving he forbade his children to follow him and issued a general interdiction to all who had not had the smallpox, which was a kindly and considerate gesture. He said further that those who had had the disease might pay their court to him at Meudon, or stay away if they felt nervous or were discommoded.

The Saint-Simons' country house, La Ferté Vidame, near Dreux, not far from Chartres.

Several guests were sent away to make room for the King's suite, whom he strictly limited to personal attendants and ministers, so that he might work as usual. Only the Chancellor did not sleep at Meudon. The ladies who remained were Madame la Duchesse and the Princesse de Conti with their maids of honour, Mlle de Lillebonne and Mme d'Espinoy, Mlle de Melun because she was deeply devoted to Monseigneur, and Mlle de Bouillon, who did not wish to leave her father, the grand chamberlain. They all dined with the King, but he supped alone, as at Marly. I have not yet mentioned Mlle Choin, who had been there since the Wednesday, nor Mme de Maintenon, who drove out from Versailles with Mme la Duchesse de Bourgogne. The King firmly refused to allow the latter to enter Monseigneur's apartments and ordered her rather abruptly to return. That is how matters stood when Mme de Saint-Simon's courier arrived at La Ferté.

I shall continue to speak of myself with the same frankness that I have used in speaking of others, and with all possible truth. In the situation that I then was regarding Monseigneur and his circle, you may readily imagine how the news affected me, for I understood that for better or worse the matter would soon be decided. I was very comfortable at La Ferté, and therefore, resolving to wait for further reports, I returned the courier to Mme de Saint-Simon, asking her to send another on the following day. All that day I spent in a state of flux, alternately gaining and losing ground as I tried to keep the Christian on guard against the courtier. At this critical time, many other thoughts occupied my mind, persuading me to foresee a speedy and unexpected deliverance under the happiest auspices for the future.

Thus I waited impatiently for the courier to return, which he did, early in the afternoon of the next day, Low Sunday. I then learned that the smallpox had declared itself and that things were going as well as could be expected. This seemed to be confirmed when I heard that Mme de Maintenon, who never left her room when she stayed at Meudon, had gone early that morning to Versailles, had dined with Mme de Caylus, and had been in no hurry to return. I therefore concluded that Monseigneur was saved and decided to stay at home; however, after taking counsel, as I have done all my life and been the better for it, I regretfully gave orders to leave on the following day, which I did, early in the morning. When I reached La Queue, fourteen leagues from La Ferté and six from Versailles, a banker named La Fontaine came up to the door of my coach as I was changing horses. He had just come from Paris and Versailles, where he had seen some of Mme la Duchesse de Bourgogne's people, and said that Monseigneur was better, giving me details that seemed to prove him out of danger. There seemed no longer any reason for fear, except the treacherous nature of that kind of illness in a very stout man of fifty.

The King took counsel and worked with his ministers as usual. He saw Monseigneur every morning and evening and sometimes in the afternoon as well, sitting for long periods by his bedside. He dined early on the Monday when I arrived, and drove out to Marly, where Mme la Duchesse de Bourgogne went to meet him. As he passed through the Versailles gardens, Messeigneurs his two grandsons were waiting to speak to him, but he would not let them approach and only called out, 'Good day', as he drove by.

The King was never happy except in his own houses. He detested being anywhere else. That is why he paid only short visits to Meudon, on rare occasions and purely out of courtesy. Mme de Maintenon disliked being there still more. Everywhere that she went, her room was kept strictly private, accessible only to the ladies of her intimate circle; yet in spite of this, she always insisted on having some other absolutely inviolable sanctuary, where only Mme la Duchesse de Bourgogne might come occasionally, for a few moments and alone. Thus, when at Versailles and Marly she had Saint-Cyr, at Marly she also had Le Repos, and, at Fontainebleau, a house in the town was reserved for her. Now that Monseigneur was so much better and the visit to Meudon seemed likely to last a long time, the King's decorators were ordered to furnish Chaville as a retreat for her. This was a house which Monseigneur had purchased from the late Chancellor, Le Tellier, and had enclosed within the park. At this time things seemed to be going so well that the King decided to hold a review on the Wednesday.

As soon as I arrived at Versailles, I wrote to M. le Duc de Beauvilliers, asking him to inform the King that I had returned when I learned of Monseigneur's illness, and that I should have gone to Meudon, only that I had not had the smallpox and felt myself to be included in the general prohibition. He sent word back that my return had been well received, and again told me on behalf of the King that I was not to go to Meudon, either alone or with Mme de Saint-Simon. This personal interdiction did not distress me in the very least, Mme la Duchesse de Berry had had smallpox and unlike Mme la Duchesse de Bourgogne was forbidden to see the King, and neither of their husbands had ever had it. The interdiction, except as regarded the two Sons of France, who were very properly included, only covered the royal family in as far as the King thought it best.

Meudon itself was full of contrasts. The Choin was confined to her attic. Mlle de Lillebonne and Mme d'Espinoy never moved from Monseigneur's bedroom, but the recluse was only allowed there when the King was away and Madame la Princesse de Conti, who was equally devoted, had gone to bed. This lady, however, realized that Monseigneur would be cruelly frustrated if he were allowed no freedom in that respect and acted with great kindness. On the very morning after the King's arrival, the day after she herself had come, she told Monseigneur that she had known for some time that someone was at Meudon, that she herself could not stay away from the château in her present anxiety, but that it was not fair to allow her affection to inconvenience him. She therefore begged him to send her away whenever he chose and promised never to enter his room without first discovering whether she might see him without embarrassment. Monseigneur was delighted by her consideration, and the princess kept her word, quietly accepting hints from Mme la Duchesse and her daughters when it was time for her to leave the room, and never appearing disconcerted or ill-humoured. In all this she deserved true praise.

Of course the someone referred to was Mlle Choin. She and Père Le Tellier figured at Meudon in the most extraordinary manner. Both were there incognito, each lived secluded in an attic, eating their meals alone, seen only when strictly necessary, yet making everyone aware of their presence. There was this essential difference between them; whereas the lady saw Monseigneur daily and nightly and never set foot elsewhere, the confessor went to the King's apartment and all others, excepting only Monseigneur's room and those adjoining. Mme d'Espinoy carried polite messages backwards and forwards between Mme de Maintenon and Mlle Choin. The King did not see her. He believed that Mme de Maintenon had done so, and when he later made enquiries and discovered that she had not he did not approve. Mme de

Drawing of the Château de Versailles, from the ministers' lodgings outside the inner gates. By Perelle.

Maintenon then sent Mme d'Espinoy to Mlle Choin with her excuses, saying that she hoped they might soon be able to meet, an odd remark considering that the message was sent from one room to another under the same roof. In fact, they never did meet afterwards.

Versailles presented a very different spectacle. Mgr and Mme la Duchesse de Bourgogne openly held court there, and that Court was like the dawn of a new day. All the courtiers had congregated there, all Paris came flocking and, since prudence and tact are not virtues of the French, all Meudon came as well, and were believed when they maintained that they had not entered Monseigneur's rooms. The times to pay one's court were during the *levers* and *couchers*, dining and supping with the ladies, in the general conversation after meals, or walking in the gardens. The state apartments could not contain the crowds. Couriers arrived every quarter of an hour bringing reminders of Monseigneur. The illness was progressing as well as could be expected; there was every reason for hope and confidence, a general eagerness to please at the new Court, and a stately and soberly cheerful bearing on the part of the young prince and princess, who had a gracious welcome for all and took care to say a few words to each individual. The crowds themselves were full of amiability, there was general satisfaction all round, with the Duc and Duchesse de Berry practically nonentities. Five days passed in this way, each person thinking of the future and trying to adapt his behaviour to suit any eventuality.

On Tuesday, April 14th, the day after my return to Versailles, the King, who was finding Meudon very dull, held the usual Conseil des Finances in the morning and, against his custom, a Conseil des Dépêches in the afternoon. I met the Chancellor on his return from the latter and he assured me that Monseigneur's condition was good and that Fagon had actually said that things were going as well as could be wished and beyond what they had dared to hope.

RIGHT The Paris fishwives at the market of Les Halles. Gouache for a fan.

148

The Chancellor appeared exceedingly confident and I believed him all the more because he was intimate with Monseigneur and did not banish all cause for anxiety, although he expressed none other than was reasonable in an illness of that kind.

Monseigneur's devoted friends, the Paris fish-wives, who had figured once before when an acute attack of indigestion was mistaken for apoplexy, again distinguished themselves by arriving at Meudon that morning in several hired coaches. Monseigneur had insisted on admitting them to his room, and they had flung themselves upon the foot of his bed, kissing it repeatedly. Then, overjoyed at the good reports, they had vowed that they would go back to make all Paris glad and to have Te Deums sung in all the churches. Monseigneur, who was never insensible to popular affection, thereupon had given orders that they should be shown the house, entertained to dinner, and sent away with presents of money.

In the meantime, as I was returning from meeting the Chancellor and was crossing one of the courtyards at Versailles to go to my own apartment, I saw Mme la Duchesse d'Orléans walking on the terrace of the new wing. She called out to me, but Mme de Montauban[1] was with her so I pretended not to see or hear and continued on my way full of the latest news from Meudon. My rooms were in the upper gallery of the new wing, almost next to those of M. and Mme la Duchesse de Berry, who were giving a supper-party that night for M. and

[1] Saint-Simon describes her earlier as hunchback, lopsided, hideous, raddled with paint and patches, debauched, avaricious, wicked, 'a kind of monster'. No one would speak to her on the rare occasions when she came to Court.

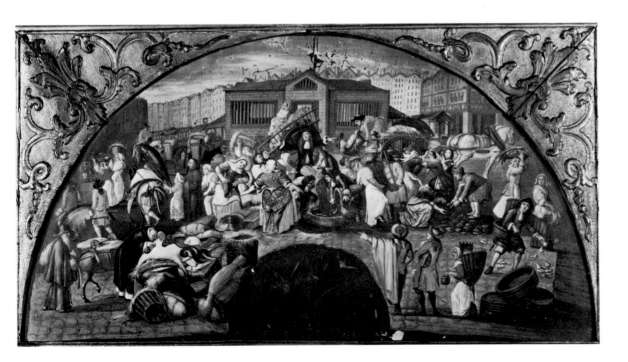

Mme la Duchesse d'Orléans and some of the ladies, including Mme de Saint-Simon, but she had excused herself because she was slightly indisposed.

I had been in my study only a very short time when they announced Mme la Duchesse d'Orléans, who had come for an hour's chat before supper. I received her in Mme de Saint-Simon's room, although she happened to be out, but she returned before long and made a third in the conversation. The princess and I had been itching to see one another and gossip about the whole situation, regarding which we thought alike. She had returned only an hour earlier from Meudon and had seen the King. It was now eight o'clock.

In talking to me, she used the very same words as Fagon, when he was speaking to the Chancellor; described the confidence that reigned at Meudon, praised the skill and care of the doctors, who neglected nothing, not even the little homely remedies, which were usually despised. She expatiated upon the success of their treatment and, to speak frankly, albeit to our shame, both she and I lamented that Monseigneur, with his age and corpulence, should be escaping so dangerous a disease. She reflected sadly in the witty, languishing manner of the Mortemarts, that after such a purging he would not retain even the tiniest little likelihood of apoplexy, and that the chance of indigestion was irretrievably ruined now that he had taken fright and delivered his system into the doctors' hands. We concluded even more gloomily that we should now have to resign ourselves to the idea that he might live and reign a very long time. From that point we proceeded to predict the fatal consequences of his reign and the vanity of trusting even the most reliable symptoms regarding Monseigneur's health, which had seemed so desperate, yet had found continuance and new strength in the very heart of death. In short, we fairly let ourselves go, although not without some scruples intervening occasionally to interrupt this fascinating conversation, which Mme la Duchesse d'Orléans, in her drolly plaintive fashion, always brought back to the point. Mme de Saint-Simon, all goodness, tried to check our more outrageous remarks, but the brakes were off, and there ensued the oddest struggle between the expression of sentiments that, humanly speaking, were very natural to us, and the feeling that they were not Christian.

Two hours passed in this way, very quickly as it seemed to us, and then we were interrupted by supper-time. Mme la Duchesse d'Orléans went to her daughter, and Mme de Saint-Simon and I to my room, where company had collected and we supped.

While everything seemed so settled at Versailles and even Meudon, a change was actually in progress. The King had seen Monseigneur several times that day, for such tokens of affection and kindness were much appreciated, but during the visit after dinner he had noticed a great swelling of the face and head, which had shocked him so much that he stayed only a little time and shed a few tears as he left the room. They had done their best to reassure him and after the council was over he had gone for a walk in the gardens. Nevertheless, Monseigneur had already failed to recognize Mme la Princesse de Conti, and

Boudin was alarmed. The prince himself had never ceased to be so. Courtiers had been seeing him one after another; some of the more intimate had never left his room, and he had asked them continually whether his sensations were usual symptoms of the disease. At moments, when he believed their reassurances, he had high hopes of recovery, and at one such time he had said to Mme la Princesse de Conti that he had been feeling unwell for a long while but had not liked to say so, and that on Holy Thursday he had been hard put to it to hold his prayer book.

At about four o'clock in the afternoon he grew so much worse that Boudin suggested to Fagon that they should send to Paris for other advice, since, as Court physicians, they themselves never saw infectious diseases and had no experience of treating them. Fagon thereupon flew into a rage, refused to listen to argument and stubbornly refused to send for anyone. He said that nothing would be gained by disputation and conflicting opinions, maintained that they could do as well if not better without outside interference, and although Monseigneur's condition worsened hourly, decided to keep secret the true state of affairs. By seven o'clock, even some of the courtiers had noticed the deterioration, but they were terrified of Fagon's presence, and none dared to warn the King and Mme de Maintenon. Mme la Princesse de Conti and Mme la Duchesse de Bourgogne were equally helpless and tried to comfort one another. What was extraordinary was that they decided to let the King sit down to his supper before alarming him with talk of desperate remedies and he finished his meal without receiving any kind of warning. Indeed, on the strength of Fagon's reports and from the general silence he believed that Monseigneur was at any rate no worse, although because of the change and the swelling he had been troubled about him earlier in the evening.

While the King was thus calmly eating his supper, panic had broken out in the bedroom of Monseigneur. Fagon and the other doctors had tried one remedy after another without waiting for any to take effect. The curé of Meudon who called to inquire every evening, had found the doors standing wide open and the footmen distracted. He entered the room, and when he saw the truth, so belatedly recognized, ran to the bed, took Monseigneur by the hand, spoke of God and, seeing that he was still conscious though almost speechless, extracted some sort of confession (which no one had thought of) and suggested certain acts of contrition. The wretched prince managed to utter a few words distinctly and to mumble some others, touched his breast, clasped the curé's hand, seemed imbued with proper sentiments, and received absolution with apparent eagerness and repentance.

By now the King had risen from table, and almost fell over backwards with astonishment when Fagon appeared before him completely distraught, crying out that all was lost. You may imagine the horror that seized everyone in this sudden transition from perfect confidence to the last degree of despair. The King had hardly recovered himself before he immediately started towards Monseigneur's apartments, cutting short tactless efforts to restrain him and saying that he wished to make sure that no remedy had been left untried. As he was about to cross the threshold, however, Mme la Princesse de Conti, who had flown to Monseigneur's side in the short interval since the end of supper, appeared to prevent his entering. She even went so far as to press him back with both hands, saying that he must now think only of himself.

After that, the King, almost swooning from this sudden and complete reversal, sank down upon a sofa near the door of the ante-room. He asked for news from all who came out of the bedroom, but few had the courage to answer him. On his way down to Monseigneur he had sent for Père Le Tellier, who had already gone to bed, but hastily redressed and was soon in the bedroom. By then it was too late, at least so all the servants said, but that Jesuit, perhaps to reassure the King, maintained that he had found good and sufficient grounds to give absolution. Meanwhile, Mme de Maintenon had hurried to the King's side and was sitting on the same sofa, endeavouring to weep. She made efforts to take him away, for his coaches were ready in the courtyard, but could by no means persuade him to go until after Monseigneur had expired.

The coma lasted for nearly an hour after the King had entered the ante-room. Madame la Duchesse and Mme la Princesse de Conti divided their attention between the dying man and the King, to whom they often returned. As for the others, the doctors were bewildered, the servants distracted, the courtiers murmuring. They jostled against one another so that there was constant movement with scarcely any change of position. At last the dreadful moment came and Fagon left, which allowed it to be generally known.

The King had been profoundly distressed and shocked at the absence of a proper confession, and he lashed out at Fagon before he allowed Mme de Maintenon and the two princesses to lead him away. The apartment was on the ground floor, level with the courtyard. As he came out to get into a carriage he noticed that the one in front of him was Monseigneur's own berline, and he signed for them to bring up another because the sight of that one upset him. Yet he was not too affected to notice Pontchartrain, and he called out, telling him to warn his father and the other ministers to come later than usual to Marly next day, for the Wednesday meeting of the council of state. I shall not comment on his extraordinary self-control, but merely say that the witnesses were astounded, and so were all who heard of it. Pontchartrain answered that since the only questions concerned current affairs, the meeting might well be postponed for a day until the King was less harassed. To this the King consented. He got with difficulty into the coach, supported on either side; Mme de Maintenon got in after him, followed by Mme la Princesse de Conti, who sat on the front seat. A crowd of the officers of Monseigneur's household had flung themselves upon their knees, lining the entire length of the courtyard on both sides of the King's way, imploring him with terrible cries to have compassion on them, for they had lost all and would die of hunger.

Whilst Meudon was thus providing a scene of horror, everything was quiet and peaceful at Versailles. We had finished our supper, the guests had retired some time later, and I was chatting with Mme de Saint-Simon as she undressed to go to bed, when suddenly one of our former footmen, whom she had given to Mme la Duchesse de Berry and who served her at table, entered in a great state of alarm. He said that bad news must have come from Meudon, because Mgr le Duc de Bourgogne had whispered something to M. le Duc de Berry, whose eyes had filled with tears. He had left the table precipitately, and when an urgent second message had come, the entire company had risen and had gone into the drawing-room. So sudden a change amazed me, and I hurried off to Mme la Duchesse de Berry's apartment, where I found no one. They had gone in a body to Mme la Duchesse de Bourgogne and I followed as quickly as I could.

I found all Versailles assembled there, the ladies out of their court-dresses, most of them ready for bed, the doors all wide open, and everything in a turmoil. I soon learned that Monseigneur had received Extreme Unction, that he was now unconscious, his condition regarded as hopeless. I also heard that the King had sent word to Mme la Duchesse de Bourgogne that he was on his way to Marly and that she was to wait for him in the avenue between the two stables as he wished to see her when he passed.

Amid the thoughts and sentiments that came crowding into my mind, I concentrated all the attention that I could spare upon the scene before me. The two princes and the princesses were in the little ante-room behind the alcove, where the toilet accessories had been laid out ready for the *coucher* in Mme la Duchesse de Bourgogne's bedroom. She herself went backwards and forwards between the two rooms, filling in the time until she had to go to meet the King. She bore herself as graciously as usual, but there was a look of compassion and stress about her, which many people mistook for grief. When people spoke to her as she passed, she answered their inquiries or said a few brief words. The expressions on the faces of the bystanders were truly eloquent; one needed only to have eyes, not the least knowledge of the Court, to read the desires of some, whilst the countenances of those who had nothing to gain remained perfectly blank. Some were self-possessed; others seemed cruelly affected, or else highly serious, and careful to reveal nothing of their joy and relief.

My first action was to inquire from several persons, but I did not place much reliance on their words, nor on the spectacle before me, for I feared that there might be all too little cause for so much excitement. Then I brought myself to reflect on the common lot of man and that I too should one day find myself at the gates of death. None the less, joy kept on breaking through these passing thoughts of religion and common humanity, by which I was striving to remember the proprieties. My own deliverance seemed so vast, so unlooked for, that from evidence which boded better than the reality, I believed that the State had everything to gain from this death. Among such reflections, however, I could not help feeling slightly afraid that the patient might still recover, and then I was mortally ashamed of myself.

Deeply immersed, as I was, in my own thoughts, I did not forget to send word to Mme de Saint-Simon that she had better come, nor to keep a surreptitious watch on each face, appearance, and action. Thus I indulged my eager curiosity, confirmed my first impressions (they have never proved wrong) of every important person present, and drew the proper conclusions from those first impulsive movements that are rarely mastered and are therefore sure signs, to those who know the Court and their fellow-men, of attachments and sentiments that are invisible in more settled times.

I saw Mme la Duchesse d'Orléans arrive, but her set, dignified countenance told me nothing. She entered the little ante-room and shortly afterwards returned with M. le Duc d'Orléans, whose manner, agitated and confused, reflected the general excitement rather than any deeper emotion. They then left together. A few moments later, I noticed M. le Duc de Bourgogne in the distance, near the door of the ante-room. He seemed profoundly moved and distressed, but the searching glance which I shot at him could detect no tender feelings, only the intense preoccupation of a man absorbed in his own thoughts.

The footmen and valets were already weeping noisily, their sorrow showing how much such kind of people stood to lose. At about half-past midnight news was received from the King, and I saw Mme la Duchesse de Bourgogne come out of the little ante-room with Mgr le Duc, who seemed now even more affected and returned immediately. The princess took her shawl and hood from the dressing-table; then, erect, purposeful, and almost dry-eyed, she crossed the room, her inner turmoil betrayed only by the furtive, questioning glances which she cast to right and left. Followed only by her ladies, she went down the grand staircase to her coach.

When she had left, I took the opportunity to go to Mme la Duchesse d'Orléans, for I was itching to be with her, but as soon as I entered I learned that they had gone to Madame's apartment, and pushed my way through the crowd in pursuit of them. I met her as she was returning and she asked me very gravely to come with her; M. le Duc d'Orléans was still with his mother. Having regained her own room she sat down, and the Duchesse de Villeroy, the Maréchale de Rochefort, and five or six ladies of her circle gathered round her. I was twitching with impatience at finding so much company, and Mme la Duchesse d'Orléans, no less exasperated, took a candle and stepped into the back of the room. I then wished to say something into the ear of the Duchesse de Villeroy, for she and I thought alike in the present circumstances, but she gave me a little push and told me in a whisper to control myself. It nearly choked me to have to keep silence amid the ladies' conventional expressions of pity and amazement, but at that moment M. le duc d'Orléans appeared at the door of his study and called me to come in.

I followed him downstairs to his inner study that leads into the great gallery, he, almost swooning, and I, with my legs trembling because of all that was happening around and within me. By chance we sat facing one another, and I saw at once to my intense astonishment that tears were falling from his eyes. 'Monsieur!' I exclaimed, rising to my feet. He understood at once and

Drawing for one of the royal coaches; the passengers all faced forwards, none had their backs to the horses. By Van der Meulen.

answered in a broken voice, now actually weeping, 'You may well be surprised, indeed so am I; but such scenes are moving. He was a good man and I have known him all my life; when they let him alone, he treated me well and was good to me. I know that my grief will be short, and in a few days' time I shall see every cause to console myself, considering the bad feeling that they created between us. At present, kinship, pity, humanity, are all involved, and one does feel moved.' I praised his sentiments, but expressed my intense surprise, on account of his bad relations with Monseigneur. At this he rose, put his head in a corner, nose towards the wall, and began to weep and sob bitterly, a thing I never would have believed had I not seen it with my own eyes. After a short silence, I urged him to control himself, saying that he would soon have to return to Mme la Duchesse de Bourgogne's apartment, and that if he were seen with red eyes everyone would ridicule him for a piece of arrant humbug, for the entire Court knew on what sort of terms he had been with Monseigneur. He then did what he could to patch up his eyes, and was still at that work when word came that Mme la Duchesse de Bourgogne had returned and that Mme la Duchesse d'Orléans was about to go to her apartment. He went to join her and I followed.

Mme la Duchesse de Bourgogne had waited only a short time in the avenue between the two stables before the King drove up. She had stepped down from her coach to greet him at his carriage door, when Mme de Maintenon, who was sitting on her side, called out, 'What are you thinking of, Madame? Do not come near, we are pest-ridden!' I never learned what gesture the King made, but I know that he did not kiss her, on account of the contagion. The princess immediately stepped back into her coach and returned to the château.

The fearful secrecy with which Fagon had concealed Monseigneur's real condition deceived everybody so completely that the Duc de Beauvilliers, who had been sleeping at Meudon throughout the illness, actually returned to Versailles after the Conseil des Dépêches. He usually retired about ten o'clock because he was a very early riser, and that night he had gone to bed without the least anxiety. It was not long before a messenger arrived summoning him to Mme la Duchesse de Bourgogne's apartment, where he found the two princes and Mme la Duchesse de Berry waiting in the ante-room.

When the first embraces were over, after Mme la Duchesse de Bourgogne's return, which, in itself, told all, the Duc de Beauvilliers noticed that it was stifling in that little room and persuaded them to go through the bedroom, into the drawing-room that separates it from the great gallery. The windows were opened and the two princes, each with his princess by his side, sat down on a sofa that stood near the windows, with its back to the gallery. The whole company in this room was dispersed, standing and sitting in great disorder, and the ladies of the intimate circle sat on the floor near the foot of the princes' sofa.

From then onwards in that room and, indeed, in the whole apartment countenances might be read like open books. Monseigneur was dead. Everyone knew it, everyone spoke of it; no one now held back out of deference, and these first moments revealed first impulses in a true light, and for once free of the constraints of good manners. Yet people behaved discreetly amid the anxiety, excitement, shocks, crowding, and general confusion of that eventful night.

In the outer rooms smothered groans could be heard from servants in despair at losing a master who had suited them to perfection and dreading the prospect of inheriting another (the King) whom they greatly feared. Among them were strangers, the more intelligent footmen of the chief personages at the Court, who had hurried to hear the news and plainly showed by their manner to which clique their masters belonged.

Farther on were crowds of courtiers of every description, the greater number, the fools, drawing sighs out of their very heels, while with dry eyes and roving glances they praised Monseigneur with one voice and for one virtue only, kindness, and pitied the King for losing so excellent a son. The cleverest, or the most prudent among them, pretended anxiety about the King's own health, congratulating themselves on remaining cool amid so much confusion, and leaving no one in doubt by their constant repetition. Others seemed truly distressed, and the members of the stricken cabal[1] wept bitterly, or controlled themselves by an effort as obvious as any sobbing. The hardest, or the most cunning, kept their eyes on the ground, or meditated in distant corners on the probable outcome of this totally unexpected event, and still more on their own futures. There was little or no conversation between the variously afflicted; although every now and then someone would let fall a remark which was echoed by his neighbours, words dropping at the rate of one every quarter of an hour. Faces were melancholy or haggard, gestures more frequent than intentional and for the rest, almost absolute stillness. Those who were merely curious or indifferent remained almost impassive; only the fools chattered and

[1] What Saint-Simon called the Cabal of the Nobles; those who had been relying on Monseigneur's accession.

asked questions, adding to the distress of the mourners and being an embarrassment to the others. Those who were glad tried in vain to increase their appearance of gravity by looking sad or stern; yet all that they could achieve was a thin veil through which keen eyes might discover their real feelings. Such people stood as motionless as those who were most affected, on their guard against public opinion, curiosity in others, complacency in themselves, or impulsiveness, but nevertheless the excitement in their eyes made up for their bodies' stillness. A change of attitude, as of men sitting uncomfortably or tired of standing, a particular care to avoid one another or even to prevent eyes from meeting, tiny incidents that arose from such encounters, an indescribable hint of release in the whole deportment of these people, shone through their efforts to be calm and controlled. A liveliness, a kind of glitter distinguished them from the rest, making them conspicuous in spite of all their efforts to the contrary.

The two princes with their princesses sitting beside and comforting them were exposed to every eye. Mgr le Duc de Bourgogne wept in all sincerity, quietly shedding tears of compassion, piety, and long endurance. M. le Duc de Berry was equally sincere, but he seemed to be weeping tears of blood, so bitterly he cried; indeed, it was not merely sobs that came from him, but shrieks and howls, even bellowings. Sometimes he was quiet, but only when he was choking, and then his cries would break out again, so loud, so monstrously loud that it was like the uncontrollable trumpeting of deep despair. Many others joined in these heartrending outbursts, goaded into weeping either by emotion or by a sense of the proprieties. At last, he reached such a pitch that they were forced to undress him there and then, to have remedies prepared, and to call for the doctors. Mme la Duchesse de Berry was beside herself; you shall soon discover why. The bitterest despair was imprinted on her face. You could see as plainly as though it were written a perfect paroxysm of uncontrollable woe, not from grief or affection, but from pure selfishness. There were intervals when she was dry-eyed, but sullen-looking and angry. Then came torrents of tears and gestures, involuntary yet restrained, that betrayed deep bitterness of spirit, resulting from her preceding meditations. The cries of her husband often interrupted her, and then she was quick to support and embrace him or to offer him smelling-salts; you could see her eagerness to minister to him. Then, just as swiftly, she would relapse into her own thoughts, then into a storm of weeping that helped her to stifle her sobs. Mme la Duchesse de Bourgogne also comforted her husband, and found it easier to do so than to give any appearance of needing consolation herself. She paraded no false emotion, yet one could see that she did her utmost to produce the tears, which she felt decency required, and which often will not come when they are most needed. A frequent use of her handkerchief reflected the sobs of her princely brother-in-law and a few tears, occasioned by the scene around her and carefully husbanded, were encouraged by artful rubbing to smudge her face and make her eyes red and swollen; but all the time, her furtive glances wandered over the bystanders and scanned the faces of each one in turn.

The Duc de Beauvilliers stood beside them, looking as cool and detached as though nothing were happening, or the scene were an everyday event. He quietly attended to the princes, giving orders to allow few to enter, although the doors stood open, and sending for all that was needed without any bustle or misjudgment, behaving, in fact, as though he were at an ordinary *lever* or *petit couvert*. His composure was unruffled, for since his conscience forbade him either to be glad or to conceal the little grief that he felt, he was able to preserve a truthful appearance to the end.

Madame again put on Court dress,[1] and arrived shrieking, not rightly knowing why she did either. She drowned with her tears all whom she embraced and made the palace re-echo with her cries, presenting the remarkable spectacle of a princess putting on formal attire in the middle of the night, and coming to weep among a crowd of women in their nightgowns, or almost in fancy dress.

Mme la Duchesse d'Orléans had left the princes and was sitting near the fireplace with her back to the gallery, among a group of ladies; but she was very silent and they gradually went farther off, which pleased her very much. Only the Duchesse Sforza, the Duchesse de Villeroy, Mme de Castries, and Mme de Saint-Simon remained, who were thankful to be left alone and drew into a little knot beside one of the camp-beds. They pulled the curtains together, and as all were of the same mind regarding the event that had assembled so large a company, they began to talk freely in low voices.

For reasons of security, a number of these camp-beds were set up at night for the use of the Swiss guard and floor-polishers in all the state apartments, and they had been arranged as usual before the bad news had come from Meudon. In the middle of the conversation, Mme de Castries, who was touching the bed, felt something stir, which terrified her, because she was nervous of everything although she had plenty of courage. The next moment, a great naked arm pulled open the curtains, and the ladies saw a huge Swiss guard between the sheets, only half-awake, yawning, and staring fixedly at the people round him, whom he was very slow to recognize. Then, obviously thinking it unsuitable to get out of bed in such exalted company, he buried himself once more between the sheets and pulled his curtains. The fellow had apparently gone to bed before any news had come and had slept so soundly that he had only just wakened. The most ridiculous incidents do sometimes relieve the most solemn spectacles, and this one made several of the ladies laugh, although Mme la Duchesse d'Orléans feared lest they might have been overheard. On reflection, however, they were reassured by the man's sleepiness and evident stupidity.

As for myself, I endeavoured to keep an open mind. Although everything seemed to prove what had happened, I refused to believe it until I found some responsible person who would confirm the news, and I happened to see M. d'O, who told me facts, over which, when I learned them, I tried not to rejoice openly. I am not sure how far I succeeded, but one thing is certain, that

[1] On the following day, April 16th, Madame wrote as follows to her aunt, the Duchess of Hanover, 'Those who imagined that they were harming me by alienating Monseigneur le Dauphin's affections, may perhaps have saved my life, for had he and I been on the same terms as before Monsieur's death I might have died from fright and grief, or have remained inconsolable, whereas at present I can support the affliction patiently and grieve only for the King. I do indeed pity Monseigneur le Dauphin, but I cannot be as much distressed at the loss of one who did not love and had entirely forsaken me, as I might have been had he remained my friend.'

neither joy nor sorrow abated my curiosity, and whilst I was careful to preserve the decencies, I did not think it necessary to pretend to any grief. I no longer feared repercussions from Meudon, nor persecution by its relentless garrison, and since the King was away at Marly, I felt unconstrained and could study the crowd freely, allowing my eyes to dwell on those who from different motives were much or little affected.

Thus, I followed the movements of certain personages and endeavoured stealthily to penetrate their inmost thoughts, for indeed, to one who knows the inner life of a Court, these first moments after some extraordinary event are intensely gratifying. Each face reminds one of the cares and intrigues, the laborious efforts to advance a private fortune, or form and strengthen a cabal, the cunning devices designed and executed for that purpose, the attachments at varying degrees of intimacy, the estrangements, dislikes, and hatreds, the ill-turns played and favours granted, the tricks, petty shifts, and baseness of some individuals, the dashing of the hopes of some in mid-career, the stupefaction of others at the summit, who had thought their ambitions fulfilled and, at the same blow, the importance given to their adversaries in the opposing cabals, the force of the recoil, which in that self-same instant brought the affairs of some (myself included) to a successful conclusion and consequently to extreme and unlooked-for joy, and the fury displayed by the rest, in spite of all their concern to hide it. At such a time one's glances fly from face to face, trying to penetrate the very soul in those first moments of shocked surprise and sudden upheaval. One takes stock of all that one sees, realizing one's astonishment at not finding expected qualities in some, for want of intelligence or courage, and in others, seeing more than one had dared to hope. Such an amalgamation of ambitious people and critical events is a delight to those who understand and, ephemeral though it may be, it provides one of the greatest pleasures to be enjoyed at Court.

It was to this pursuit, then, that I gave myself wholly up, and with all the more alacrity because whilst I myself had been accorded a very real deliverance by this death, I was closely bound up and conjoined with the illustrous personages who could not force tears into their eyes. Thus I rejoiced in the unalloyed gain to them, and their gratification increased my own, raising my hopes and promising me the peace of mind of which, before this sad event, I had had so little prospect, for I had never ceased to mistrust the future. On the other hand, as an opponent of the cabals and almost a personal enemy of their leaders, I realized at my first keen glance and with inexpressible delight, all that was slipping from their grasp and all the troubles that would crush them. I knew so well the affairs of the different cabals, their leaders, and degrees of leadership, their ramifications and sub-divisions, that several days of meditation would not have told me these things half so clearly as that first sight of faces, which reminded me of others, not then seen, but none the less delectable morsels for my mind to feed upon.

I stayed for a little while to consider the scene in that vast and now chaotic state apartment. The tumult had lasted for fully an hour, but the Duchesse du Lude, who was in bed with the gout, did not appear. Finally, it was the Duc de Beauvilliers who decided that it was time to deliver the two princes from their distressingly public situation. He suggested that M. and Mme la Duchesse de Berry should retire to their own apartments and allow the Court to leave those of Mme la Duchesse de Bourgogne. His advice was accepted immediately. M. le Duc de Berry slowly moved forwards, partly alone, partly with the support of his wife. Mme de Saint-Simon attended them with a handful of the officers of their household; I followed, but at a distance, so that my curiosity was not noticeable. The prince wished to go to his own room to sleep, but Mme la Duchesse de Berry would not consent to leave him, indeed, he was so much congested and she also, that a complete faculty of doctors, all furnished and equipped, was asked to remain with them.

The whole of that night they spent in weeping and sobbing. From time to time M. le Duc de Berry asked for news from Meudon, apparently refusing to understand the reason for the King's departure to Marly. Sometimes he inquired whether there was no longer any room for hope, and then he wished to send for further news. Only much later in the morning was the tragic veil drawn from his eyes, so hard it is for nature and self-interest to accept absolute disaster. I cannot describe his state when final realization came. The condition of Mme la Duchesse de Berry was not much better, but that did not prevent her from taking all possible care of him.

The night of Mgr and Mme la Duchesse de Bourgogne passed more quietly, and they went to bed in reasonable peace. Mme de Levis whispered to the princess that since she had no cause for affliction it would be dreadful to see her make a pretence. She answered, most unaffectedly, that without any pretence she was moved by compassion and by the scenes she had witnessed, and that she was restrained by a sense of the proprieties, nothing more. Indeed, she kept within those limits with sincerity and dignity. They asked that some of the palace ladies should spend the remainder of the night in armchairs in their room. The curtains were left open and before long the room became like the palace of Morpheus. The prince and princess promptly fell asleep and woke once or twice, but only for an instant. As a matter of fact, they rose early and without fuss. The fountains had dried up within them; from then onwards they wept seldom and gently, when occasion demanded. The ladies who had watched and slept in the room told their friends what had occurred. No one was surprised, and since Monseigneur was no more, no one was scandalized. Mme de Saint-Simon and I then spent two hours alone together. Finally, it was common sense rather than a desire to sleep that persuaded us to go to bed, and we slept so little that I was up and dressed by seven in the morning. Nevertheless some insomnia is sweet and such awakenings are delectable.

At Meudon, in the meanwhile, horror reigned. When the King left, such attendants as remained with him followed, piling themselves into whatever vehicles came to hand. In a moment Meudon was a desert and Mlle de

Lillebonne and Mlle de Melun went up to Mlle Choin, who, isolated in her garret, was only beginning to feel the transports of despair. She knew nothing, for no one had thought of bringing her the bad news, and she had only realized her misfortune from the sound of lamentations. Her two friends bundled her into a hired coach that happened to be available and took her away with them to Paris.

A crowd of officers and servants of Monseigneur's household, and many others, spent the night wandering about in the gardens. Some of the courtiers slipped away singly and on foot. There was a complete dispersal. One or two valets, at the most, stayed by the body, which was a most laudable action, and La Vallière,[1] the only courtier who had not abandoned him in life, remained with him in death. He had much difficulty in finding anybody to send to fetch the Capuchins to pray beside the corpse. Decomposition set in so suddenly and so violently that it was not enough to open the doors and windows wide upon the terrace; La Vallière, the Capuchins, and the few remaining servants were forced to spend the night outside.

Everything had seemed so quiet before the crisis that no one dreamed of the King's going to Marly that night. Nothing, therefore, was ready to receive him, the door-keys were missing, there were only a few night-lights and no candles at all. In these circumstances the King and Mme de Maintenon were forced to sit for an hour or more in the ante-room to her apartment, with Madame la Duchesse, Mme la Princesse de Conti, and Mmes de Dangeau and de Caylus, the latter having hurried from Versailles to be with her aunt.[2] The last two ladies, however, stood discreetly here and there, and only for short intervals; others, who arrived later, stayed in the salon in spite of the disorder, for they did not know where else to go. For a long time they groped about in the dark, without even a candle, and when at last the servants did manage to find the keys they were so distraught that they mixed them up. Gradually the boldest of those in the salon began to show their faces in the ante-room, and then all made an appearance, partly out of curiosity, partly from a desire to show zeal. The King sat in a far corner between Mme de Maintenon and the princesses and wept for long stretches at a time; but at last Mme de Maintenon's door was opened and he was relieved from that uncomfortable situation. He entered the room with her alone and remained for another hour. He then went to bed—it was nearly four o'clock—and left her a breathing-space in which to recover. After his departure, the rest of the company were free to find lodging for themselves. . . .

Summing up the details of Monseigneur's character, it appears that he was a man without vice or virtue, knowledge or understanding, and totally incapable of acquiring any. He was vastly lazy, with no imagination or creative ability, without taste, decision or discernment. He was capable only of being bored and infected others with his ennui. Nature fashioned him to be like a ball that is rolled hither and thither at the will of others. Stubborn, and in all things very mean, incredibly gullible and easy to prejudice, a prey to most pernicious

[1] Charles-François de la Beaune-le-Blanc, Duc de La Vallière. He was a nephew of Louis XIV's mistress and first cousin of the Princesse de Condé.

[2] Mme de Maintenon.

influences, yet unable either to escape from them or to realize their vileness, immersed in his fat and his gloom; albeit with no desire for wrong-doing, he would have made a most abominable king.

He died of the smallpox, but the purples and the rapid decomposition that resulted therefrom made it useless as well as dangerous to open his body. Some say that he was prepared for burial by the grey sisters, others, by the floor-polishers of the château, or perhaps by the workmen who made the coffin, over which was thrown an ancient pall, belonging to the parish church of Meudon. There was no other retinue except the few who had remained, that is to say, La Vallière himself, some junior officials, and the Capuchins of Meudon, who took turns to pray by the coffin, without funeral hangings or any lights, except for a few candles.

It was about midnight that he died, between Tuesday and Wednesday. On the Thursday, he was taken to Saint-Denis in one of the royal coaches, not in mourning, and with the front window removed to allow room for the foot of the coffin. The curé of Meudon and the chaplain-in-residence travelled in the same coach, which was followed by another, also out of mourning, in which sat the Duc de la Trémoïlle and M. de Metz, the lord high almoner, on the back seat; and in front, Dreux, the grand master of ceremonies, and the Abbé de Brancas, who afterwards became Bishop of Lisieux. These two carriages, with footmen and twenty-four of the royal pages carrying torches, formed the whole of the very short procession that left Meudon at six or seven in the evening, crossed the bridge at Sèvres and through the Bois de Boulogne, and arrived at Saint-Denis by way of the Saint-Ouen plain. The body was then lowered into the royal vault without ceremonial of any kind.[1]

Such was the end of a prince who for nearly fifty years allowed others to plan, whilst he, who stood upon the steps of the throne, led a life that was private, not to say obscure, so much so, indeed, that nothing in it was remarkable except the estate of Meudon and what he did to beautify it. He hunted without pleasure in the chase, and was a near-voluptuary, but without discrimination. At one time he gambled heavily in order to win, but after he began to build, he used to stand in a corner of the salon at Marly, whistling through his teeth, drumming on his snuff-box, staring vacantly around him without really seeing anything, without conversation or amusements, I am inclined to say without either thoughts or feelings. Yet, because of this high estate, he was the head and centre, the soul, the very life of one of the strangest, most sinister, most secret, and, in spite of its ramifications, most united cabals that have emerged since the Peace of the Pyrenees put an end to the revolt of the King's minority. I have dwelt too long on this prince, whose character is almost beyond definition, because only the superficialities of it are known. It would take an eternity to describe them all. Nevertheless, the subject is interesting enough to have warranted my enlarging on this so little known Dauphin, who himself was nothing, who counted for nothing in his long, vain expectation of the crown, and with whom, at last, that cord was broken, on which had depended so many hopes and fears.

[1] In fact, the King requested 3,000 masses from Cardinal de Noailles, and two hundred from the Quinze-Vingts, the famous hospital for the blind of Paris, not to mention public prayers.

Death of Mme la Duchesse de Bourgogne

On Monday, January 18th the King went to Marly. The Dauphine had arrived there early in the morning with a face hugely swollen and had immediately retired to bed. She rose again at seven o'clock because the King wished her to preside in the drawing-room, but she played cards in morning dress and with her head muffled in a hood. She went to see the King in Mme de Maintenon's apartment shortly before his supper and then returned to bed, where she ate her own meal. On the 20th the swelling had subsided; she was somewhat prone to inflammation of the gums, for her teeth were badly decayed, but she felt better and for the next few days was able to lead her ordinary life.

Taking snuff. By Rosalba Carrieri.

On Friday, February 5th, the Duc de Noailles presented her with a beautiful snuff-box filled with fine Spanish snuff, which she tried and thought excellent. This occurred towards the end of the morning and afterwards she placed the box on a table in her private boudoir, where no one ever went. That same evening she was seized with a feverish chill, retired to bed, and did not get up again, not even to go to the King's room after supper. She had a bad night, but rose at her ordinary time on the following day and went about her business as usual. That evening, however, the fever returned. She was unwell during the whole of the night, but slightly better on the Sunday. At six that evening she was seized with a sudden pain below the temples, not greater in size than a six-sous piece, but so violent that she implored the King not to enter her room when he came to visit her. This maddening pain lasted without intermission until Monday 8th, and was not relieved by smoking and chewing tobacco, nor by quantities of opium and two bleedings from the arm. When the pain grew less the fever increased. She said that she suffered more even than in childbirth.

The violence of the illness gave rise to rumours about the snuff-box which the Duc de Noailles had given her, for she had spoken of it to her ladies when she went to bed on the first day of her illness, and had praised both the box and its contents; but when Mme de Levis went to fetch it from the table in her boudoir it was not there and, to make a long story short, it was never seen again. The disappearance seemed strange enough when it was first discovered, but the long and fruitless search, followed by such sudden and terrible events aroused the darkest suspicions.[1] They did not actually point to the giver of the box, or were so carefully generalized that they did not reach his understanding. The rumour, indeed, was minimized even in that small circle, where so many hopes were fixed on that adored princess, on whose life depended the fortunes of her small group of intimates. The fact that she took snuff was unknown to the King, but this did not make her nervous, because Mme de Maintenon knew; nevertheless, there would have been a dreadful to-do had he discovered, and that was why they were afraid to mention the strange disappearance of the snuff-box.

On the Monday night, the Dauphine was very drowsy. All that day, during which the King came often to her bedside, she had been in a high fever with short periods of delirium. Some spots began to appear on her skin, which made the doctors hope that the disease might turn out to be measles, which was very prevalent at that time and many people had had attacks, both at Versailles and Paris. The Tuesday night was harder to bear because by then the hope of measles had faded. Early the following morning, the King came to see her and found that she had been given an emetic, but although the result was everything that could be desired, it brought her no relief. At this point they persuaded the Dauphin, who had never left her side, to go into the garden for the fresh air, but he was so anxious that he returned almost at once. Towards nightfall she became worse and about eleven o'clock the fever increased. It was a very bad night. The King came to the Dauphine at nine o'clock in the morning of February 11th, and Mme de Maintenon was with her the entire time, except during his visits. By this time, the princess was so bad that they decided to speak to her of the Sacraments, but although so weak, she seemed surprised and questioned them about her condition, and they reassured her as best they could, but continued gently to press the suggestion, urging her not to delay. She thanked them for their frankness and said she would prepare herself.

A little later, they feared that there might be a sudden change, and her confessor, Père La Rue,[2] a Jesuit, whom she had always appeared to like, came

[1] Saint-Simon suspected that the Duc and Duchesse de Bourgogne were poisoned. It is now believed that they and later their eldest son died of the measles and mistreatment by the doctors.

[2] Charles de La Rue, one of the most fashionable preachers of that day.

up to the bed and urged her to wait no longer. She looked at him, answered that she understood him perfectly, but did no more, and when La Rue proposed to hear her there and then, she did not answer. Being a man of intelligence, he realized that something was amiss and tactfully changed his manner of approach. Saying that she might perhaps have some personal reasons for not wishing to confess to him, he bade her not to be afraid but to name a priest and he would take all responsibility upon himself and go himself to fetch him. She then said that she would like M. Bailly, priest of the mission of the parish of Versailles, a man of high reputation, who confessed the more orthodox members of the Court, and was not free of all suspicion of Jansenism, although that was a rare thing among those missioners. Unfortunately Bailly had gone to Paris. The Dauphine seemed distressed when she heard the news and desired to wait until his return, but Père La Rue told her that she had better not waste precious time, which the doctors could profitably use after she had taken the Sacraments. She accordingly asked for a Franciscan friar, Père Noel, whom Père La Rue immediately went to fetch and brought to her.

You may imagine the excitement that was caused by this sudden change of confessor at so dreadful a moment, and all the suspicions that were aroused. I shall return later to this subject, for I cannot now interrupt a tale of such tragic interest. The Dauphin was by that time overcome with grief. He had hidden his distress as long as possible in order to remain by the bedside, but the fever could no longer be concealed, and the doctors wished to spare him the dreadful scenes which they foresaw. With the King's approval, they therefore did everything to persuade him to stay in his own room and sustained him with lying reports of his wife's true condition.

The Dauphine's confession was a very long one, and immediately afterwards Extreme Unction was administered and she partook of the Last Sacraments, which the King went out to greet at the foot of the grand staircase. An hour later, she asked for the prayers for the dying, but they told her that the time had not yet come, and comforted her, urging her to try to sleep. Throughout all this time, the King and Mme de Maintenon remained in the drawing-room, where the doctors were summoned to consult in their presence. There were seven of them altogether, some attached to the Court, others sent for from Paris. They unanimously recommended that she should be bled from the foot before the fever returned and that an emetic should be given in the early hours of the morning if the bleeding did not produce the desired effect. When the fever returned it was less violent than before, but the night was cruel. Next morning, the King came very early and the Dauphine was given an emetic at nine o'clock, but with very small result. As the day went on, new symptoms appeared, each more distressing than the last, and she was conscious only at rare intervals. Towards evening, her servants became distraught, so that many strangers were admitted to the room even although the King was present. He left only a few moments before she died and, stepping into his carriage at the foot of the grand staircase, was driven away to Marly with Mme de Maintenon and Mme de Caylus. Both of them grieved so bitterly that they could not summon up strength to visit the Dauphin.

No princess coming so young to a foreign Court was ever better prepared and instructed. Her wise father had known the modes of our Court and had described them perfectly to her, teaching her the only way in which she could be happy with us. He was greatly assisted in his task by her natural quickness and intelligence, and she had many lovable qualities which won people's affection. Moreover, her personal relationships with her husband, the King, and Mme de Maintenon caused her to be regarded with respect and approval by men of ambition. From the moment of her arrival, she strove to achieve that end, and throughout her whole life she persisted in this useful labour, from which she reaped continual benefits. Gentle, shy, but none the less shrewd, she was so kind that she dreaded causing the slightest pain to anyone, and though she was lively and pleasure-loving, she was capable of forming her own opinions and could act upon them consistently and for long periods at a time. The constraints, which bordered on torture, of the Court life, bore down upon her with all their weight, but they seemed not to affect her. Kindness came naturally to her, and she showed it to all, even to her own household.[1]

In appearance she was plain, with cheeks that sagged, a forehead too prominent for beauty, an insignificant nose, and thick sensual lips; but the line of her chestnut hair and eyebrows was well marked, and she had the prettiest, most eloquent eyes in all the world. Her few remaining teeth were badly decayed, which she was the first to laugh at and remark on. She had, however, a fair complexion, a beautiful skin, a small but admirable bust, and a long neck with the suspicion of a goitre, which was not unbecoming. The carriage of her head was noble; she was very stately and gracious in her manner and in the expression of her eyes, and she had the sweetest smile imaginable. She was long-waisted, slender but not angular, very supple. Altogether, she had a beautiful figure and she walked like a goddess upon clouds. Her charm was beyond description; it showed in her impulsive ways and gestures and coloured her most ordinary remarks. She always appeared natural and unaffected, sometimes a little childish, but with a touch of wit. She delighted all who met her because through her own graciousness she had the knack of putting everyone else at their ease.

She loved to be pleasant, even to the most ordinary and undistinguished people, but seemed to make no effort to be popular. When you were with her, you were tempted to believe that she was wholly and solely on your side. The whole Court was enlivened by her youth and high spirits, she flitted hither and thither like a nymph, like a summer breeze, she seemed to have the gift of being in many places at once and brought life and gaiety wherever she passed. Every entertainment was graced by her presence, for she was the life and soul of all the balls and plays and fêtes, besides enchanting everyone by the elegance and neatness of her dancing.

She enjoyed playing cards, even for low stakes, for she was easily amused,

[1] Other people took a less kindly view of her character. In 1698, the Venetian ambassador wrote, 'The little Duchesse de Bourgogne is sly and spiteful. She has a deadly hatred, for no good cause, for her lady-in-waiting, the Duchesse du Lude, mimics her and makes her look ridiculous. On the other hand, she fawns most abjectly over Mme de Maintenon, and when they are in private calls her "Grandmamma".'

The Duchesse de Bourgogne,
by Jean-Baptiste Santerre.

but she preferred playing high; she was quick and clear-headed, the finest gambler imaginable, and could see through her opponent's game in a moment. But she was as cheerful and as much pleased to spend an afternoon in quiet reading, sewing, and conversation with her 'serious ladies', as she called the older palace ladies. She never spared herself, not even for her health's sake, and never forgot the least little thing that might please Mme de Maintenon and, through her, the King. In that respect her versatility was amazing; it never flagged for a moment, although she tempered it with the caution which long experience had taught her, for she knew exactly when to be discreet, and when bold. Her personal wishes, her pleasures, even, I repeat, her health, she sacrificed for them and thus she became familiar with them in a way that none of the King's children nor even his bastards was able to approach.

Her manner in public was serious, reserved, reverential towards the King, and shyly formal with Mme de Maintenon, whom she called 'Aunt', in a pretty mingling of affection and respect. When they were in private, she chattered, skipped, and frolicked around them, sometimes perching on the arm of their chairs, sometimes upon their knees. She used to fling her arms around their necks, kissing and hugging them, rumpling them and taking hold of them by the chin. She would rifle their writing-tables, rummaging among the papers, unsealing their letters and sometimes, when she saw that it would amuse them, insist on reading them aloud, commenting on what she read. The King's private apartments were open to her at all times, even when couriers brought important dispatches or during the meetings of the council, and she was always ready to oblige, to assist by smoothing away difficulties or to do a kindness, except for someone for whom she had taken a violent antipathy, as she did for Pontchartrain, whom she sometimes spoke of to the King as 'your one-eyed monster'. She was so bold, indeed, that one evening when the King and Mme de Maintenon were speaking affectionately of the English Court—it was at a time when they hoped to make peace with Queen Anne—she said, 'Aunt, you say that the queens in England are better than the kings, but do you know why?' and skipping all the time about the room, she continued, 'It is because when there is a king, the women rule, but under the queens men do so.' The wonder was that they both burst out laughing and agreed that she was perfectly right.

Were these Memoirs more solemn, I could scarcely bring myself to relate the following anecdote, but it does serve to illustrate to what point she was free to say and do as she pleased with them. I have already described how she shared the informal private life of the King and Mme de Maintenon. One evening there was to be a play at Versailles and she was chattering about this and that when Mme de Maintenon's old nurse, Nanon, came into the room. Instantly, arrayed as she was in full Court dress, with her jewels, she went and stood with her back to the fireplace and leaned on a little screen, placed between two tables. Nanon, who seemed to have one hand in her pocket, slipped quietly behind her and went down on her knees, whereupon the King, who was nearest to them, asked what they were doing. The princess burst out laughing and said

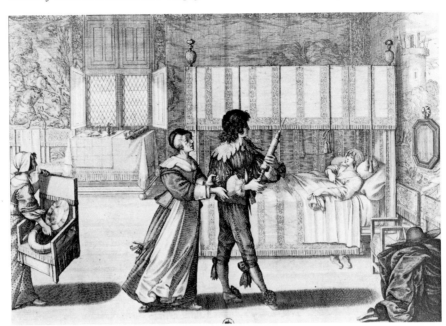

Ladies find enemas vastly refreshing. Engraving by Abraham Bosse.

that she was only doing what he often did before a play, but the King persisted. Then she said, 'Must I really tell you, since you have not seen for yourself? The truth is that I am having an enema.' 'What?' said the King, in an explosion of laughter. 'You are not seriously telling me that you are having an enema at this moment?' 'Indeed, I am', she said. 'But how?' asked the King, and they all four laughed until their sides shook. And in very truth, Nanon had brought the syringe all prepared, hidden under her petticoats, and had lifted up the princess's skirts while she pretended to warm herself. Then she had inserted the nozzle, the skirts were pulled down, and Nanon carried the syringe away underneath her own petticoats. In this way everything was discreetly hidden. The King and Mme de Maintenon paid no particular attention, thinking that Nanon was rearranging some part of the princess's dress. Thus they were taken completely by surprise and found the whole episode intensely amusing. What is extraordinary is that she used to go to the play holding the *lavement* and in no hurry to be quit of it. Sometimes she held it throughout the entire time of the King's supper and afterwards. She said that she found it refreshing and that it prevented her from getting a headache in the stuffy theatre. After being found out, she did not alter her ways, for she knew them through and through, and could not help realizing what Mme de Maintenon and Mlle Choin once had been.

One evening, when she was about to join Mgr le Duc de Bourgogne in bed, and was sitting on her chaise-percée, where she often talked confidentially, she told Mmes de Nogaret and du Châtelet, who repeated it afterwards to me, that she marvelled at the good fortune of those two sirens. She then added, laughing, 'I should like to die before M. le Duc de Bourgogne, so as to see what happens afterwards. I am sure that he will marry a grey sister, or the portress of the Filles de Sainte-Marie.' She tried as hard to be charming to him as to the King himself, but she often went too far, and was over-confident of his passion for her, although she was greatly concerned to uphold his rank and personal honour. As for the King, he could not bear to be without her. When her pleasure parties, which in his affection for her he encouraged, drove her from his side, his life was empty, and even at his public suppers when she was absent, as rarely happened, a cloud seemed to descend upon him and he was more solemn and silent than usual. Consequently, although she enjoyed her parties, she was very quiet about them, and only arranged them when expressly bidden to do so. She always made a point of visiting the King when she left and returned, and if she happened to be kept late at night by a ball in winter, or a picnic in summer, she always managed to be there to kiss him when he woke and to amuse him with her tittle-tattle.

I have said enough already of her disapproval of Monseigneur and the members of his private court. I shall say no more now, except that she took care to hide her feelings from the Court, in general, for she masked them under an appearance of being on pleasant terms with him, and perfectly serene among them all whenever she was at Meudon. Nevertheless she felt deeply embarrassed by the situation, and promised herself that she would be revenged after Monseigneur's death.

One evening, at Fontainebleau, when the princesses and their ladies were with the King in the drawing-room after supper, and she had been diverting him by pretending to chatter in half a dozen different languages, and other such nonsense, she suddenly noticed that Madame la Duchesse and Mme la Princesse de Conti were eyeing one another and contemptuously shrugging their shoulders. As soon as the King rose and went into his inner study in order to feed his dogs, the Dauphine seized Mme de Saint-Simon and Mme de Levis by the hand, and pointed to Madame la Duchesse and Mme la Princesse de Conti, who were only a few feet away. 'Did you see them? Did you see them?' she cried. 'I know as well as they do that I act nonsensically, that it is all very silly; but he has to have a bustle about him and that kind of thing diverts him.' And then, swinging on their arms, she began to dance and sing, 'Oh! it makes me laugh, oh! I can jeer at them, because I am going to be their queen. I need not care for them now or ever, but they have to reckon with me, for I'm going to be their queen', and she shouted and jumped and laughed as loud and as high as she could. Mme de Saint-Simon and Mme de Levis whispered to her to be quiet because the princesses would hear her and the entire company think that she had taken leave of her senses, but she skipped and sang the more, 'What do I care for them, for I'm going to be their queen!' and she only ceased when the King returned.

Alas! sweet princess, she believed what she said, and who could have thought otherwise? But for our sins, it very shortly afterwards pleased God to arrange matters differently. So far was she, indeed, from imagining her approaching end, that on Candlemas Day, when she was alone with Mme de Saint-Simon in her bedroom, the other ladies having gone before her into the chapel, she began to speak of the numbers of people about the Court whom she had known and who were now dead, of what she would do when she grew old, and how no one but Mme de Saint-Simon and Mme de Lauzun would be left from the days of her youth, and she had run on in this way until it was time to go to hear the sermon.

In spite of so many good and agreeable qualities, however, there was another side to her character, both as a princess and a woman; not, indeed, where the keeping of secrets or loyalty to friends was concerned, for in that she was like a deep well, nor in her care for the interests of others; but she had small failings that marred her perfection. She gave her friendship to acquaintances, when she saw them often, either because they amused her, or merely because she happened to need them (indeed, so far as I am aware, Mme de Saint-Simon was the only exception), and she confessed to this dangerous weakness with a grace and candour that made it almost seem tolerable in her. As I have already said, she liked to please everyone, and she could hardly be blamed if some pleased her in return. When she first came to the Court, she was kept strictly apart, and had then been surrounded by ancient gallants, whose romantic inclinations were no whit reduced because decrepitude prevented their enjoyment of them. Then, as time went on and she came more into the world, she chose companions of her own age less for their virtues than for their good looks. She was naturally adaptable and apt to like the people whom she saw day by day, although (and this was never made sufficient use of) she took as much pleasure in serious reading and conversation with the older ladies of her household, as in the lighter, less proper gossip of the rest, who often led her further than she cared to go—for shyness and some remains of modesty still restrained her. Nevertheless, she did go to very great lengths, and a princess less lovable and less beloved might have found herself in serious trouble on several occasions. The manner of her death revealed some of these mysteries and showed, too, the extreme tyranny which the King exercised over the members of his family. Both he and the Court received a shock when, in those awful moments when the present vanishes and only the future is feared, she desired to change her confessor and repudiated the entire Order to which he belonged, before receiving the Last Sacraments.

With her death all joy vanished, all pleasures, entertainments, and delights were overcast and darkness covered the face of the Court. She was its light and life. She was everywhere at once, she was its centre; her presence permeated its inner life, and if, after her death, the Court continued to subsist, it merely lingered on. No princess was ever so sincerely mourned, none was ever more worth regretting. Indeed, mourning for her has never ceased, a secret, involuntary sadness has remained, a terrible emptiness that never can be filled.

171

Death of Mgr le Duc de Bourgogne

The King and Mme de Maintenon were pierced with sorrow, the only real sorrow that had ever entered into his life. As soon as they arrived at Marly, he went straight to Mme de Maintenon's apartment, then dined alone in his own room and stayed only a short while afterwards in the study with M. le Duc d'Orléans and his natural children. The Duc de Berry, who was full of his own sincere grief, and felt even more deeply for that of Monseigneur his brother, had stayed at Versailles with Mme la Duchesse de Berry. She was beside herself with joy at being thus delivered of one who was greater and better loved than herself, and to whom she owed everything; but she forced her mind to rule her feelings, so far as she was able, and managed to keep up the appearances. On the morning of the following day they went to Marly in time for the King's *lever*.

The Dauphin, ill, and stricken as he was with the most bitter personal suffering, did not leave his room at Versailles and would see no one but M. le Duc de Berry, his confessor, and the Duc de Beauvilliers. The latter had been lying ill for the past week at his town house, but he made the effort to leave his bed and go to his pupil, and so was able to admire the great qualities which God had given him, for the Dauphin never appeared so noble as in that last terrible day and throughout all those that followed until his own death. This must certainly have been the last occasion on which they met in this world.

On the morning of February 13th, they managed to persuade the Dauphin to go to Marly, so as to spare him the anguish of hearing noises in the room above, where the Dauphine had died. He left at seven in the morning by the back door of his apartment and flung himself into one of the blue chairs[1] in which they carried him to his coach. A few courtiers, more lacking in tact than curious, were standing beside it and he courteously acknowledged their bows. When he reached Marly, he stopped at the chapel and heard mass, and was then carried to a window of his private apartments, through which he entered, and Mme de Maintenon went at once to visit him. You may imagine the anguish of that interview, indeed, she could not endure it for long and returned quickly to her own rooms. He was also obliged to see the princes and princesses, but they were considerate and stayed only for a few moments. Even Mme la Duchesse de Berry called on him, attended by Mme de Saint-Simon, to whom he gave a look expressive of sorrow shared. Afterwards he spent some time alone with M. le Duc de Berry.

It was then nearly time for the King's *réveil*, and when the three pages went in to announce it, I ventured to enter with them, and the Dauphin let me perceive that he had noticed me, turning on me so gentle and loving a glance

[1] A fleet of chairs with carriers dressed in the blue of the royal liveries, which were at the service of the courtiers in the gardens of Versailles.

that I was deeply moved. None the less, I was horrified at his appearance, for his eyes looked wild and glazed, his face was changed, and there were spots upon it, livid rather than red in colour. I noticed a fair number of them, some large, and other people in the room also perceived them. At that time he was standing, but when, a few moments later, they came to announce that the King was awake, the tears which he had held back for so long brimmed over his eyelids. He turned away without saying anything but did not move otherwise.

The mourning catafalque for the Duc and Duchesse de Bourgogne. Engraving after Jean Berain.

Mausolée pour la Cérémonie funèbre de tres haut et tres puissan. Prince, Loüis de Bourbon, Duc de Bourgogne, Dauphin de France; decedé le 18 Fevrier 1712, et de tres haute et tres puissante Princesse Marie Adelaïde de Savo...

With him were only his three pages, myself, and Du Chesne; they suggested once or twice that he should go to the King, but he neither moved nor answered. Then I approached him and motioned to him to go; I also spoke to him in a low voice, but seeing that he still did nothing, I dared to take him by the arm, saying that he would have to see the King sooner or later, for he was waiting and certainly longing to see and embrace him, and that it would be gracious in him to delay no longer. Then, gently urging him on, I took the liberty of giving him a little push. He gave me such a look as nearly broke my heart and left the room. For a little way I followed him and then went to recover myself. I never saw him again. God grant that I may meet him in that eternal life to which His mercy will surely have called him.

The whole company at Marly, very few at that time, were assembled in the great drawing-room, and the princes and princesses and those who had the *grande entrée* were in the small room between the King's apartments and those of Mme de Maintenon. She was in her bedroom, but when they announced the King's *réveil* she went in to him alone, passing through the little room and the people gathered there, who shortly afterwards followed her. The Dauphin, who had entered by way of the offices, found all this company in the King's bedroom, but the King, as soon as he saw him, called him and kissed him long, lovingly, and repeatedly. These first touching moments were interrupted by broken sentences, tears, and sobs.

After a while, when the King had had time to look well at the Dauphin, he, too, was alarmed by the same symptoms which we had observed in the other room, and all who were present were equally dismayed, and the doctors more than anyone. The King ordered them to take his pulse, which was very bad, or so they afterwards said, although at that time they were content to say that it was not quite normal but that all would be well if he would go to bed. The King then embraced him again, urged him very affectionately to take good care of himself, and told him to go to his bed, which he did, and never rose again.

By this time it was late in the morning. The King had spent a wretched night and his head ached. While he was dining he saw the few great nobles who presented themselves, and afterwards went to visit the Dauphin, whose fever had increased and whose pulse was worse than ever. He then went to Mme de Maintenon, supped in his own room, and spent only a very short time in his study with those who were accustomed to be there. From then onwards, the Dauphin saw no one but his pages and the doctors, his brother for short periods, his confessor for rather longer, M. de Cheverny,[1] for a little while. His day was spent in prayer and sacred reading. The list for Marly was made up on the spot and the company was notified, as had been done at Monseigneur's death so short a time before.

The next day, Sunday, the King spent as he had the previous day. Anxiety for the Dauphin increased. He did not disguise from Boudin, in the presence of Du Chesne and M. de Cheverny, that he had no expectation of recovery and that, by what he felt, Boudin's information would prove to be correct. He

[1] His old friend and gentleman-in-waiting, owner of the beautiful château, not far from Blois.

174

repeated this more than once with the utmost unconcern, showing much contempt for the world and its vanities and an inestimable love and fear of God. It would be impossible to describe the general dismay.

On Monday 15th, the King was bled and the Dauphin was no better. The King and Mme de Maintenon saw him separately more than once, but no one else was admitted, except M. le Duc de Berry for a few moments only, his pages scarcely at all, M. de Cheverny occasionally. He continued to read and pray.

On Tuesday 16th, he was worse. He complained of a consuming fire which did not correspond with the external appearance of the fever although the pulse was hard to find, most abnormal, and very alarming. As the day wore on there was a deterioration in his condition and also a disappointment, because the spots spread from his face over his entire body and were mistaken for measles. This gave rise to some hope, but the doctors and the more thoughtful members of the Court remembered that similar marks had appeared on the Dauphine's body, although this was not generally known until after her death.

By Wednesday 17th, the illness had increased considerably. I received news continually through Cheverny, and also through Boulduc, who came to speak to me whenever he found it possible to leave the bedroom. This Boulduc was an excellent apothecary, attached to the King, and after his father died he had become ours and was devoted to us. He knew quite as much as the best doctors, as we had discovered for ourselves, and, moreover, had much courage, honour, discretion, and wisdom. He hid nothing from Mme de Saint-Simon and myself, had already told us what he suspected about the Dauphine, and had spoken very plainly to me from the second day of the Dauphin's illness. Thus I no longer hoped, but some people, it seems, will go on hoping to the end, against all expectations.

The pains that were like a devouring flame increased during the day, becoming more and more violent. Late in the evening, the Dauphin sent to ask the King's permission to take communion very early in the morning, with no ceremonial and without spectators at the mass, which would be said in his bedroom. But no one heard about this on that night, it was only generally known in the course of the next morning. On that same Wednesday evening, I went quite late to visit the Duc and Duchesse de Chevreuse, who had their lodgings in the first pavilion, and we were in the second, both on the side of Marly village. I was by then in a state of utter misery; I saw the King scarcely once a day and went out only to hear news, and then only to M. and Mme de Chevreuse, for thus I could be sure of seeing none but those who were as much affected as myself, with whom I could be perfectly frank. Mme de Chevreuse had no more hope than I, but M. de Chevreuse, always calm, ever optimistic, ever seeing life through rose-coloured glasses, tried to prove to us, with talk of good constitutions and remedies, that there was more reason to hope than fear, all with an equanimity that exasperated me and caused me to round upon him somewhat uncivilly, but it gave some relief to Mme de Chevreuse and the few who were with us. I then returned and spent a very wretched night.

Early in the morning of Thursday, February 18th, I learned that the Dauphin had waited impatiently for midnight to come, had taken the Sacrament immediately afterwards, had then spent two hours in close communion with God, and that his head was now much confused. Mme de Saint-Simon told me later that he had received Extreme Unction, and had died at half-past eight o'clock. These Memoirs are not intended to be a record of my personal sentiments; if ever, long after I am dead, they should be published, readers will understand only too well my feelings and the state that I was in, and Mme de Saint-Simon also. Suffice it now to say that we could scarcely bring ourselves to appear in public, even for a moment, during those first days; that I wished to give up everything and retire from the Court and society, and that it was only the wisdom and good guidance of Mme de Saint-Simon that prevented me. Even so she had a hard task.

That prince, first the presumptive, then the apparent, heir to the throne was born with a violent temper and in his early youth was alarming. Hard and choleric to the last degree, subject to transports of rage even against inanimate objects, wildly impetuous, unable to brook the slightest opposition, even from time or the weather, without flying into such a passion that one feared his whole body would break, stubborn beyond measure, mad for pleasures of every kind, he was a woman-lover and at the same time, which is rare, had an equally strong fancy in another direction. He loved wine and good eating just as well, was passionately fond of hunting, and listened to music in a kind of ecstasy. Cards he delighted in, but so hated to be beaten that it was dangerous to play against him. In sum, he was subject to all the passions and loved all the pleasures.

Often tyrannical and naturally inclined to cruelty, he was ruthless in sarcasm and exposed fools with a devastating realism. From his celestial height, he thought of other men, no matter who they were, as of atomies bearing no resemblance to himself, and although he and his brothers were supposed to have been brought up in perfect equality, he regarded them, at best, as go-betweens twixt himself and the human race. He was extremely intelligent and quick-witted, and even in a rage his replies were astonishing, for when most angry his arguments were reasonable and well-founded. Acquiring abstract knowledge was child's play to him, but his varied and lively interests prevented him from concentrating on any one subject at a time, so that he never became proficient. They were forced to allow him to draw during his lessons, otherwise he would not learn, but although he had great taste and aptitude, this practice may have contributed to ruining the shape of his body.

He was short rather than tall, with a long, brown face, the upper part of which was exceedingly handsome, and he had the finest eyes imaginable. His look was alert, moving, memorable, very aristocratic, usually rather kind, always penetrating; his expression was pleasant, noble, sensitive, and so

The Battle of Oudenarde (Tapestry)

Building the Château de
Versailles

The Duc de Bourgogne by Hyacinthe Rigaud, 1703

intelligent that it inspired others. The lower part of his face was less good, for it was too pointed, and the nose, long, high-bridged, but not well shaped, did not become him. His chestnut hair was too thick and curled so tightly that it frizzed. The mouth and lips were pleasant enough when he was not talking, and his teeth were not decayed, but the upper jaw jutted out so far that it almost enclosed the lower, which gave a most unhappy effect. Apart from the King himself, he had the finest legs and feet that I have seen in any man, but they and his thighs were too long in proportion to the rest of his body.

When he left the nursery, his back was straight, but it was soon noticed that it had begun to curve, and they made a collar and cross of iron, which he wore at all times in his apartments, even when there was company, and neglected none of the games and exercises designed to straighten such deformities. Nature, however proved to be stronger and he grew hump-backed, and so much more so in one shoulder that he limped, not because his legs and thighs were unequal, but because when the shoulder dropped there was no longer the same distance between his hips and the ground, so that instead of standing upright he leaned to one side. This did not make him walk less comfortably, nor less far, nor less quickly or gladly, for he still enjoyed going for walks and riding, although he did that very ill. What was surprising was that for all his clearsightedness and intelligence, and in spite of all the virtues to which he later attained and his real and notable piety, the prince never learned to see his body as it really was, or would never acknowledge it. This was a failing that caused great anxiety to others lest they should be thoughtless or indiscreet, and a great

1691 drawing of a hunting scene by the Duc de Bourgogne when he was nine years old.

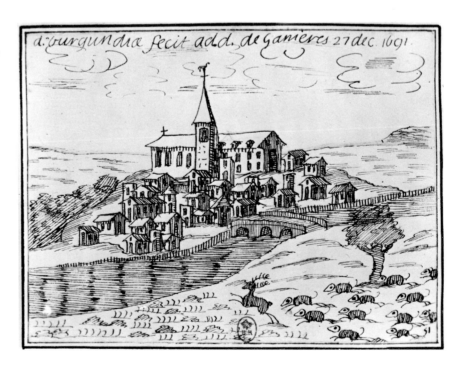

deal of trouble to his valets when they dressed him and arranged his hair, for they had to try to conceal the defect as much as possible and yet be very careful not to appear to see what was visible to all. From this we must conclude that it is given to no man to reach perfection here below.

The prince never completely mastered his intellectual capacity, but like the bee he gathered his honey from the finest and sweetest blossoms. He endeavoured to meet men of learning and to extract from them the knowledge and ideas for which he sought. Occasionally, he would confer with some of them, but as it were casually and on some special topic or, more rarely, he would see them in private to obtain necessary information, but such interviews were never repeated nor habitual. I have never heard, and surely it would not have escaped me, that he ever worked continuously with any one person, excepting with the ministers, including by that term the Duc de Chevreuse and certain prelates. Apart from them, I was the only person to have free and frequent access to him, either at my request or his, and when I was with him, he spoke his mind of the present and the future, confidently, without constraint, yet discreetly. He would expatiate on the plans he thought necessary and on general topics, but was more reserved about private matters and individuals. At the same time he would try to extract everything that he could from me. I adroitly gave him the opportunity for such outpourings, and often successfully, for he came to feel more and more confidence in me.

A whole volume would not suffice to recount all the conversations that took place between the prince and myself. What love of goodness! What unselfishness! What learning! What fine results! What detachment! Dare I say it? what a clear reflection of the Divinity appeared in this pure soul, so strong, so simple, so candid, who, so far as is permitted here below, retained the image of its Creator! In him one saw the shining marks of an education that was laborious, active, virtuous, wise and Christian, exemplified in a brilliant pupil, who was born to command.

The debasement of the nobility was odious to him, for he thought it intolerable that all should be considered equal. This latest innovation, only waived for holders of offices, which ranks noblemen, gentilshommes, and seigneurs on the same level, seemed to him to be the final injustice, and the resulting lack of degrees an immediate danger to a military State. He remembered that at the times of greatest peril, under Philippe de Valois, Charles V, Charles VII, Louis XII, François I, his grandsons, and Henri IV, France owed her salvation entirely to the old nobility, who knew their places and acknowledged their different grades. They were thus able and willing to march to their country's aid by companies and provinces, because no one stepped out of his place or objected to obeying those greater than himself. He saw that this defence had been destroyed, for there was not a man who did not now claim equality with all others, and consequently there was no organization, no commanding, no obedience.

In the present situation he was deeply moved at the ruination of the

The robes of a duc et pair.

aristocracy and shocked at the steps, which had already been taken and still continued, to bring them to destruction and to hold them down. He saw the degeneration in courage, character, morals, and humanity, which had been brought about by poverty and mixed blood, for more and more low marriages had become necessary in order to avoid starvation. He was indignant that the French nobility, once so famous, so illustrious, should have been reduced to a class almost indistinguishable from the common herd. For indeed, the only difference is that commoners have the right to work in every profession, including arms, whereas the nobility must choose between a deadly, destructive idleness that renders them unfit for anything, mocked and censured by all, or death in the wars, after being exposed to insults from secretaries of secretaries of state and secretaries of intendants. Even the very greatest among the nobles, whose birth and dignities alone should place them above the rest, cannot avoid unemployment, or humiliation from the quill-drivers when they serve with the armies. Above all, he could not stomach the wrongs done to the profession of arms, on which this kingdom has been founded and maintained; for example, that a veteran officer several times wounded, a lieutenant-general, perhaps, retiring from the army with honours, reputation, possibly with a pension, should, unless he belongs to the nobility, be subjected to the same taxes as all the peasants in his parish and be classed in every way on a level with them. This I have seen happen to aged knights-captain of Saint-Louis, pensioners, and they had no hope of exemptions, whereas exemptions are granted by the score to the lowest grades of pettifogging bank clerks.

That noble and Christian maxim that kings are made for their peoples, not peoples for their kings, was so firmly imprinted on his heart that splendour and warfare were hateful to him. That was why he sometimes argued too warmly against war; he was carried away by truths too hard for the ears of worldly men, and people often said maliciously that he did not care to fight. His justice was blindfolded with the completeness that is her only security. He took great trouble to study the various cases that came up for the King's decision at the Conseils de Finance and Dépêches, and if any great matter were concerned, he worked with specialists, consulting their expert knowledge but not slavishly adopting their opinions. Every fortnight, at least, he took communion with most notable quietness and reverence, and always wore the collar of the Order of the Holy Spirit, with the mantle and bands. He saw his Jesuit confessor once or twice a week, sometimes for long periods at a time, but later, although he went more often to communion, he did not stay with him so long.

He perfectly understood the King, respected him and, towards the end, loved him as a son. He paid homage to him as a subject, but always with a proper sense of his own position. Mme de Maintenon he cultivated with all the civility that their respective situations required. While Monseigneur lived, he was careful to render him his due, but one felt the constraint, still more so with Mlle Choin, and his entire disapproval of the inner life of Meudon. I have so often described the reasons for his embarrassment that I shall not repeat them now. The prince, like most other people, failed to understand how Monseigneur, who for all his sensuality had plenty of pride, who never learned to tolerate Mme de Maintenon and only visited her out of politeness when he could not avoid so doing, should yet keep his own Maintenon in Mlle Choin and force his children to accept her just as the King subjected his to Mme de Maintenon. He loved his brothers tenderly and his wife passionately. His sorrow at losing her broke his heart and only by the most prodigious effort did his religion survive. It was a sacrifice which he made without reservation; it killed him, yet in that terrible affliction he showed nothing mean or common, nothing unworthy. Onlookers saw a man, driven frantic with grief, who still wrung out of himself the strength to preserve a calm exterior but died in the struggle. His days were soon brought to a premature close.

It was the same throughout his last illness, for he never believed that he would recover and maintained that opinion against his doctors, not concealing the reasons on which it was based. Indeed, what he felt from first to last confirmed them! What an appalling thing to have reached such a conviction regarding his wife's death and his own! But, Great God! what an example Thou hast given us in him! The inmost, most sublime secrets may not yet be revealed, and Thou alone knowest the price which he had to pay! What an imitation he gave of Jesus Christ upon the Cross! I speak not only of death and suffering, but of his gentle tolerant outlook, his supreme unselfishness! Such thankfulness that he was not called on to reign and to render an account of his kingship! How humble he was; how excellent! How dearly he loved God; how clearly saw his own unworthiness and sins! How wonderful his sense of the divine mercy! How holy his fears! How temperate his hopes! What peace of mind! How continually he read and prayed! How eagerly he longed for the Last Sacrament! How deep his self-communion! How invincible his patience; how good he was; how thoughtful for all who came near him! How pure the love that urged him to go to God! In his death, France suffered her final chastisement, for God showed her the prince whom she did not deserve. Earth was not worthy of him; he was ripe already for the joys of Paradise.

1712

The King is Bored

The King grew bored in Mme de Maintenon's apartment in the intervals of working with his Ministers, for the void left by the Dauphine's death could scarcely be filled by the diversions of that very small circle of elderly ladies who were occasionally admitted. Musical entertainments were given increasingly often, but they had begun to pall for that very reason, until someone thought of enlivening them with short scenes from Molière's comedies, acted in costume by the King's musicians.

Mme de Maintenon then had the Maréchal de Villeroy recalled for no better reason than that he amused the King with old tales of their past youth. He alone was allowed into the intimate circle at these modest entertainments, in order to animate them with his tittle-tattle; but he was well under her thumb at all times and knew that he owed his return to favour to her. She made him useful in many ways, for instance in broaching certain subjects that did not come within the scope of the ministers and about which she wished the King to consult with her. Thus she was able to urge her views in some matters with greater delicacy and assurance because the topic did not seem to originate with her.

The Princes of the Blood had died leaving only children; the two Dauphins and the Dauphine were dead; M. le Duc d'Orléans had been reduced to nothing by black and subtle calumny, and the agonies of fear which M. le Duc de Berry already felt in the King's presence were being carefully fostered. Thus a vast new field lay open to the limitless ambition of M. le Duc du Maine and the mad partiality of his one-time governess. The Maréchal de Villeroy, a vile courtier, no more, was the finest possible instrument to serve their object, and Mme de Maintenon made sure of having him at hand in case he should be needed.

1713

Brissac Plays a Prank

Old Brissac, who had been living in retirement for several years, was another who died at a great age. He was a lieutenant-general, governor of Guise, and had been adjutant of the Gardes du Corps for a long time. A gentleman of very small standing, he had risen through all the ranks by attracting the King's notice for his keenness, his attention to detail, and his devotion to the King and none other. He gained such a reputation for knowing everything about the Gardes du Corps that even the captains, all of them great nobles and general officers, felt that he needed to be handled with care and tact, and how much more so the junior officers. To speak truth, he was a coarse, common man, exceedingly disagreeable and abominably spoilt by the King, but he was a man of honour and good principles, honest and worthy, and was esteemed as such. At the same time many people hated him, and everyone, even the courtiers, even the great ones, dreaded having dealings with him, for he was dangerous. He was the only man who ever dared to attack Fagon about medicine, and barked at him in the King's presence in a way that put Fagon into a rage, and made the King and the bystanders laugh until their sides ached. Fagon, himself a man of no little wit, and fiery tempered, gave back as good as he got and caused much amusement; but at the same time, he could not endure to see Brissac or even to hear him mentioned without losing his temper.

One anecdote about this adjutant of the Gardes du Corps will give a little sketch of the Court. Every evening at Versailles there were public prayers at the end of the day, followed by evening service, and benediction on Sundays and Thursdays. In wintertime, the service was at six o'clock, and at five in summer, so as to allow time for going out of doors afterwards. The King always attended on Sundays, and rarely missed on Thursdays during the winter. At the end of prayers, one of the blue footmen on duty in the tribune would run to warn him, so that he arrived a moment before benediction. But whether he was expected or not, the service always began at the proper time, and guards were always posted in the tribune, where the King stood. The ladies made a point of filling the bays between the tribunes, and in wintertime they took care to make

RIGHT Louis XIV receives Dangeau's oath as Grand Master of the united Orders of Mont Carmel and Saint Lazare, in the chapel of Versailles. By Antoine Pezey.

themselves conspicuous by holding the little candles, which they carried to light their prayer books, in such a way as to throw a beam full upon their faces. Regular attendance was accounted a merit; thus all the ladies, young as well as old, endeavoured to be seen by the King and Mme de Maintenon.

Brissac grew tired of seeing so many ladies present who had no reputation for eagerness to hear benediction, and one day he laid a plot with the officers of the Gardes du Corps. Towards the end of prayers, he entered the royal tribune, rapped with his staff, and cried out with a loud voice, 'Gardes du Corps, you may withdraw! The King is not coming to benediction.' Everyone obeyed the order, the guards went away, and Brissac hid himself behind one of the pillars. Then a great whispering began in the other tribunes which were full of ladies, and a moment afterwards each one snuffed out her candle and vanished, leaving only Mme de Dangeau and two others of no great standing.

All of this occurred in the old chapel. The officers, having been forewarned, posted the guards on the staircase to Blouin's[1] room and in the back passages, where they were well hidden, and when Brissac had given the ladies ample time to get out of earshot, the guards were reposted. It was all timed to perfection, so

[1] The King's head valet.

that the King appeared and benediction was begun only a moment afterwards. He always ran his glance around the tribunes to see who was there, and being used to seeing them filled to capacity he was extremely surprised to discover no one but Mme de Dangeau and the two other ladies. When he came away he spoke about it and expressed his astonishment. Then Brissac, who always walked near him, began to laugh and told the whole story of the joke he had played on those pseudo-saints, because he was tired of seeing the King duped. The King laughed heartily, and his courtiers still more. They soon found out who the ladies were who had blown out their candles when they heard that the King was not coming, and some of them were so furious that they would have liked to scratch out Brissac's eyes. Indeed, he almost deserved it for the scathing remarks that he made about them.

1714

The King's Will

It is now time to speak of the King's will, which made its appearance amid the most extraordinary precautions to keep the entire contents secret and the document itself inviolably secure.

The King was at last showing his age; not that there was any change in his way of life, but those nearest him were beginning to fear that he had not long to live. This is not the place to give details of a constitution that for so long a time had been remarkably strong; suffice it to say that there had been ominous signs. For very many years, he had been accustomed to master his fate, but lately he had suffered a series of bitter defeats and his family tragedies had wounded him still more. His legitimate children had all died before him, leaving him a prey to the most sinister suspicions, and every moment he expected to meet the same fate himself. Yet instead of receiving comfort from the intimate circle whom he saw every day, he found there only fresh cause for anxiety.

Maréchal, the chief surgeon, was the only one who strove to allay his fears. All the rest, Mme de Maintenon, M. du Maine, Fagon, Blouin, and the confidential servants who were all creatures of the bastard and his former governess, endeavoured only to increase his doubts, and to speak truly, they had no great difficulty. Everyone suspected poison, no one could seriously think otherwise. Maréchal was equally certain of it, although he said otherwise because he wished to save the King from useless worry. M. du Maine and Mme de Maintenon (because she hated the Duc d'Orléans and wished to serve one whom she loved better) had too many interests at stake not to endeavour to increase the King's alarm by allowing suspicion to fall on the one remaining royal prince who was old enough to oppose them. Indeed they had determined

A wax portrait of Louis XIV
by A. Benoist, 1706.

to ruin him. You may imagine the mental state of the King who daily, at his meals and in his study, was confronted by that prince who, so they assured him, had committed such appalling crimes.

Besides the loss of his own children he had suffered the death, in the same cruel manner, of an irreplaceable princess, the life and light of his Court, his joy, his darling, his great delight at the times when he was not engaged with public business. Never, since he first entered the world, had he felt at ease with anyone but her, and I have already described to what lengths he went in his relaxation. Nothing could fill so vast an emptiness, and his sorrow was all the greater because he could find no other distraction. In this wretched state he took what comfort he could find, and abandoned himself more and more to Mme de Maintenon and M. du Maine. He found their seemingly unending devotion and their restraint a reassurance. They had long since managed to persuade him that M. du Maine, although sufficiently intelligent to be consulted over the final details of public business (and final details were the King's foible), was without aims and ambitions and incapable of having any. The King pictured him as engrossed in family affairs and only interested in grandeur in so far as it reflected that of a monarch whom he loved simply, honestly, transparently, and above all else. He imagined him after a day spent dutifully working to please the King, and after giving much time to his prayers and meditations, going off to hunt alone, or exercising his charm and wit in the bosom of his family, often quite ignorant of the affairs of the Court.

Such an opinion pleased the King immensely and made him feel perfectly at ease with M. du Maine who, in any case, was his favourite, constantly beside him, amusing him with jokes and anecdotes. Indeed, of all the good conversationalists I have ever known, M. du Maine was the most accomplished. He could be charming and so easy that one was almost tempted to trust him; yet at the same time he was clever at being spiteful and could mock absurdities most cruelly. His words were always carefully considered; he suited the occasion and the King's humour, which he understood to perfection.

He and Mme de Maintenon being thus firmly established in the King's heart and confidence, it had become merely a question of making the best use of a precious time which they thought could not endure long. If the crown itself were not their immediate objective, which seems hard to believe in view of the edict[1] that had made the bastards capable of the succession, they were at least determined to keep what they had gained, to make sure of greatness in the future, and to force the future Regent to reckon with them.

Fortune seemed to smile upon their atrocious designs. They themselves had prepared and smoothed the way for success by abominable slanders, most artfully and perseveringly sustained, in order to blacken the reputation of the one prince whose right to the regency was incontrovertible. With great skill and cunning manoeuvres, they convinced the ignorant and put doubts into the minds of others, thus rendering M. le Duc d'Orléans suspect in Paris and the provinces, and especially at the Court, where no one cared or dared to approach

[1] Edict of July 1714, registered in the Parlement on August 2nd of the same year. It admitted to the succession of the crown of France, M. le Duc du Maine, M. le Comte de Toulouse, and their male descendants should there be no Prince of the Royal Blood available. It was also laid down that the bastards and their descendants should enjoy the same ranks, honours and privileges as the Princes of the Blood and rank immediately after them.

him. How could a friendless prince defend himself in that deplorable situation to which they had reduced him? How could he disprove a negative, especially one of that particular kind? And what could he do to clear himself in the eyes of a king whose mind was thus bedevilled? M. du Maine could scarcely have held better cards, and he felt this so strongly and Mme de Maintenon also, that they determined there and then to reap all the benefits that they desired for the present and the future.

For them it was no longer a matter of appointments, high office, governorships and reversions, still less one of rank and honours. What they now wanted was something far greater, to make themselves what no man can become, to take what no subject, although crowned, can assume, namely, the Divine Right. They wished to defraud the Princes of the Blood of that sublime birthright that distinguishes them from all other kinds of men, to introduce the most tyrannical and pernicious of precedents, to destroy the holiest and most ancient law, thus making a mockery of the crown and trampling upon the nation. Worst of all, to perform this dreadful act, they chose a man who could not change nature, nor make that which is not become what is, a man who, as head of a unique line, should have been doubly anxious to preserve its sanctity, since he was King solely by right of inheritance. They caused the King of this most loyal and obedient nation to dishonour and overthrow its most sacred laws in order to make possible the crowning of the offspring of a double adultery. Louis XIV was the first King of France to raise from nothingness what all other nations, including the savages, have kept hidden from the beginnings of time. The plot was vast enough, but it would have ended in failure had it even been mooted, for its authors would have perished amid the general ruin and have lost all that they had gained.

As they thought then, however, their only concern was to have a will drawn up by the King at their dictation. By this means, because of the respect paid to the wishes of that testator, they hoped to establish their new position and gain more far-reaching powers in the future. M. du Maine had so successfully convinced the King and the bulk of the nation of the criminality of M. le Duc d'Orléans that it only remained for him to gather his fruit. This was to persuade the King for conscience's sake, for the safety of his one remaining legitimate heir and the security of his kingdom, to reduce as far as possible the power of the prince who had become suspect, by dividing his power as future Regent and making M. du Maine the keeper and absolute governor of that precious infant, the future King.

One other no less difficult point remained, how to ensure the safety of the will once the King had been brought to make it, for it must be secured beyond all doubt and such extraordinary precautions taken that would increase the respect ordinarily felt for such a document. It must, moreover, be so arranged that the executing of it should become a proper matter for the Parlement, and some means be found to overcome the King's dislike for that body. To those who knew him, his obstinate clinging to his principles, his never broken habits, and his extreme sensitiveness regarding his absolute authority even in the distant future, made the task seem impossible. But Providence decreed otherwise. In punishment, perhaps, for the scandal offered to the world by the double adultery, the King, fully realizing the wickedness of the act in all its shame and significance, was yet driven to perform it, step by step, against his will, and came at last, groaning in bitterness of soul and despair at his weakness, to crown his crime with this most terrible apotheosis.

We have already seen from the King's unguarded words when he told M. du Maine what he had done to include him in the line of succession, and from his tone and manner of speaking, how unwillingly that outrageous concession had been wrung from him.[1] We shall now see how that monarch, who was usually a master of self-control, betrayed his true feelings no less plainly in the matter of his will.

A few days before the news broke, when the King was still full of that monstrous thing, he was in his study with the two bastards, d'O, d'Antin, and some of the confidential servants. He turned to M. du Maine, and speaking with a sour, resentful air, said sternly, 'You would have it so, but remember, however great I make you in my lifetime, when I am dead you are nothing. It is for you to make good use of what I have done, if you can.' All present trembled at this thunder-clap, so sudden, so totally unexpected, so foreign to the King's nature and habits. It clearly revealed M. du Maine's ultimate ambitions and the violence which he had done to the King in his weakness, for the latter obviously reproached himself for his own failing and the bastard for his ambition and arrogance.

Then it was that the curtain began to be raised before that small circle of the inner household, who had been so troubled and baffled by the changes that were taking place. M. du Maine's dismay at the outburst, for which he had been quite unprepared, was so intense that the spectators held their breath and gazed fixedly at the floor. A long silence ensued that lasted for an appreciable time. It was only broken when the King had gone into his dressing-room and everyone could breathe again.

The King's heart was very heavy because of what he had been made to do, but that was only the beginning. Like a woman who gives birth to twins, he had produced one monstrosity, but still had to be delivered of a second, and he felt all the anguish without any relief from the suffering caused by the first. Two days later, a second event completed the raising of the curtain.

The Court was at Versailles at that time. On Sunday, August 26th, after the *lever*, the King sent for Mesmes, the premier président, and Daguesseau, the procureur général, who had already seen the Chancellor[2] and agreed upon a means of safeguarding the precious document. You may be sure that as soon as M. du Maine became certain of it, he had discussed it thoroughly with his tool, the premier président. When they were alone, the King unlocked a drawer and took out a large packet sealed with seven seals—I do not know if M. du Maine, when he so sanctified it, was thinking of that mysterious Book with the Seven

[1] In his study, surrounded by the courtiers and officers of his household, the King had said, sighing deeply, that he had now done everything in his power for M. du Maine and his brother the Comte de Toulouse, but that the higher he raised them the more they had to lose. They must try to make themselves worthy of their new rank, which after his death could be sustained only by their merits.

[2] Daniel François Voysin (1654–1717). He had become Chancellor of France in 1714.

Seals that is mentioned in the Apocalypse. This he handed to them saying, 'Messieurs, this is my will. No one but myself knows its contents. To your care I consign it for safe keeping by the Parlement, to whom I can show no higher proof of my trust and esteem. The fate of the wills of earlier kings and of my royal father makes me well aware what may become of it. But they would have it so. They have pestered me. They have allowed me no peace, no matter what I said. Now I have purchased my rest. Here it is! Take it away! Come what may, I shall at least have peace and quiet and hear no more about it.' Then, turning on his heel with a curt nod, he went into another room, leaving them almost petrified with fright. They looked at one another terrified by what they had just heard and by the King's glance and expression, and as soon as they had come to their senses they withdrew and went back to Paris.

It was not generally known until after dinner that the King had made a will and given it into their keeping. As the news spread, the whole Court was filled with dismay, although the toadies, who at heart were as much shocked as the rest, surpassed themselves in praises and congratulations.

[1] Mary of Modena, widow of James II.

On the following day, the Queen of England,[1] who as usual was staying at Chaillot, came to visit Mme de Maintenon. The King went in to see her, and as soon as he caught sight of her, exclaimed in an exasperated tone, 'Madame, I have made a will, they badgered me into so doing. I know how futile it is. We do what we choose whilst we are alive, but after we are dead we have less power than ordinary individuals. You have only to think of what became of my royal father's will, and that immediately after his death, and of the wills of many other Kings. I am well aware of all this, but they have insisted on it. They gave me no peace or rest until it was done. Well! Now it is done, Madame. Perhaps it may have some influence. At least they will stop pestering me!'

Such words, expressive of outraged feelings and of a long and bitter struggle before he yielded, are so plain and so momentous that they require equally clear proof of authenticity. Here it is! What the King said to the premier président and the procureur général, I learned from the former who could never forget it. It is also true, for I must be accurate, that he told me a long time afterwards, but he repeated the speech word for word, exactly as I have written it down. What the King said to the Queen of England was much more direct and emphatic, partly because he was more familiar with her and partly, perhaps, because he was in the presence of Mme de Maintenon, on whom he intended his reproaches to fall. I heard it two days later, from M. de Lauzun, to whom the Queen told it in her first astonishment, and she did not need pressing. So full was she of the King's dire speech that she repeated it to M. de Lauzun, word for word, as he reported it to me, and just as I record it here.

As soon as the premier président and the procureur général reached Paris, they sent for workmen and took them into a tower behind the robing-room of the great chamber and the former's office. There they bade them hollow a large opening in the wall, which is very thick in that place, and in that hole they placed the will. They then closed the opening, first with an iron door, then with

codicille 1

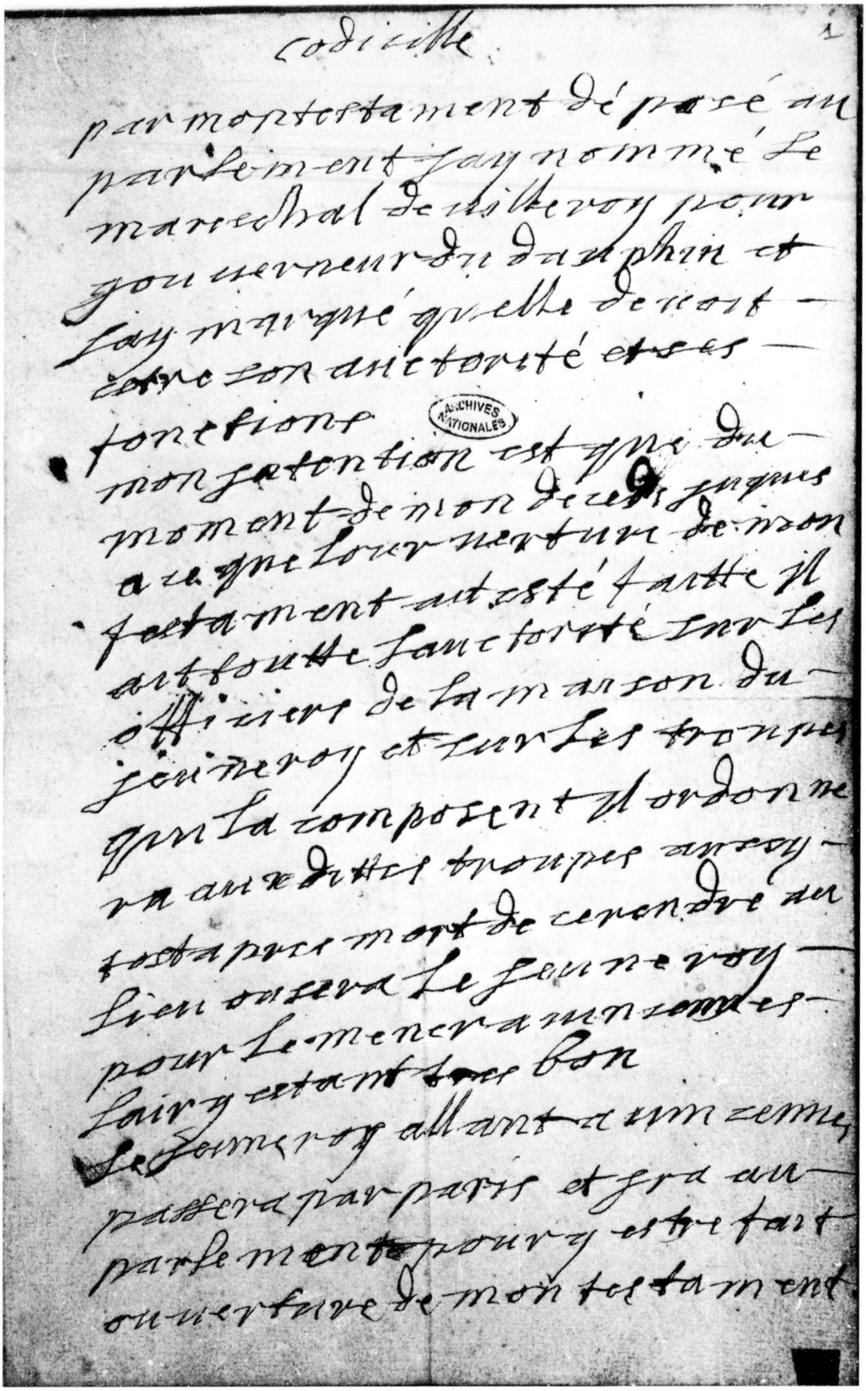

par mon testament déposé au
parlement j'ay nommé le
marechal de villeroy pour
gouverneur du dauphin et
j'ay marqué quelle devoit
estre son autorité et ses
fonctions
mon intention est que du
moment de mon decés jusques
a ce que louverture de mon
testament ait esté faitte il
ait toutte lautorité sur les
officiers de la maison du
jeune roy et sur les troupes
qui la composent il ordonne
ra aux dittes troupes aussy-
tost apres mort de se rendre au
lieu ou sera le jeune roy
pour le menera vincennes
lair y estant bon
le jeune roy allant a vincennes
passera par paris et ira au
parlement pour y estre fait
ouverture de mon testament

Codicil to the King's Will, 1715.

an iron grille, and finally walled it in. The door and the grille were fitted each with three locks, in such a way that three keys each opened two of the locks. The premier président and the procureur général each kept a key and the third they gave to the chief clerk, so as to prevent jealousy between the second président à mortier and the doyen. The Parlement happened to be sitting at that time, and the premier président at once gave a most flattering account of the King's respect and esteem, and his confidence that the will would be kept safe and its provisions put into effect when the time came.

I have already said that consternation was very great when the existence of a will became known. It was always M. du Maine's fate to obtain what he wished, but with public abhorrence, and this was so in the matter of the King's will. When he realized the general opinion he became frantic, Mme de Maintenon was furious, and both redoubled their efforts to prevent any whispers reaching the King. They set themselves more than ever to keep him happy and amused, and saw to it that he heard nothing but praise, joy, and general congratulations for his great, wise, generous, and necessary gesture, one that was calculated, so they said, to maintain order and extend the glories of his reign beyond the span of his lifetime. It was indeed natural that the public should feel dismayed; but M. du Maine himself had been deceived and found himself in difficulties. He was indeed fully persuaded of having prepared and smoothed his path by making M. le Duc d'Orléans hated and suspect. He had, in fact, partly succeeded, but not so well as he believed, for his own desires and his spies had exaggerated his success, and when instead of applause he received the opposite, he became utterly discomfited.

People saw very clearly that the will must be aimed against M. le Duc d'Orléans, for had there been no desire to hinder him, there had been no need to make a will, matters would have taken their normal course. The doubts and suspicions so carefully cultivated were not diminished, but whatever people may have thought privately, or however much they disapproved, no one was so blind as not to realize that the Duc d'Orléans must needs become Regent because of his incontestable birthright. No provisions in any will could weaken that right, unless some new power were set up equal to his own. But to do that would be to create two parties, which the rival leaders would support by every possible means. Everyone would then be forced to choose a side, and in such choices lie a thousand dangers and no good hopes.

What the people desired was that the King, during his lifetime, should establish the government that he wished to continue after him, bring into his councils and businesses those whom he intended to leave in power, and at once give them their functions and offices. Thus, whilst still retaining authority, he would train the future Regent and those who served under him in a new administration. In fact, the King would be executor of his own will, so that after his death there would be no sudden change, but all continue smoothly as he had directed and arranged.

M. le Duc d'Orléans was stunned by the blow. He felt how nearly it touched

191

him, but saw no remedy in the King's lifetime. A deep, respectful silence seemed to him the only possible course, for any other would have led to precautions being redoubled. I shall leave the matter there. This is not the time to enter into the prince's ideas and plans for the future. The King avoided all speech with him on the subject, except for a bald statement after the event. M. du Maine the same. M. le Duc d'Orléans therefore contented himself with a monosyllable of acquiescence, like a good courtier who never comments, and even refrained from discussing it with his wife. I was the only one to whom he dared to speak openly. With all others he took pains to appear as usual and avoided looking displeased or laying his mind open to prying eyes. His utter isolation at the Court and in society saved him from overhearing casual remarks, for nobody came near him.

1715

Character of M. le Duc d'Orléans

The reign of Louis XIV has now been brought almost to its close and nothing more remains to tell, or only the events of the final month. These are so very important that they must be recorded with the utmost exactness and clarity and in their proper order, for they are closely linked with all that followed immediately after the monarch's death. It is no less essential, however, to describe the plans, thoughts, and problems that were revolving in the mind of that prince who, in spite of the endeavours of Mme de Maintenon and the Duc du Maine to strip him of all but the bare title of Regent, would inevitably become head of the State during the minority of the future King. Now therefore the time has come to disclose many things, after which I shall return to the events of the last month of the King's life.

Before venturing upon that thorny path, I think it best to describe, if I can, the nature of the leading figure, his private and official difficulties, and his personal characteristics. I say 'if I can', for never in all my life have I met a man so perfectly inconsistent as M. le Duc d'Orléans. I knew him intimately for very many years, during which time he never tried to conceal his nature from me, indeed, during the latter part of that time I was his only friend, the only one to whom he could speak freely, and he did so speak, openly, trustingly, and, indeed, of necessity. Yet, in spite of this, I never learned to know him; neither did he fully know himself.

M. le Duc d'Orléans was, at the very most, of medium height, stout, without being gross, with an easy aristocratic bearing, a large pleasant face, red complexion, black hair and a black wig.[1] He always was an abominable dancer, and had not succeeded at the Academy, but he possessed such natural charm of

[1] Madame described him as follows: 'When my son was only about fourteen or fifteen years old he was not ill-looking, but the suns of Spain and Italy so bronzed his skin that his complexion turned a dark red. He is not tall, but in no way gross. His bad sight causes him sometimes to squint a little, and he carries himself badly. I love him with all my heart, but I can understand that women should not be attracted by him, for he is ungallant with them and has no tact.'

The Duc d'Orléans, Regent
of France, 1715–1722. French
School, 17thC.

manner and expression that it coloured and enhanced all his actions, even the
most commonplace. When nothing crossed him, he could be gentle, cordial,
frank, easily approachable, with an agreeable voice and a most original turn of
phrase. He could converse clearly and fluently on any subject, never hesitating
for words, and always surprisingly interesting. What is more, he could talk just as
sensibly and eloquently on the abstract sciences, government business, finance,
the law, military matters, and the affairs of the Court, as engage in polite
conversation or discuss the arts and engineering. He knew the histories and
memoirs of great men and could put them to good use. He was familiar with the
lives of leading personalities in other periods and the intrigues of ancient courts
as well as those of his own time. To hear him speak you would have thought
him vastly well-read. Not so indeed, for he was a skimmer; but his memory was
so good that he forgot nothing, not even names and dates, which he could quote
accurately. His understanding was so admirable that in glancing through a
book he took in as much as though he read it carefully, and he excelled in
impromptu speeches, being very witty with his sallies and repartees. I never

193

flattered him, for which he used to reproach me, as others did, but I did praise him often for a quality which few possess and which he had abundantly, namely great intelligence combined with excellent good sense. Had he followed his first instincts in every matter he would have made no mistakes. He sometimes took this praise of mine as though it were meant in reproach, but although he was sometimes wrong, it was none the less true. With all these talents, he never gave himself airs or paraded superior knowledge, but argued with each man as an equal and often surprised scholars by his cleverness. In society he was never pompous nor overbearing, but retained a proper sense of his rank and position so that no one forgot himself in his presence, yet everyone felt at ease because he placed himself on their level.

He was particularly careful to keep his place with the Princes of the Blood. No one was more respectful in speech and bearing, no one more dignified in his attitude towards the King and the Sons of France, for he inherited through Monsieur inordinate pride in his royal ancestry. Although not prone to say ill-natured or spiteful things he was a dangerous critic of other men's courage. He never boasted of his own, and, indeed, was unusually modest and silent about events in which he had played a leading part. He gave others due credit, but found it hard not to round upon those whom he described as not pulling their weight and he made his dislike and scorn very evident.

Another of his weaknesses was to believe that he greatly resembled Henri IV and to imitate his ways and sayings. He even managed to convince himself that he looked like that monarch in face and figure, and no flattery pleased him more. But this I would never stoop to, for I was too much assured that he tried to copy that great king's vices as well as his virtues and that he admired both equally. As a matter of fact, he did resemble Henri IV in being by nature good, kind, and compassionate. They have accused him of most inhuman crimes, yet I never met a man more violently opposed to murder, none more averse even to causing pain. You might reasonably say that he carried humanity and tolerance too far, for I maintain that he made a vice of the sublime virtue of forgiving enemies, and that his indiscriminate generosity verged on carelessness and caused him much annoyance and trouble in later years, as will be seen.

I remember, for example, that about a year before the King died I was at Marly and went up soon after dinner to pay a call on Mme la Duchesse d'Orléans, whom I found in bed, suffering with a migraine. M. le Duc d'Orléans was with her alone, sitting in an armchair by the bedside. No sooner had I seated myself than Mme la Duchesse d'Orléans began to tell me of the Cardinal de Rohan's part in the plot against the duke, and of his support of Mme de Maintenon and M. du Maine in their efforts to substantiate the abominable imputations which were then so fashionable. I exclaimed all the more emphatically because M. le Duc d'Orléans, for some unknown reason, had always favoured the Cardinal and his brother and thought of them as friends. 'What do you think of M. le Duc d'Orléans?' she continued. 'He knows that this is true beyond dispute, yet he goes on treating them with the

The Regency Council, of which Saint-Simon was a member.

same kindness.' I looked at the duke lolling in his chair and saying nothing beyond a word or two in confirmation, and I said, 'To speak truth, Monsieur, I think that since Louis the Meek (*le Débonnaire*), there has never been anyone as meek as you.' At these words he leapt up, scarlet with rage to the very whites of his eyes, and began to splutter angrily at me, accusing me of spite and malice, while the duchess egged me on and laughed at him. 'Well done, Monsieur', I said. 'Go on scolding your friends and making much of your enemies. I am delighted to see you so angry. It shows that I have put my finger on an abscess; when I press it the patient screams. I wish I could squeeze all the poison out of your system, you would be a better man and better respected.' He growled at me a little longer and then subsided. This was one of the only two occasions when he was really vexed with me, the other I shall proceed to relate.

It occurred two or three years after the King's death, when I was talking one day in a corner of the long gallery at the Tuileries, waiting for the Conseil de la Régence to begin, and M. le Duc d'Orléans was speaking to someone in one of the window recesses at the other end of the room. I heard my name called from one to another and was told that he wished to speak to me, as often happened before the meetings. I accordingly went to the window, where I found him looking grave, thoughtful, and angry, which surprised me much. 'Monsieur', he said abruptly, 'I have much to reproach you with; I had hitherto thought you my friend.' 'With me, Sir!' I exclaimed, yet more astonished. 'Pray, what have I done?' 'What you have done', he answered, 'is something which you cannot deny, verses, Sir, which you have written against me'. 'Verses!' said I. 'Who on earth has been telling you such nonsense? You have known me for forty years and must be aware that I cannot string two lines together, let alone write verses.' 'Disgraceful', he said. 'But you cannot deny these', and bursting into laughter, he there and then began to sing a street-song with the refrain, '*Notre Régent est débonnaire, là! là! il est débonnaire*'. 'What!' I exclaimed, 'you have not forgotten that incident? Well, since you have had your revenge, remember to make good use of it.' And I, too, laughed heartily. He was still laughing when he sat down at the council table. I do not hesitate to record this trifling incident, because it describes him so well.

He truly loved liberty, as much for others as for himself. One day he praised the English to me because they had no exiles and no *lettres de cachet*, and because their King could forbid no one anything but the entrée to his palace and could keep no one imprisoned. He then told me with great relish (all our princes were alive at that time) that King Charles II had had many lesser mistresses besides the Duchess of Portsmouth, and that the Grand Prieur,[1] young and charming in those days, once went into England when banished for some foolishness, and was given a warm welcome by the English King. By way of showing his gratitude, he managed to seduce one of those lesser mistresses, to whom the King was so passionately devoted that he begged for mercy, offered bribes of money, and promised to smooth matters so that his rival might return to France. The Grand Prieur refused to yield up the lady. Charles forbade him the palace, but he cared nothing for that and took his conquest every night to the play, sitting opposite to the King. Finally, the King of England, not knowing how to get rid of him, so pestered King Louis for his recall that that was ordered. But the Grand Prieur still stayed on, pretending that he was very comfortable in England and pursuing his love-affair openly. Then, in indignation, King Charles went so far as to tell the King in confidence of the situation in which the Grand Prieur had placed him, which procured so swift and peremptory an order to return, that back he went forthwith. M. le Duc d'Orléans seemed to admire him for this episode, and I am not sure that he himself would not have liked to have been in the Grand Prieur's shoes. I said that for my part it astonished me that the grandson of a King of France should have lent himself to so insolent a manoeuvre and that speaking as a subject who, like him, had no claim to the throne, I thought it more than scandalous and most worthy of punishment. But the Duc d'Orléans would not have it so, and went on telling the story with enormous gusto.

He had no desire himself to reign or govern, and although he did do a very foolish thing in Spain,[2] it was solely because someone else put it into his head.

[1] Philippe de Vendôme, brother of the duke.

[2] In 1708 the Duc d'Orléans, commanding the French army in Spain, was accused of attempting to dethrone Philip V in order to succeed to the Spanish throne.

As a matter of fact he had never seriously considered ruling the country until forced to choose between exercising his birthright or being dishonoured, and as for reigning, I can truthfully say that he never aspired to it. Had the necessity arisen, he would have been troubled and embarrassed. What did he want? you will say. To command the armies so long as the wars lasted, and for the rest of the time, to find amusement, without restraint on himself or others.

That was really what suited him best. By nature he was calm and courageous, able to foresee difficulties and apply the proper remedies. He had great aptitude for campaigning, making plans and executing them, mustering his resources, taking full advantage of them, and making prompt use of any good opportunities that might occur. It is not too much to say that he was a most able commander, engineer, and commissary-general. He knew the effective strength of all the troops under his command, the names and capabilities of the officers and the particular merits of the different regiments. The troops adored him; he kept them under strict discipline and inspired them to fulfil the most difficult tasks although they lacked for everything. Both his military and his governmental plans were remarkably wise and practical. It was really amazing to see how well he could grasp the details of different courses of action, never confusing the issue, but weighing the advantages and disadvantages and explaining them most lucidly to others. In short, he had fine and varied capabilities and knowledge, but never paraded them, for truly he had no very great opinion of himself.

What a man! So superior, so well-informed! So fit to bring happiness to France when he came into power! Moreover he had one other excellent qualification for ruling; he was more than thirty-six years old when the two Dauphins died and nearly thirty-eight at the death of the Duc de Berry. During the whole of that time he lived as a private individual, an ordinary subject, with no idea of ever taking the helm. Like the other courtiers, he was buffeted by all the storms and tempests and learned to know all those who were leading personalities and many who were not. Thus he had the advantage of leading a private life, and gained a knowledge of the world which he would not otherwise have acquired. That is the good side of him, and very good it is, no doubt, and very rare. Unfortunately there is another, which must be mentioned at the risk of repeating what has already been said.

The prince had been intended to be the fruit and perfect example of a good education, but he was not lucky in his masters. When he gained his freedom, he was young, healthy, and virile, but resentment at his marriage, lack of employment, and inevitable boredom bred in him an admiration for men of fashion and that desire to copy them which is so often fatal at an early age. Tempted into promiscuous love-affairs, influenced by bad companions who pleased their vanity or ambition by encouraging him to live like them, he grew so accustomed to debauchery and excitement that eventually he could not exist without them and found pleasure only amid noise, turmoil and licentiousness.

After Monseigneur died he came more frequently to the Court, where he

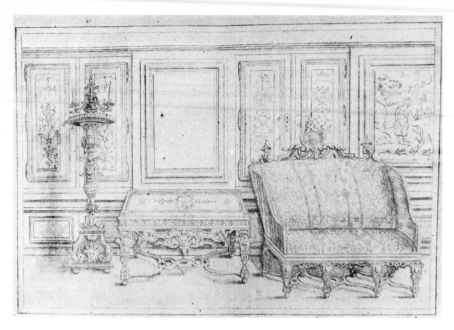

Furniture and panelling at Saint-Cloud, in the study of the Duc de Chartres (later Duc d'Orléans and Regent of France).

was bored to tears. He then plunged into those scientific experiments which I have mentioned earlier and which were used so spitefully against him. It is difficult to realize how incapable he was of gathering a circle of friends, how totally unsuited to hold his Court, even before the fiendish plots of Mme de Maintenon and the Duc du Maine had isolated him entirely. In spite of his apparent unconcern, society embarrassed and wearied him,[1] yet in his own home he was without resources, although his many talents should have provided him with endless interests. He was born bored and by this time had become so accustomed to outside amusements that he found his own company intolerable and would not even try to distract himself. He lived only amid the hustle and bustle of affairs, when, for instance, he was with the army supplying the needs of a campaign, or amid the excitement of some debauch. As soon as the noise and tumult ceased he began to flag and found it hard to pass the time. When his passion for chemistry was exhausted or destroyed by the unkind things that were said, he flung himself into art. He painted during nearly the whole of every afternoon when he was at Versailles or Marly, knew a good deal about pictures, loved them, and made a collection as fine and as large as that of the King. He also liked compounding strong perfumes, but there I used to discourage him, because the King hated them, and he nearly always smelt of them. Never was any man so gifted, yet no man's life was ever so flat, vain, and empty.

Madame, who loved fairy-stories, used to tell how all the fairies were invited to his christening and how each gave him the present of a talent so that he possessed them all. Unfortunately, one old fairy had lived in retirement for so

[1] Madame wrote: 'I wish my son would take more pleasure in the company of men of quality, and consort less with actors, artists and doctors. When he is with the latter he will talk, whereas when men of quality visit him he hangs his head, bites his nails, and does not utter, so that they are vexed when they leave him.'

long that she was forgotten. She arrived late, in a fury, leaning on her little stick, but when she heard what had been done and that the fairies had already made their gifts she became even angrier, and nullified them all by decreeing that although he might possess all the talents he should be incapable of making use of any. In truth, I must admit that the portrait is on the whole a speaking likeness.

One of the prince's chief misfortunes was to have so little perseverance that he scarcely knew the meaning of the word. Another of his weaknesses, as I have already mentioned, was his insensibility to affronts, even dangerous or deadly slanders, and, since the instinct and origin of love and hatred, gratitude and revenge, are one and the same, and since he lacked that instinct, the consequences were many and pernicious. He was by nature undecided, and he knew it and was ashamed, so that he pretended to the contrary and boasted of his firmness. The truth is, however, that as everyone realized when he came into power, nothing could be gained from him, neither favour nor justice, without importuning him or acting on his fears. He would try to escape by making promises, with which he was very liberal, but only the strongest could force him to keep his word. At last, he broke so many pledges that his word ceased to mean anything, for he often promised to several people what he could grant only to one. There was much discontent and he ceased to be respected. In the end he was not believed even when he spoke in good faith and his glibness of speech weakened his actions. Finally, the low company that he sought, and from among whom he chose those boon companions whom he openly referred to as his 'rascals', drove better men from his side and did him infinite harm, even after he had risen to power.

We often spoke of religion, for so long as I had any hope of reclaiming him I took great pains to discuss it with him from different angles so as not to weary him. I never could discover what convictions he held, if any, and I ended by deciding that he remained uncertain, having formed none. Like his boon companions, he longed to persuade himself that God did not exist, but was too intelligent to be an atheist, a far rarer type of lunacy than most people imagine. This glimmer of enlightenment worried him; he did his best to extinguish it, but was never entirely successful. It would have comforted him to have believed that he had no soul, but he could not be convinced in spite of all his efforts. The idea of a living God and an immortal soul greatly distressed him, yet he was unable to blind himself to the fact that both do exist. I was only able to discover what he was not; I never found in him any positive feelings towards religion. Yet I do know his extreme discomfiture regarding that great mystery, and I think that had he incurred some dangerous illness and been given time, he would have required no urging to put himself into the hands of all those priests and friars whom he made such a parade of despising and ridiculing. His besetting sin was to pride himself on irreligion and to try to out-mock the most brazen scoffers.

I remember one Christmas Eve at Versailles when he accompanied the

King to matins and the three midnight masses and astonished the Court by appearing to be absorbed in a book that looked like a prayer book. Mme la Duchesse d'Orléans' head ladies' maid,[1] who was devoted to them both and like all old retainers very free in her speech, was so much overcome with delight that she congratulated him in public on his piety, before Mme la Duchesse d'Orléans and a large company. M. le Duc d'Orléans was pleased to indulge her for a time, and then said, 'You are a great ninny, Mme Imbert. Do you want to know what I was reading? It was my Rabelais. I brought it with me for fear of being bored.' You may imagine the effect of this answer. And it was a fact, but done out of sheer bravado, for beyond all comparison of subjects and places, the music in the chapel was far beyond any at the opera, or indeed anywhere else in Europe. Moreover, as matins, lauds, and the three Christmas masses lasted a very long time, the music was even finer than usual. In any case nothing could have been lovelier than the decoration of the chapel and the way in which it was lighted. It was always crowded, even the bays between the tribunes were filled with the ladies of the Court, not indeed in full court-dress, but none the less glamorous for that. The spectacle was therefore as beautiful as could be and the music enchanted the ears. M. le Duc d'Orléans loved music. He composed a little himself, and even wrote a short opera for which La Fare supplied the libretto, and it was sung before the King. Listening to the music in the chapel would have been quite enough to occupy his mind most delightfully; he would not have needed his Rabelais. But he had to make a show of being a mocker and free-thinker.

[1] Henriette Prieur Imbert, wife of Pierre Imbert, the duke's family-doctor.

The Regent loved the theatre. A performance at the Opera, by Bonnart, 1710.

Character of Mme la Duchesse d'Orléans

Mme la Duchesse d'Orléans was quite another kind of person. She was tall and in every way dignified, with an admirable complexion, bosom, and arms, fine eyes, a mouth that was not ill-formed, and beautiful if rather long teeth. Full, pendulous cheeks spoiled her a little, but did not prevent her from being a woman of beauty. The most unbecoming feature was the arch of her eyebrows, for there the skin looked red and as though it were peeling, and the hairs were scanty. On the other hand, she had good eyelashes and her hair grew prettily. Although neither lame nor in any way misshapen, one of her sides was bigger than the other, which made her walk crabwise, and this physical defect matched another that was more of a handicap in society and troublesome even to her, as I shall describe.

She had as much intelligence as M. le Duc d'Orléans, and even better, for she possessed a greater sense of continuity. Words came easily to her, with a gift for choosing the apt and unexpected phrase that always came as a delightful surprise. What is more, she used that enchanting idiom to which none but Mme de Montespan, her sisters, and those brought up in her household possessed the key. Mme la Duchesse d'Orléans was capable of saying what she pleased and how she pleased with point, tact, and charm. She could also speak without uttering a word and could make her meaning plain to the precise degree that she chose. But her speech itself was so thick and hesitant, so hard upon unaccustomed ears that this disability, although she seemed not to regard it as such, took much of the charm from what she said.

Reserve, propriety, good manners were innate in her. She was the very essence of pride and fastidiousness. You will scarcely believe me when I tell you, what is no more than the exact truth, that at the bottom of her heart she felt that she had conferred a great honour upon M. le Duc d'Orléans by marrying him, and often let slip an almost imperceptible hint to that effect. She had too much sense not to perceive that such an attitude would not be tolerated but too much pride to discard it entirely. She was relentless, even with her own brothers, in keeping the rank into which she had married and remembered that she was a Granddaughter of France even upon her chaise-percée. M. le Duc d'Orléans used often to laugh about it, and when he was alone with her called her Mme Lucifer, which she allowed she did not mind. Moreover, she was fully conscious of the advantages and favours which, at the time of Monsieur's death, had accrued to M. le Duc d'Orléans on account of his marriage. Her annoyance at his behaviour towards her, although in public he was most punctilious, came not from jealousy but from resentment that he would not treat her like a goddess. On the other hand, she never made a step towards him,

Françoise Marie de Bourbon,
youngest daughter of the
King by Mme de Montespan.
Married, 1692, the Duc de
Chartres (later Duc
d'Orléans). Portrait after
Antoine Coypel.

nor did anything to please him or win his affection, nor did she ever refrain
from doing what she saw he disliked. Never did she show him any kindness,
nor those little liberties which women take who live happily with their
husbands. She received any advances from him coldly, with a kind of
patronizing superiority. This was one of the main causes of their estrangement,
and after their reconciliation all the endeavours of M. le Duc d'Orléans
counted less with her than politics.

As for her Court, for that is how one had to speak of her household and the
company who went to her, she preferred to be worshipped rather than courted.
Indeed, I think I can truthfully say that in all her life she found only the

202

Duchesse de Villeroy and myself, who were not ready to bow down before her, but always did and said to her as we thought right. Yet at the same time Mme la Duchesse d'Orléans was painfully nervous. The King needed to look at her only a little sternly and she felt ill at once; possibly Mme de Maintenon had the same effect upon her. At any rate she trembled before them both, and even in public on the most banal subjects could only stammer her answers and look terrified. I say answers because it would have required more courage than she possessed to speak to them first, especially to the King.

For the rest, although she enjoyed excellent health, her life was very boring—solitude and reading until dinner-time, needlework for the rest of the day, and company between five and six in the evening; but there was neither amusement nor relaxation because she did not know how to put people at their ease. She had no intercourse, except very formally, with Mme la Duchesse du Maine, and M. du Maine visited her seldom and almost never during her visiting hours. As for me, I never saw her when she had company, but nearly always tête-à-tête, or with M. le Duc d'Orléans, sometimes, but very occasionally, with M. le Comte de Toulouse, never with M. du Maine. Neither of the latter ever set foot in M. le Duc d'Orléans' apartments except on state occasions, for they did not care for him. Self-interest apart, M. du Maine had very little inclination to care for anyone. He afterwards adopted Mme de Maintenon's likes and dislikes, and you have seen what endeavours he later made to steal away M. le Duc d'Orléans' birthright and seize the sovereign power. The Comte de Toulouse, unfeeling by nature, led a different life and disapproved of that of M. le Duc d'Orléans; he sympathized with his sister's vexations, and held aloof because of the King's displeasure. Yet in the events that followed, I never found him otherwise than truthful, honourable and prudent, fulfilling his duty towards M. le Duc d'Orléans, although never becoming friendly or affectionate.

When the Court entirely abandoned M. le Duc d'Orléans, leaving him in the wilderness, his wife, whose pride and laziness were extreme, was disinclined to make the slightest approach towards anyone. She seemed perfectly prepared to wait for society to pay her homage, without herself taking any trouble, and thus their lives became wearisome, ignominious, unsuited to their rank and despised. That was one of the first conditions which they had to remedy. Both of them realized this, but it must be allowed that once her mind was made up, Mme la Duchesse d'Orléans set herself to the task with much more courage and perseverance than her husband. I say courage advisedly, because her pride had to suffer many hurts in the long struggle to extricate herself from that unhappy situation.

The ladies whom she invited to her dinner-parties were fertile in inventing excuses. They dreaded being seen in company with M. le Duc d'Orléans, and the most cunning among them waited for one of his excursions to Paris in order to dine with his wife, and then considered themselves exempt for several months to come. They also feared the King, which is to say Mme de

Maintenon and, for those most in the know, the Duc du Maine. For a long time it was fashionable to refuse at first and then to be persuaded into going, on the excuse that continual invitations gave one no further grounds for escape. Men were a more difficult problem for her than women, because her rank as a Granddaughter of France allowed her to invite only noblemen to her table.

Once Mme la Duchesse d'Orléans had convinced herself of the need to break down this most unseemly barrier that separated her from society on account of her husband, she did not flinch. Realizing that she could not entice people to her unless they were also reconciled with him, she assumed, so far as she was able, an amiable and gracious manner in order to melt the ice and make her apartments and table alluring. The labour was odious to her and very hard, but she persisted and finally succeeded. People began to grow bolder, following the example of others, and little by little the numbers increased after the manner of a snowball.

The food and wine at her table were delicious, and after a while the constraint became less obvious although respect for rank and the proprieties was strictly observed. M. le Duc d'Orléans became more guarded in his speech and gradually began to converse on general topics, such as public affairs, in a way that did not embarrass others or himself. Card-tables were often arranged after the meal, so that the company were detained until it was time for the King's supper. After a while people began to praise these dinner-parties and to express surprise that they should ever have been shunned. The lack of interest shown by the King and Mme de Maintenon reassured them and they began to feel ashamed of having feared their disapproval. None the less, those who

The King gives a dinner at the Court for the princes and princesses, 6 July, 1710.

'Appartement'. Card playing in the second room, at the King's weekly receptions at Versailles—Monseigneur's table.

frequented the King's salon did not soften towards M. le Duc d'Orléans. At the dinner-parties one dined in the apartment of the King's bastard-daughter, her husband only happened to be there in the position of a guest. In the King's salon, where most of the gentlemen had not been to the dinners, he was still kept at a distance and was avoided even by many who had just left his table. This state of affairs did not change until the King's last illness.

Mme la Duchesse d'Orléans was well aware that M. le Duc d'Orléans confided in me and that I had much influence in his thoughts and plans for the present and the future. This she had known for a long time, and realized more clearly than outsiders could do that I was the only man to whom he could speak frankly on matters of importance. She also knew that I had my own opinions and ideas of the changes that would follow after the present reign; she was very anxious to learn of them and tried to lead me on about people and future events in the course of our many conversations. I was careful about both, less so perhaps about people, for she already knew my mind in most cases. As regards events, I escaped into generalities, and as time went on I emphasized the carelessness, irresponsibility and idleness of M. le Duc d'Orléans, who acted as though the present situation would last for ever. Perhaps I may have exaggerated somewhat in my complaints to her, but indeed, it was only too true, for as you will see my criticisms were well-founded.

1715

Death of the King

On Friday August 9th Père Le Tellier instructed the King at some length on the registration in the Parlement of the Bull *Unigenitus*,[1] entire, as it stood. The the King saw the premier président[2] and the procureur général,[3] whom he had summoned on the day before. After dinner, he went stag-hunting, driving his own calash himself for the last time in his life, and returned home exhausted. That evening there was *grande musique* in Mme de Maintenon's apartment. On the Saturday, he walked before dinner in his gardens at Marly, and about six o'clock returned to Versailles for the last time in his life, never again to contemplate that monstrous work of his creation. In the evening he worked with the Chancellor in Mme de Maintenon's rooms. Everyone thought him looking gravely ill. On Sunday August 11th, he held the council of state, and in the afternoon walked to the Trianon. He never went out again.

On the following day he took physic in the ordinary way and led the life to which he was accustomed in those days. It was reported that he complained of sciatica in the leg and thigh. He had never before suffered from sciatica, nor from rheumatism; he had never had even a cold and for a long time past had

[1] The Bull issued by Pope Clement XI in 1713 condemning Jansenism. It caused a fierce struggle between the Jansenists and the Jesuits during the early part of the eighteenth century.

[2] M. de Mesmes.

[3] Henri François Daguesseau.

205

had no attacks of gout. That evening they had *petite musique* at Mme de Maintenon's, and that was the last time he ever walked.

On Tuesday August 13th, he made a last effort, on returning from mass in his chair, to give the final audience, standing without support, to that dubious ambassador from Persia.[1] His weakness did not allow him to repeat the splendours of the first audience and he had to be satisfied with receiving him in the throne room, where nothing happened out of the ordinary. This was the last of the King's public engagements, one in which Pontchartrain played vilely upon his vanity in order to press his court. Indeed, he was shameless enough to conclude the farce with the signing of a treaty, whose results amply demonstrated the fraudulence of the whole affair. The audience was long and tiring, but after it was over the King would not rest although he must have longed to do so. He held the Conseil des Finances, dined in private, and was carried to Mme de Maintenon's rooms, where there was *petite musique*. As he was leaving his study, he stopped to allow the Duchesse de La Rochefoucauld to present her daughter-in-law, the Duchesse de La Rocheguyon, the last lady ever to be presented to him. She took her tabouret that night at the King's supper, the last time that he ever ate in public. Afterwards he worked alone with the Chancellor, and on the following day he sent gifts, including some jewels, to that fine ambassador, who, two days later, was escorted to the house of a merchant at Chaillot and shortly afterwards left for Hâvre-de-Grace, where he re-embarked.

The King's health had been failing for more than a year. The personal valets

Audience to the Persian Ambassador Extraordinary, Mehemet Reza Beg, in the Salle de Glaces, 19 February, 1715. By Antoine Coypel. Louis XIV on his silver throne, and the famous Persian carpet with a gold background.

[1] Pontchartrain was accused of 'manufacturing' ambassadorial rank for a vulgar impostor in order to give the King the satisfaction of appearing in splendour, perhaps for the last time. 'Only the King was duped', says Saint-Simon.

had been the first to notice it, and had observed every symptom without daring to speak. Then the bastards, especially M. du Maine, also perceived it and with the assistance of Mme de Maintenon acted with all dispatch. Fagon, now weak in body and mind, was the only one in all that great household who noticed nothing. Maréchal, the chief surgeon, often reminded him, but was harshly rebuffed. At last, out of duty and attachment to the King, Maréchal was driven to go to Mme de Maintenon to warn her how completely Fagon was mistaken. He assured her that the King, whose pulse he had often taken, had for a long time been suffering from a slow internal fever, that his constitution being so robust there would be no danger with proper care and remedies, but that if it went unchecked, the evil might soon prove fatal. Mme de Maintenon lost her temper, so that what his loyalty led him to tell her only served to make her angrier still. She said that only Fagon's personal enemies believed such tales about the King's health, and that the chief physician's skill, wisdom and experience could not be deceived. Maréchal told me indignantly he felt there was nothing more that he could do. From that moment he began to mourn for the death of his master. Fagon had indeed once been the first physician in all Europe, but for a long time past his health had prevented him from broadening his experience, and his unlimited authority and favour with the King had spoilt him. He would brook neither argument nor discussion, continued to treat the King's health as in earlier days and, by his stubbornness, killed him.

Because the King had once suffered from prolonged attacks of gout, Fagon continued to swaddle him every night in a great mass of feather pillows, so that he had to be changed and rubbed down every morning before the grand chamberlain and first gentlemen of the bed-chamber could enter. Instead of the champagne to which he had been accustomed all through his life, they had of late years made him drink watered-down burgundy, so old that it had lost its potency. He sometimes said laughingly that foreigners felt swindled when they asked to be allowed to taste the royal wine. Never at any time did he drink his wine unwatered, and he had never been accustomed to take sweet wines, nor even tea, coffee, nor chocolate. When he rose, instead of eating a little bread with wine and water, he had for a long time past been used to having two cups of sage and veronica. Between meals, and always at bedtime, he drank more than one pint-size glass full of water flavoured with orange-flowers, and all his drinks were iced. Even on days when he took physic he drank, and always at his meals, and he never ate anything between meals except for a few cinnamon lozenges, which he used to put into his pocket at dessert, with many dry biscuits for the setter-bitches in his dog-room.

When during the last years of his life he became increasingly constipated, Fagon made him begin his meals with iced fruit, such as mulberries, melons, and figs, often half-rotten with over-ripeness, and he ate still more fruit for dessert, with an astonishing number of sweetmeats. He ate an immense deal of salad for his supper, all the year round. His soups, of which he drank several different kinds morning and evening, taking a full cup of each regardless of what was to come, were made of strong meat juices, exceedingly rich, and all that was served to him was highly spiced, at least twice the normal quantity, and very hot. Fagon did not approve of the spices and sweetmeats and often made a face when he saw the King eating them, but he dared not say anything, except once in a way to Livry and Benoist, who told him that it was their business to make the King eat and his to purge him. He never touched venison nor water-fowl, but with those exceptions he ate everything, on feast and fast days alike, apart from Lent, which he had kept for the last twenty years, although only for a few days. In that last summer he had increased his consumption of fruit and drinks.

In the end, so much fruit taken after soup flooded his stomach and took away his appetite, which never before had failed in the whole of his life, although he never felt hungry, even when his meals were unavoidably delayed. At the first spoonful of soup his appetite came, as I have many times heard him say, and he ate prodigiously of solid meals each morning and evening, and so steadily that one never grew accustomed to watching him.[1] So much water, so much fruit, unrelieved by any alcohol, turned his blood gangrenous by lowering the vital spirits, and weakened his digestion by nightly sweating. They finally caused his death, as was proved when his body was opened, for all the vital parts were found to be so perfectly healthy and strong that he might well have lived more than a century. His stomach and bowels were particularly remarkable because their size and capacity were double that of any ordinary man, which explains why he was so huge and regular an eater.

No one had thought of applying remedies until it was too late, because both Fagon and Mme de Maintenon refused to admit that the King was ill, although she took care to safeguard her own future at Saint-Cyr, and M. du Maine's as well. The King himself was one of the first to realize his condition and sometimes spoke of it to his personal valets, but Fagon always reassured him and did nothing. The King listened to what he said but remained unconvinced, nevertheless his friendship for Fagon and more especially Mme de Maintenon's influence restrained him from taking action.

On Wednesday August 14th they carried him to mass for the last time, and he afterwards held the Conseil d'État, ate a full meal, although it was a fast day, and went to the *grande musique* at Mme de Maintenon's apartment. He supped alone in his room and was seen by the Court at his dinner-time. He stayed only a short time in his study among his family and retired to bed soon after ten o'clock. . . .

On Saturday 17th he had another bad night. He remained in bed for the Conseil des Finances, received the company at dinner, rose immediately afterwards, and went to Mme de Maintenon, where he worked with the Chancellor. That night was the first when Fagon slept in his room.

Sunday August 18th was like other days, Fagon still pretending that the King had no fever. He held a Council of State, afterwards worked as usual with Le Peletier[2] on the fortifications, and then went to Mme de Maintenon for the

[1] Madame wrote: 'I have often seen the King consume four full plates of different kinds of soup, a whole pheasant, a partridge, a large dish of salad, two great slices of ham, mutton served with gravy and garlic, a plate of sweet cakes, and on top of that, fruit and hardboiled eggs.'

[2] Le Peletier de Souzy, directeur général des fortifications.

Reza Beg is entertained to dinner by the King's household after his audience.

music. It was clear, however, that he could not be expected to last for more than a few days in that condition, about which Maréchal told me more truly than Fagon. I then remembered Chamillart, who was receiving a retirement-pension of 60,000 livres from the King and immediately went to M. le Duc d'Orléans to beg for its continuance. I received his promise with permission to write to Chamillart to that effect, which I accordingly did. The latter was much moved at hearing of the King's illness, but showed very little emotion at my other news. None the less, he was agreeably surprised at my having written to him and very grateful for my thought; he had had none for himself. He also sent me a formal letter of thanks to be transmitted to M. le Duc d'Orléans. Nothing that I have ever done has given me greater pleasure. The thing remained a secret until after the King's death, but as soon as the Regency had begun, I lost no time in publishing the news.

The night and the morning of Friday 23rd were as usual. The King worked with Père Le Tellier, who was trying unsuccessfully to persuade him to appoint nominees for the many important benefices then vacant. Père Le Tellier was secretly hoping to have the disposal of them himself, so as not to leave them to M. le Duc d'Orléans, indeed, it cannot be denied that as the King grew worse he pressed him ever more urgently. He feared to lose these rich prizes and with them the chance of securing a loyal following, for he made his bargains with intrigues, not with money. None the less, he failed. The King declared that seeing he was so soon to appear before God, he had enough accounts to settle without further burdening himself with appointments and he forbade Père Le Tellier to mention them again. He then dined standing in his room, wearing a dressing-gown, and afterwards went into the study with the two bastards (M. du Maine very assiduous), Mme de Maintenon, and some ladies of the circle. The evening was as usual.

Here I must pause to describe the arrangement in the King's apartments now that he no longer went out. The entire Court spent the whole day in the great gallery. No one remained in the ante-chamber nearest the bedchamber except the personal valets and the dispensers, who heated whatever was necessary. People merely passed quickly through the room from one door to another. Those who had the entrée entered the private apartments by the mirror-door that gave on to the gallery and was kept shut. It was only opened when one scratched at it and was closed again immediately. Ministers and secretaries of state also entered by that door and waited in the study adjoining the gallery. Not even the Princes of the Blood nor the King's daughters were allowed nearer, unless the King asked for them, which never happened. The Maréchal de Villeroy, the Chancellor, the two bastards, M. le Duc d'Orléans, Père Le Tellier, the curé of Versailles,[1] also Maréchal, Fagon, and the first valets (when they were not required in the bedroom) waited in the council chamber between the King's room and that other room where the Princes and Princesses of the Blood, the entrées, and the ministers were assembled.

The Duc de Tresmes, whose year it was as first gentleman, stood by the open door between the two rooms and never entered the King's bedroom unless his duty made it absolutely necessary. During the daytime, no one entered except those in the council chamber, the valets and dispensers who waited in the first ante-room, Mme de Maintenon, and the ladies of the household, and, for dinner and supper, such officers and courtiers as were permitted. M. le Duc d'Orléans carefully limited his appearances to, at the very most, twice a day, once when the Duc de Tresmes entered the bedroom, and once again at the door leading into the council chamber, where the King could see him from his bed.

On Saturday 24th, the night was scarcely more distressing than usual, for it was always a bad time, but the leg seemed much worse and gave him more pain. Mass was said as usual, dinner was served in bed, where he was seen by the principal courtiers who had not the entrée; then followed the Conseil des Finances, after which he worked alone with the Chancellor. Mme de Maintenon and the ladies later came to him and he supped standing in his dressing-gown in the presence of the Court for the last time. I noticed that he swallowed only fluids and that it annoyed him to be stared at. He was unable to finish and asked the courtiers to go on, that is to say, to leave the room. He then desired to be put to bed. They examined the leg and found black spots. He sent for Père Le Tellier and confessed. By now confusion reigned among the doctors. They had tried milk, and quinine with water, now both were discontinued and no one knew what to do next. They admitted that he had had a slow fever since Whitsun, but excused themselves on the grounds that he disliked remedies, and that they had not thought him very bad.

[1] Claude Huchon.

Sunday August 25th was the feast of Saint-Louis and the night was much worse. No secret now was made of the danger, which was suddenly realized to be great and critical. Nevertheless, the King would allow no change to be made in the order of the day.[1] The drums and fifes stationed beneath his windows still struck up as soon as he woke, and the four-and-twenty violins played in the ante-room as usual during dinner. He then spent some time alone with Mme de Maintenon, the Chancellor and, for a little while, with the Duc du Maine. Paper and ink had been sent in to him on the previous evening when he was working alone with the Chancellor, and they were again ordered when he was closeted with Mme de Maintenon. It therefore must have been on one of those two days that the Chancellor wrote the codicil at his dictation. Mme de Maintenon and M. du Maine, who never ceased thinking of themselves, had decided that not enough was being done for them in the King's will and were determined to remedy this by a codicil, which shows the wicked advantage taken of the King in his extremity and the lengths to which inordinate ambition can lead. Under this codicil, the King's entire establishment, both civil and military, were to be subjected to the Duc du Maine forthwith, without reserve, and under him to the Maréchal de Villeroy. These two would thus become absolute masters of the King's households and residences, of the city of Paris (because two regiments of guards and two companies of Musketeers were quartered there), and of all the service departments, bedchamber, wardrobe, chapels, kitchens, and stables. Thus no shadow of authority would remain to the Regent. He would be at their mercy, in constant danger of arrest, or worse, should he happen to displease the Duc du Maine.

Soon after the Chancellor left, Mme de Maintenon, who had remained with the King, sent for the ladies of the household and for the orchestra, which arrived at seven o'clock. But he fell asleep during the general conversation and woke confused, which frightened the ladies and caused them to summon the doctors. In the meanwhile he had recovered his senses, but the pulse was so weak that they did not hesitate to advise him to take the Last Sacraments without delay. Père Le Tellier was accordingly summoned, and Cardinal de Rohan, who was at home with company, his thoughts quite otherwise occupied. The orchestra, who had already arranged their books and instruments, were dismissed, and the ladies departed.

It chanced that I was walking through the great gallery at that precise moment, on my way to Mme la Duchesse d'Orléans's apartment from my own rooms in the new wing. I noticed some of the remaining musicians and thought that the rest had entered the ante-room, but one of the ushers came up and told me what had occurred. I found Mme la Duchesse d'Orléans in bed with the remains of a migraine, surrounded by ladies making conversation and suspecting nothing. I went up to the bed and told her the news, but she would not believe me, saying that the orchestra was playing at that very moment and that the King was no worse. Then, after I had whispered to her, she asked the ladies whether they had heard anything; but they knew nothing and Mme la

He is supposed to have said: 'I have lived among the people of my Court and I desire to die among them. They have followed the whole course of my life; it is only right that they should witness my end.'

Duchesse d'Orléans was reassured. I told her the facts a second time, insisting that I was certain of them and thought that she should at least send to inquire and, in the meantime, dress. Then she did believe me and I went in to M. le Duc d'Orléans and warned him also, but he rightly thought it more prudent to remain where he was since no one had sent for him.

In a quarter of an hour all was prepared. Père Le Tellier confessed the King whilst Cardinal de Rohan went to the chapel for the Host and sent for the curé of Versailles and the Holy Oils. Two of the King's almoners walked before the Cardinal, together with eight of the blue footmen carrying torches, two lackeys belonging to Fagon, and one in Mme de Maintenon's service. This very small escort accompanied the Cardinal up the narrow staircase into the King's chamber, while Père Le Tellier, Mme de Maintenon and about a dozen of the household, lords and valets alike, went out to greet or follow the Holy Sacrament. The Cardinal said a few words to the King about this tremendous final act, during which he seemed to be resolute and much moved. When he had received Our Lord and the Holy Oils, everyone left the room in procession, either before or following the Host; only Mme de Maintenon and the Chancellor remained. Then, immediately, and this was most dreadful in the circumstances, they put a book or small table upon the bed and the Chancellor laid the codicil upon it, after which the King added four or five lines in his own hand, and it was removed.

The King then asked for a drink, called to the Maréchal de Villeroy, who was standing by the door leading into the council chamber, and spoke with him for nearly a quarter of an hour. He sent also for M. le Duc d'Orléans and spoke with him privately, expressing his esteem, confidence, and affection and, what was most terrible, with Jesus Christ still upon his lips, assured him that he would find nothing in the will but what would content him, and recommended to his care the State, and the person of the future King. Not half an hour had elapsed between his receiving Extreme Unction and this conversation. He cannot have forgotten the vile provisions which they had extracted from him with so much difficulty, moreover, in that short interval he had added words in a codicil that placed a knife at the throat of M. le Duc d'Orléans and its handle in the grasp of the Duc du Maine. One strange result of this interview was the rumour that the King had already given the Regency to M. le Duc d'Orléans.

The night of Monday August 26th was no better. The King dined in bed in the presence of the household. As the meal was being cleared away, he bade them approach and said these words, which were written down within the hour. 'Gentlemen, I ask your pardon for the bad example which I have set you. I have much to thank you for the manner in which you have served me and for your constant devotion. It grieves me that I have not done all I could have wished for you; the fault lies in the hardness of the times. I shall ask you to show the same attachment to my great-grandson; that child may right many wrongs. Let your example be a guide to my other subjects. Obey my nephew's orders, for he will govern the kingdom. I trust that he will do it well. I also trust that you will remain united, and that should one of you break away the rest will endeavour to reclaim him. I feel that I begin to be moved to tears and that I am moving you, I ask your pardon. Gentlemen, farewell, I hope that sometimes you will remember me.'

Shortly afterwards he desired the Duchesse de Ventadour to fetch the Dauphin. He made the child come to him, and said these words before Mme de Maintenon and the closest of the household, who later repeated them. 'My child, you are about to become a great King. Do not imitate my love of building nor my liking for war, but try, on the contrary, to live at peace with your neighbours. Render to God all that you owe Him; recognize your duty towards Him; see that He is honoured by your subjects. Always follow good counsellors; try to comfort your people, which it grieves me that I was unable to do. Never forget the debt of gratitude which you owe to Mme de Ventadour.' 'Madame', said he, turning to her, 'let me kiss him', and as he did so, he said, 'My dear child, I give you my blessing with all my heart.' As the little prince was being lifted from the bed, the King again asked for him, embraced him once more and, raising his hands and eyes to heaven, blessed him again. It was a most moving spectacle. Mme de Ventadour then hastened to remove the Dauphin and took him back to his apartment.

On Tuesday August 27th, the King said to Mme de Maintenon that he had heard how hard it was to reconcile oneself to dying, but now that he himself approached that awful moment he did not find it difficult to submit. She replied that it was always exceedingly painful when people retained old attachments or hatreds, or had reparations still to make. 'Oh!' said the King, 'as for debts to individuals, I have none; as for what I owe the State I put my trust in the mercy of God.' The night that followed was most distressing. He was seen many times to clasp his hands, and they heard him recite the prayers to which he had been accustomed when he was well, and he beat his breast at the *Confiteor*.

On Wednesday August 28th, he made an affectionate remark to Mme de Maintenon which she did not at all relish and did not answer. He said that he was consoled at leaving her by the thought that at her age the parting would not be for long.[1] Then he sent for Père Le Tellier. As they were speaking of God, he saw reflected in the mirror above the chimney-piece two of the pages who were weeping at the foot of the bed. He said to them, 'Why do you weep? Did you think that I was immortal? I have never thought so, and considering my age, you should have been prepared to lose me.'

A very rough, common sort of peasant from Provence learned of the King's illness as he was on his way from Marseilles to Paris, and appeared that same morning at Versailles with a remedy which he said was a certain cure for gangrene. By this time, the King was so ill and the doctors so desperate that they accepted it without demur, in the presence of Mme de Maintenon and the Duc du Maine. Fagon did try to make an objection, but the peasant, whose

[1] Mme de Maintenon thus describes the King's three farewells to her: 'The first time he assured me that his only regret was in leaving me; "But," he said, sighing, "we shall meet again before long." I entreated him to think only of God. The second time, he asked my forgiveness for not having lived better with me and for not having made me happy, but said that he had indeed always loved and esteemed me. Then, feeling that he was near weeping, he asked me to see that we were not overheard, and added, "But no one could be surprised at my loving you." On the third occasion, he said, "What will become of you? You have nothing." I exhorted him again to think only of God; then, reflecting that I did not know in what manner the princes would treat me, I begged him to recommend me to M. le Duc d'Orléans.'

213

name was Le Brun, turned upon him so fiercely that Fagon, who usually bullied everyone until they were terrified of him, was struck perfectly dumb. They gave the King ten drops of the medicine in a glass of alicant at eleven in the morning. For a little while he felt stronger, but the pulse weakened and nearly failed entirely; then they offered him a further dose at about four o'clock, saying that it would revive him. As he took the glass, he said, 'For life or death, as God pleases.'

In the meantime, Mme de Maintenon left the King's room with her hood drawn down, and was conducted by the Maréchal de Villeroy past her apartments, which she did not enter, as far as the foot of the grand staircase. There, raising her hood, she embraced him dry-eyed; said, 'Adieu! M. le Maréchal'; stepped into the King's coach, which she always used, and where Mme de Caylus awaited her, and drove away to Saint-Cyr, followed by her own coach, containing all her women. That same evening in his apartment, the Duc du Maine made a thoroughly good story of Fagon's encounter with Le Brun. But I shall find other opportunities to describe his conduct and that of Mme de Maintenon during those last days.

The day and night before Thursday August 29th were very bad, but the removal of those who had nothing more to do beyond what had already been done left room for the high officers who until then had been excluded from the King's bedroom. No mass had been said on the previous evening and there seemed no prospect of any in the future, but the Duc de Charost, a captain of the guard, who had stolen in with the others, rightly thought this very bad, and directed one of the valets to ask the King if he would not like to hear one. When the King answered that he did so desire it, they sent for the necessary priests and objects, and thus it continued during the following days. He had seemed stronger that morning and there was a ray of hope which was immediately exaggerated. Good news flew in all directions. He had even been able to take two small biscuits in a glass of alicant, and had seemed to enjoy them.

At about two o'clock in the morning I went to M. le Duc d'Orléans's apartments, which had been so swarming with courtiers for the past week at every hour of the day and night that, truthfully speaking, you could scarcely have dropped a pin between them, and I found no one. As soon as M. le Duc d'Orléans saw me, he burst out laughing, telling me that I was the first person he had seen that entire day, for his rooms had been utterly deserted. That is society!

I seized upon this quiet moment to speak to him of many things, and it was then that I realized for the first time how he had changed his mind about summoning the États Généraux,[1] and that except for what had been agreed concerning the councils, he had not given the matter another thought. Nor had he considered many other matters, about which I had taken the liberty of speaking my mind strongly.

The late evening of the 29th did not fulfil the earlier hopes and the King said to the curé of Versailles, who came to tell him that all the people were praying,

[1] Les États Généraux. The council of nobles, prelates, and commoners, called together to assist the King in government.

that it was no longer a question of his life, but of his salvation, and for that he urgently needed prayer. On that same day, when he was giving some orders, he chanced to refer to the Dauphin as 'the young King', and noticed the sudden movement in his entourage. 'Why do you start?' he said. 'That does not trouble me.' At eight o'clock he took more of the medicine of the man from Provence, and afterwards seemed confused, saying that he felt very ill. At about eleven, they examined the leg and found gangrene in the foot and knee; the thigh was much inflamed. He fainted during the examination. It was then that he noticed with dismay the absence of Mme de Maintenon, who had not intended returning. He asked for her several times that day, until it was no longer possible to hide the fact that she had gone. He then sent to Saint-Cyr for her and she returned during the evening.

Friday August 30th was as bad as the previous night. A coma set in and in the intervals his mind wandered. From time to time they gave him a little jelly in fresh water; he could no longer take wine. No one went into his room except his personal valets, the doctors, Mme de Maintenon and, on very rare occasions Père Le Tellier, if Blouin or Maréchal sent for him. Few people waited, even in the ante-rooms; M. du Maine was not among them. The King responded readily to thoughts of religion when Mme de Maintenon or Père Le Tellier seized on moments when his mind was clear, but such intervals were short and rare. At five in the evening, Mme de Maintenon went to her apartments, distributed what furniture she possessed there among the members of her household and left for Saint-Cyr, never to return.

The King on his deathbed, 1 September 1715.

The day and night of August 31st were very dreadful. There were only short moments of consciousness at rare intervals. The gangrene spread over the knee and the whole of the thigh. They gave him medicine of the late Abbé d'Aignan,[1] which had been suggested by the Duchesse du Maine, and was an excellent remedy for smallpox, but by this time the doctors were consenting to any suggestion because they no longer had any hope. At eleven o'clock, the King was seen to be so ill that they said the prayers for the dying. The service brought him back to consciousness, and he recited the prayers in so strong a voice that it could be heard clearly above the many priests and all the other persons who had entered the room. At the end of the prayers, he recognized Cardinal de Rohan and said to him, 'These are then the last favours of the Church.' The Cardinal was the last person to whom he ever spoke. Several times he was heard to repeat the words, '*Nunc et in hora mortis*', also, 'Oh! God help me. Haste Thou to succour me.' Those were his last words. All the rest of that night he lay unconscious. His long-protracted agony ended at a quarter past eight in the morning of Sunday 1st September 1715, just three days before his seventy-seventh birthday, in the seventy-second year of his reign.

[1] François d'Aignan (nick-named 'Le Père Tranquille'), who travelled in the East as a mendicant monk and brought back the recipes for many remedies, including one called 'La Baume Tranquille' a narcotic ointment, perhaps the first mention of a 'tranquilliser'.

1715

Character of Louis XIV

He was a prince in whom no one would deny good and even great qualities, but he had many others that were petty or downright bad, and of these it was impossible to determine which were natural and which acquired. Nothing is harder to find than a well-informed writer, none rarer than those who knew him personally, yet are sufficiently unbiased to speak of him without hatred or flattery, and to set down the bare truth for good or ill.

This is not the place to tell of his early childhood. He was king almost from birth, but was deliberately repressed by a mother who loved to govern, and still more so by a wicked and self-interested minister, who risked the State a thousand times for his own aggrandisement. So long as that minister lived the King was held down, and that portion of his life should be subtracted from his reign. Nevertheless, he throve beneath that yoke for he learned to know love, and discovered that idleness is the enemy of glory. He made feeble excursions in both directions. After Mazarin's death, he had enough intelligence to realize his deliverance, but not enough vigour to release himself. Yet, that event proved one of the finest moments of his life, for it taught him an unshakable principle, namely to banish all prime ministers and ecclesiastics from his councils. Another ideal, adopted at that time, he could never sustain because in practice it constantly eluded him. This was to govern alone. It was the quality upon which he most prided himself and for which he received most praise and flattery. In fact, it was what he was least able to do.

Born with an intelligence rather below the average, his mind was very capable of development with training and education, for he could learn easily from others and not parrot-wise. He profited immensely from having always lived among people of the highest quality with the widest knowledge of life, men and women of vastly different ages and characters, but all of them personalities.

Indeed, if I may say so of a King of twenty-three years old, he was fortunate in entering the world surrounded by brilliant people of every kind. His Ministers at home and abroad were the strongest in Europe, his generals the greatest, and all were men whose names have been handed down to posterity by common consent. The disturbances that rocked the very foundations of the State after the death of Louis XIII produced a Court full of famous men and polished courtiers. The house of the Comtesse de Soissons[1] was the vastly select centre of the life of that Court. As superintendent of the Queen's household, she lodged in Paris at the Tuileries, where she reigned supreme by virtue of the remnants of her late uncle Cardinal Mazarin's splendour and her own skill and cunning. There, all the most distinguished men and women foregathered every day, making her drawing-room the centre of the Court love-affairs, the gallant intrigues and endeavours for ambition's sake — schemes in which birth counted for much, since rank was then as much prized and respected as it is now despised. Into this brilliant vortex the King was first launched, and there he first acquired that polite, chivalrous manner which he retained all through his life and knew so well how to combine with stateliness and propriety. You might say that he was to the manner born, for he stood out like a king bee amid all that crowd of people because of his height, grace, and beauty (even in the tone of his voice), and because of his princely bearing which was better than good looks. Had he been born into private life, he would still have had a genius for entertainments, pleasures, and flirtations, and would have caused innumerable broken hearts. It would have been better for him had all his mistresses resembled Mme de La Vallière, who truly loved him, was ashamed of being what she was, and still more ashamed at seeing the fruits of her love elevated and acknowledged against her will. One must allow, therefore that the King was more to be pitied than blamed when he yielded to love and that he deserved credit for having at intervals torn himself away in the pursuit of glory.

Let me repeat. The King's intelligence was below the average, but was very capable of improvement. He loved glory; he desired peace and good government. He was born prudent, temperate, secretive, master of his emotions and of his tongue — can it be believed?, he was born good and just. God endowed him with all the makings of a good and perhaps even of a fairly great king. All the evil in him came from without. His early training was so dissolute that no one dared to go near his apartments, and he would sometimes

[1] Olympe Mancini (1639–1708). In 1657 she married Eugène Maurice de Savoie-Carignan, Comte de Soissons. She was the mother of Prince Eugène.

Olympe Mancini, Comtesse de Soissons, nicknamed 'the Snipe', one of the King's early loves. She was the mother of Prince Eugène.

speak bitterly of those days and tell how they found him one night fallen into the fountain at the Palais Royal. He became very dependent on others, for he had scarcely been taught to read and write, and he remained so ignorant that he learned nothing of historical events nor the facts about fortunes, careers, ranks, or laws. This lack caused him sometimes, even in public, to make many gross blunders.

You could imagine that as king he would have loved the old nobility and would not have cared to see it brought down to the level of other classes. Nothing was further from the truth. His aversion to noble sentiments and his

218

partiality for his Ministers, who, to elevate themselves, hated and disparaged all who were what they themselves were not, nor ever could be, caused him to feel a similar antipathy for noble birth. He feared it as much as he feared intelligence, and if he found these two qualities united in one person, that man was finished.

His ministers, generals, mistresses, and courtiers learned soon after he became their master that glory, to him, was a foible rather than an ambition. They therefore flattered him to the top of his bent, and in so doing, spoiled him. Praise, or better, adulation, pleased him so much that the most fulsome was welcome and the most servile even more delectable. They were the only road to his favour and those whom he liked owed his friendship to choosing their moments well and never ceasing in their attentions. That is what gave his ministers so much power, for they had endless opportunities of flattering his vanity, especially by suggesting that he was the source of all their ideas and had taught them all that they knew. Falseness, servility, admiring glances, combined with a dependent and cringing attitude, above all, an appearance of being nothing without him, were the only means of pleasing him. Once a man left that path there was no return for him, as Louvois found out to his cost.

The poison gradually spread until it reached a degree almost unbelievable in a prince who was not unintelligent or without experience of the world. For example, although he had no voice nor ear for music, he could often be heard in his private rooms singing the verses written in his praise in the prologues of the plays and operas. You could see that he revelled in them, and sometimes even at State suppers he hummed the words under his breath when the orchestra played these tunes.

Flattery fed the desire for military glory that sometimes tore him from his loves, which was how Louvois so easily involved him in major wars and persuaded him that he was a better leader and strategist than any of his generals, a theory which those officers fostered in order to please him. All their praise he took with admirable complacency, and truly believed that he was what they said. Hence his liking for reviews, which he carried to such lengths that he was known abroad as the 'Review King', and his preference for sieges, where he could make cheap displays of courage, be forcibly restrained, and show his ability to endure fatigue and lack of sleep. Indeed, so robust was his constitution that he never appeared to suffer from hunger, thirst, heat, cold, rain, or any other kind of weather. He greatly enjoyed the sensation of being admired, as he rode along the lines, for his fine presence and princely bearing, his horsemanship, and other attainments. It was chiefly with talk of campaigns and soldiers that he entertained his mistresses and sometimes his courtiers. He talked well and much to the point; no man of fashion could tell a tale or set a scene better than he, yet his most casual speeches were never lacking in natural and conscious majesty.

He had a natural bent towards details and delighted in busying himself with such petty matters as the uniforms, equipment, drill, and discipline of his troops. He concerned himself no less with his buildings, the conduct of his household, and his living expenses, for he always imagined that he had something to teach the experts, and they received instruction from him as though they were novices in arts which they already knew by heart. To the King, such waste of time appeared to deserve his constant attention, which enchanted his ministers, for with a little tact and experience they learned to sway him, making their own desires seem his, and managing great affairs of State in their own way and, all too often, in their own interests, whilst they congratulated themselves and watched him drowning amidst trivialities.

Pride and vanity, which tend always to increase, and the flattery with which he was fed continually without his perceiving it, even from the clergy preaching before him, were the foundations on which his ministers raised themselves above all other ranks. He was cunningly persuaded that their rank was merely an extension of his own, supreme in him, in them capable of increase (since without him they were nothing), and useful to him, because it gave them as his instruments greater dignity and made them more readily obeyed. That is why secretaries of state and ministers gradually left off their cloaks, then their bands, then their black gowns and simple seemly dress, and finally came to clothe themselves like gentlemen of quality. They then began to adopt the manners and later the privileges of the nobility, rising by stages to eat with the King, their wives assuming, as by right, the same prerogatives as their husbands, dining at the royal table, riding in the royal coaches, and in every way appearing equal to ladies of the highest rank.

Personal vanity of another kind led the King to encourage this behaviour. He was well aware that though he might crush a nobleman with the weight of his displeasure, he could not destroy him or his line, whereas a secretary of state or other such minister could be reduced together with his whole family to those depths of nothingness from which he had been elevated. No amount of wealth or possessions would avail him then. That was one reason why he liked to give his ministers authority over the highest in the land, even over the Princes of the Blood and all others who held no office under the crown, and to grant them rank and privileges to match. That is why any man of consequence who possessed anything which the King had no power either to destroy or maintain was carefully kept from the ministry; he would have been a source of danger and a continual anxiety. The sole exception to this rule was the Duc de Beauvilliers. During the whole course of the King's long reign, from the death of Mazarin to the King's own death fifty-four years later, he was the only nobleman to be admitted to the council.

Therein lay the reason for the watchful, jealous attitude of his ministers, who made it difficult for the King to hear any but themselves, although he pleased to think that he was easy for any man to approach. Indeed, he considered that it enhanced his majesty and the respect and fear with which he was regarded, and which he used to snub the most noble, to give all men access to him only as he passed. Thus great lords and underlings alike

Louis XIV commanding in person at the Siege of Mons, 11 March, 1691. By Lecomte.

might speak freely to him as he went from one room to another on his way to or from mass, or stepped into his coach. The more distinguished might wait at the door of his study, but none dared to follow him inside. In fact, approach to him was limited to those moments. Any matters whatsoever had to be explained to him in a few words, very awkwardly, and always within hearing range of his entourage, or, if one knew him well, one might whisper into his wig, which was scarcely more convenient. His almost invariable answer was, 'We shall see' (*Je verrai*), very useful no doubt as a means of gaining time, but often bringing little comfort.

Private audiences in his study were rarely if ever granted, even when the matter concerned State affairs, never, for example, to envoys returning or going abroad, never to generals, unless in extraordinary circumstances; and private letters written to the King always passed through the hands of some minister, except on one or two most rare and special occasions.

Nevertheless, in spite of the fact that the King had been so spoiled with false notions of majesty and power that every other thought was stifled in him, there was much to be gained from a private audience, if it could be obtained, and if one knew how to conduct oneself with all the respect due to his majesty and habits. I, indeed, can speak from experience, for I have described already how I obtained, even compelled him to grant me one when he was most angry, and how I each time managed to over-persuade him and leave him satisfied with me; and he said as much to me and afterwards to others.

Once in his study, however prejudiced he might be, however much displeased, he would listen patiently, good-naturedly, and with a real desire to be informed. You could see that he had a sense of justice and a will to get at the truth, even though he might feel vexed with you, and that quality he retained all through his life. In private audience you could say anything to him, provided, as I have already remarked, that you said it respectfully, with submissiveness and proper deference, for without that you would have been in a worse plight. With the proper manner, however, you could interrupt him when it was your turn to speak, and bluntly deny his accusations, you could even raise your voice above his without vexing him, and he would congratulate himself on the audience and praise the person he interviewed for ridding him of prejudices and the lies he had been told; moreover, he would prove his sincerity by his subsequent attitude.

It is therefore enough to make one weep to think of the wickedness of an education designed solely to suppress the virtue and intelligence of that prince, and the insidious poison of barefaced flattery which made him a kind of god in the very heart of Christendom. His ministers with their cruel politics hemmed him in and made him drunk with power until he was utterly corrupted. If they did not manage entirely to smother such kindness, justice, and love of truth as God had given him, they blunted and obstructed those virtues to the lasting injury of his character and his kingdom.

From such alien and pernicious sources he acquired a pride so colossal that, truly, had not God implanted in his heart the fear of the devil, even in his worst excesses, he would literally have allowed himself to be worshipped. What is more, he would have found worshippers; witness the extravagant monuments that have been set up to him, for example the statue in the Place des Victoires, and its pagan dedication, at a ceremony at which I myself was present, and in which he took such huge delight. From this false pride stemmed all that ruined him. We have already seen some of its ill-effects; others are yet to come.

Louis XIV and the Court

The Court was yet another device to sustain the King's policy of despotism. Many things combined to remove it from Paris and keep it permanently in the country. The disorders of the minority had been staged mainly in that city and for that reason the King had taken a great aversion to it and had become convinced that it was dangerous to live there. He believed that with the Court residing elsewhere, even though the distance was not great, cabals with Paris would be less easy, and harder to conceal because absences would be more noticeable. He would never forgive Paris for his flight on the eve of the Epiphany,[1] 1649, nor for having witnessed, despite all his efforts, his tears at the first retirement of Mme de La Vallière.[2]

The awkward situation with his mistresses and the dangers involved in conducting such scandalous affairs in a busy capital, crowded with people of every kind of mentality, played no small part in deciding him to leave, for he was embarrassed by the crowds whenever he went in or out or appeared upon the streets. Other reasons for departure were his love of hunting and the open air, so much more easily indulged in the country than in Paris, which is far from forests and ill-supplied with pleasant walks, and his delight in building, a later and ever-increasing passion, which could not be enjoyed in the town, where he was continually in the public eye. Finally, he conceived the idea that he would be all the more venerated by the multitude if he lived retired and were no longer seen every day. All these considerations led him to take up his residence at Saint-Germain soon after the Queen-Mother's death, and it was then that he first began to attract society to him with fêtes and diversions and to let it be known that he wished often to be visited.

The liaison with Mme de la Vallière,[3] which was at first kept secret, occasioned many excursions to Versailles, then a little hunting-lodge erected by Louis XIII when he, and still more his courtiers, grew tired of sleeping in a low tavern or an old windmill, after long, exhausting hunts in the forest of Saint-Léger and still further afield. They used to cover great distances in those days, even by present standards, when the speed of hounds and the great numbers of mounted grooms and huntsmen have made hunting so short and easy. Louis XIII never, or very rarely, slept there for more than one night, and then only when it was unavoidable. His son used it to be more private with his mistress, a pleasure unknown to that most upright monarch, that worthy son of Saint-Louis, who first built the little château at Versailles.

Gradually, those quiet country excursions of Louis XIV gave rise to a vast building project, designed to house a large Court more comfortably than in crowded lodgings at Saint-Germain, and he removed his residence there

[1] The Royal family fled to Saint-Germain-en-Laye during the night of January 5–6, 1649, when the Frondeurs took Paris.

[2] Mme de La Vallière fled from the Tuileries on February 4, 1662, and sought refuge at a convent, near Chaillot, to the west of Paris. On that occasion the King went after her and fetched her back.

[3] She was addressed as Madame by courtesy after the King had made her a duchess.

altogether, shortly before the death of the Queen. Immense numbers of suites were made, and one paid one's court by asking for one, whereas, at Saint-Germain, almost everyone had the inconvenience of lodging in the town, and those few who did sleep at the château were amazingly cramped.

The frequent entertainments, the private drives to Versailles, and the royal journeys, provided the King with a means of distinguishing or mortifying his courtiers by naming those who were or were not to accompany him, and thus keeping everyone eager and anxious to please him. He fully realized that the substantial gifts which he had to offer were too few to have any continuous effect, and he substituted imaginary favours that appealed to men's jealous natures, small distinctions which he was able, with extraordinary ingenuity, to grant or withhold every day and almost every hour. The hopes that courtiers built upon such flimsy favours and the importance which they attached to them were really unbelievable, and no one was ever more artful than the King in devising fresh occasions for them. In later days, he made great use of the Marly excursions for that purpose, and Trianon, too, for although every man had the right to go there to pay his court, only the ladies ate with him, and they were specially selected for every meal. Another of his contrivances was the ceremony of the candlestick,[1] which he allowed some courtier to hold every evening at his *coucher*. He always chose from among the most distinguished persons present and called his name aloud as he went out from prayers.

Still another device was the granting of the *justaucorps à brevet*, blue, lined with scarlet, with scarlet facings and waistcoat, embroidered with gold thread and a little silver in a particular pattern. Only a certain number of these jackets were made. The King and the members of the royal family and the Princes of the Blood each possessed one, but the latter had to wait, like the other courtiers, until a vacancy occurred. The greatest persons at the Court used to beg one for themselves or another, and it was considered an enormous privilege to obtain one. Originally, they were designed for the very select few who had the right to go with the King on his excursions to Saint-Germain or Versailles without a special invitation. When these outings ceased, the jackets no longer had any special significance, but they might be worn for Court or family mourning, unless it were full mourning, or at those periods when it was forbidden to wear gold or silver. I never saw the King wear his, nor Monseigneur nor Monsieur, but Monseigneur's three sons often wore theirs, and so did the other princes. Until the King's death, there was always great rivalry among the courtiers as soon as one became available, and if some young nobleman received one it was thought to be a great distinction.

But there would be no end to describing all the different expedients that followed one after another as the King grew older and the entertainments increased or diminished in number, or to telling of the methods he employed to keep so large a Court always about him.

He not only required the constant attendance of the great, but was also aware of those of lower rank. He would look about him at his *lever* and *coucher*, at

[1] See p. 81.

meals, and while walking through the state apartments or the Versailles gardens, where none but courtiers might follow him. He saw and noticed every one of them, marked very well the absences of those usually at Court and even of those who attended more rarely, and took care to discover the reason, drawing his own conclusions and losing no opportunity of acting upon them. He took it as an offence if distinguished people did not make the Court their home, or if others came but seldom. And to come never, or scarcely ever, meant certain disgrace. When a favour was asked for such a one, the King would answer haughtily, 'I do not know him at all', or, 'That is a man whom I never see', and in such cases his word was irrevocable.

Another crime was not to go to Fontainebleau, which he regarded as a second Versailles, and if certain people did not beg for an invitation to Marly, even though he might have no intention of taking them, they needed, man or woman, a pretty good excuse to save them from disgrace. Above all, he could not bear people to go to Paris for their amusements. He did not so much mind the absences of those who loved their estates, but none the less, one needed to be moderate, or else take precautions before making a long visit.

Louis XIV took enormous pains to be well-informed about all that went on in public places, in private houses, society, family business, or the progress of love-affairs. He had spies and reporters everywhere and of all descriptions. Many of them never realized that their reports reached the King, others wrote directly to him, sending their letters by secret channels of his own devising. Their letters were seen by him alone and he always read them before proceeding to other business. There were even some who spoke privately with him in his study, entering by the back way. Through such secret informants, an immense number of people of all ranks were broken, often most unjustly and without their ever discovering the reason, for the King, once suspicious, never trusted again, or so rarely that it made no matter.

One other fault he had, that made him highly dangerous to others and, indeed, to himself, for it often deprived him of loyal subjects. Although his memory was so good that he could recognize some common man, whom he had seen perhaps once, twenty years earlier, and could learn things easily without confusing them, he could scarcely be expected to remember everything. But if he chanced to have only a vague recollection of some person, there remained imprinted upon his mind the idea that he had something against that man, and that alone was enough to exclude him. Nothing could persuade him to change his mind. No matter what his ministers, generals, or even his confessor might argue, he always answered that he could not clearly remember what there was against the man, but that he would feel more secure in choosing some other.

It was owing to the King's curiosity that the lieutenants of police assumed their dangerous power, which went on steadily increasing. These officers were more dreaded, more delicately handled, more respected during his reign even than the ministers, and even by the ministers themselves. No one in France, not even the Princes of the Blood, thought it politic to treat them disrespectfully; for apart from the official reports which they sent to the King, they amused themselves by knowing all the intrigues and the latest scandals in Parisian society.

But the cruellest of all the King's methods of obtaining information was the opening of private letters. Years passed before this practice was generally suspected; and even afterwards, many ignorant and foolish people continued to feed him, for it was almost incredible how swiftly and skilfully the letters were dealt with. He read extracts of those containing any matter which the postmasters or their minister decided that he should see, and entire letters when their contents or the importance of the persons addressed made it appear worth while. Thus it came about that the chief postmasters were in a position to impute whatsoever they chose to whomever they chose, and since it needed very little to ruin a man irretrievably, they had no need for plots or forgeries. A single word of abuse or disparagement of the King or the government, one jest, one sarcastic remark, one plausible fragment cut out of a letter was enough to finish a man's career without further inquiry. Rightly or wrongly accused, it is almost unbelievable how many people of all sorts and conditions were broken to a greater or lesser extent by such means. The veil of secrecy was impenetrable, for nothing came more easily to the King than absolute silence or dissembling. Indeed it was a talent which he carried to the verge of deceit, but never to actual falsehood, for he prided himself on keeping his word, once given. That was why he almost never gave it, and he guarded other people's secrets as scrupulously as he did his own. It even pleased his vanity to receive confidences and to be trusted, and neither mistresses, ministers, nor favourites could drag them out of him, not even when they themselves were implicated.

There is one story in particular of a certain noble lady, whose identity has never yet been discovered, who found that she was pregnant just as her husband was returning after a year's absence with the army. At last, when all other expedients had failed, she besought the King to grant her an absolutely secret audience on the most urgent business in the world. She obtained her interview and told the King that, in her extreme necessity, she had come to the man whom she could best trust in the whole of France. He advised her to let this great trouble be a lesson to live more wisely for the future, and promised her instantly to send orders to keep her husband on duty at the frontier in such a way and for so long that he would have no suspicions, and to refuse him home-leave on any pretext whatsoever. What is more, he sent Louvois instructions that very moment, and forbade him also to leave the fortress which he was to command throughout the winter, even for a single day. The husband, an officer of high rank, had never expected, and had certainly not asked, to be employed at that season on the frontier, neither had Louvois, and both were equally vexed and astonished. None the less, they could do nothing but obey and ask no questions, and when the King finally told the story many years later, he made sure that none of the people concerned would be identified, as indeed they never have been, not even by the vaguest hint.

View of Fontainebleau with Louis XIV stag-hunting. By Van der Meulen.

[1] Michel François le Tellier, Marquis de Courtenvaux. He was the son of Louvois and colonel of the Swiss Guard. Louis XIV turned upon him in a fury one day at Fontainebleau, for a blunder that exposed the King's system of spying on the Court.

No man ever distributed his favours with a better grace than the King, and in so doing he enhanced their value. No one ever put his words, his smiles, his very glances, to better advantage. Everything that he did, he made to appear precious because of his exquisite tact and majesty. When he stopped to ask a man some question on general matters, everyone turned to look at the person he addressed; it was considered a marked distinction, a cause for congratulation, and so it was with all the courtesies, favours, and preferences, which he showed by different degrees. He never allowed himself to say anything ungracious to anybody, and if he needed to check, reprove, or punish, which very rarely occurred, he always did so in a more or less kindly manner, scarcely ever harshly, and never in a rage—except for that one incident with Courtenvaux,[1] None the less, he could be angry when he chose, and sometimes looked very severe.

There never lived a man more naturally polite, nor of such exquisite discrimination with so fine a sense of degree, for he made distinctions for age, merit and rank, and showed them in his answers when these went further than the usual '*Je verrai*', and in his general bearing. Such fine gradations were perfectly displayed in his manner of giving and acknowledging salutations when one approached or left him. He was admirable for the different ways in which he took the salute at the head of the army or at reviews. But above all, he was unrivalled in his courtesy to women, for he never passed a petticoat without raising his hat, even when, as often happened at Marly, they were housemaids, whom he knew to be such. For ladies, he took his hat quite off, but more or less far, as occasion demanded. For noblemen he would half-remove it, holding it in the air or against his ear, for a few moments, or longer. For landed gentlemen, he only touched his hat. Princes of the Blood he greeted in the same way as the ladies, and if he joined a group of ladies, he replaced his hat only after leaving them. But such things occurred only out of doors, for inside the house he was never covered. All these different degrees of courtesy were easy and relaxed, but incomparably graceful and stately, even down to his manner of half rising from his chair at dinner for each 'sitting-lady'[1] as she arrived, and for no one else, not even for Princes of the Blood. Towards the end of his life, this custom tired him, but he would never give it up, and so the ladies who had the right to tabourets avoided entering after he was seated.

In the same way, he made distinctions when Monsieur, M. le Duc d'Orléans, or the Princes of the Blood served him at his *lever* or *coucher*. To the latter he simply made a civil gesture, and the same to Monsieur; to his son, some affectionate movement. The high officers he treated with graciousness and consideration.

If they happened to keep him waiting for something when he was being dressed, he was invariably patient. He was punctual to the minute[2] on his daily round and absolutely clear in his orders, but very occasionally, in bad winter weather, he could not go out and would then go to Mme de Maintenon a quarter of an hour or so before his usual time; it was a most rare event. If the captain of the bodyguard had not yet arrived, the King never forgot to tell him afterwards that it was his own fault for not warning him in time. Such unfailing punctuality made him all the better served and was vastly convenient for his courtiers.

His valets he treated with kindness, especially his body-servants, for with them he felt most at ease and could talk intimately. Their likes and dislikes had much influence so that they were for ever able to do people good or ill turns. They put one in mind of the imperial freedmen of the old Roman Empire, who were fawned upon and courted by senators and other great men. Throughout the whole of his reign, Louis XIV's valets were not less considered and spoiled. The most powerful ministers openly humoured them and so did the Princes of the Blood and even the bastards themselves, not to mention the ordinary courtiers. The duties of the gentlemen of the bedchamber were quite taken over by the head valets, and their high offices were esteemed according to how much the servants and lower officials in their departments had access to the King. Most of them were intolerably insolent; one had to make up one's mind to escape or else bear their rudeness patiently.

The King protected them all. He sometimes told us, with obvious pleasure,

[1] Only Princesses of the Blood, duchesses, and foreign princesses sat on tabourets, all the rest stood.

[2] Saint-Simon says elsewhere that if you had a calendar and a watch, you could tell exactly what he was doing at any time even though you might be three hundred leagues away.

how when he was a young man he had had occasion to send a footman with a letter to the Duc de Montbazon, then governor of Paris. The fellow arrived just as the Duke was going in to dinner, but he had insisted that this footman should eat with him and had walked with him into the courtyard, when he left — because he came from the King. Because of this, the King never forgot to ask how his gentlemen had been received, when they had conveyed his compliments or condolences to some nobleman, and would have taken it very ill if they had not been asked to sit down and escorted for some way on their return, if they were men as far as the door of their coach.

There was nothing to equal his bearing at reviews or, indeed, anywhere graced by the presence of ladies. I have already said that he had learned his gracious manner at his mother's Court and in the drawing-room of the Comtesse de Soissons. The company of his mistresses had encouraged it. He was sometimes gay, but never undignified, and never, at any time, did he do anything improper or indiscreet. His smallest gesture, his walk, bearing, and expression were all perfectly becoming, modest, noble, and stately, yet at the same time he always seemed perfectly natural. Added to which he had the immense advantage of a good figure, which made him graceful and relaxed.

On state occasions such as audiences with ambassadors and other ceremonies, he looked so imposing that one had to become used to the sight of him if one were not to be exposed to the humiliation of breaking down or coming to a full stop. At such times, his answers were always short and to the point and he rarely omitted some civility, or a compliment if the speech deserved one. The awe inspired by his appearance was such that wherever he might be, his presence imposed silence and a degree of fear.

He loved the open air and exercise so long as strength was given to him. In his youth, he had excelled in dancing, at pall-mall,[1] and at the jeu de paume, and all his life he was a superb horseman. He liked men to acquit themselves well in such pastimes; gracefulness or clumsiness in them he regarded as a virtue or discredit, for he used to say that such pursuits were unnecessary and it were better not to do them at all than do them badly. Shooting he loved and was better than the average. He liked beautiful setter bitches and always had seven or eight in his rooms and fed them with his own hands so that they learned to know him. He also loved stag-hunting, but after he broke his arm he rode in a carriage. He drove himself in a small open carriage, drawn by four ponies with five or six relays, and went alone, going full tilt with a skill that few professionals could equal and all the elegance which he habitually displayed. His postillions were children between nine and fifteen years of age, whom he trained himself.

In everything he loved magnificently lavish abundance. He made it a principle from motives of policy and encouraged the Court to imitate him; indeed, one way to win favour was to spend extravagantly on the table, clothes, carriages, building, and gambling. For magnificence in such things he would speak to people. The truth is that he used this means deliberately and

[1] A game like croquet.

The King hunting in his *calèche*, drawn by galloping ponies, which he used after he broke his arm. By van der Meulen.

successfully to impoverish everyone, for he made luxury meritorious in all men, and in some a necessity, so that gradually the entire Court became dependent upon his favours for their very subsistence. What is more, he fed his own pride by surrounding himself with an entourage so universally magnificent that confusion reigned and all natural distinctions were obliterated.

Once it had begun this rottenness grew into the cancer which gnaws at the lives of all Frenchmen. It started, indeed, at the Court but soon spread to Paris, the provinces, and the army where generals are now assessed according to the tables that they keep and the splendour of their establishments. It so eats into private fortunes that those in a position to steal are often forced to do so in order to keep up their spending. This cancer, kept alive by confusion of ranks, pride, even by good manners, and encouraged by the folly of the great, is having incalculable results that will lead to nothing less than ruin and general disaster.

No other King has ever approached him for the number and quality of his stables and hunting establishments. Who could count his buildings? Who not deplore their ostentation, whimsicality and bad taste? He abandoned that lovely Saint-Germain and did nothing to improve or embellish Paris, except out of sheer necessity, as when he built the Pont Royal. Even so, for all its splendid prospect, Paris remains inferior to many towns in other parts of Europe.

When, for instance, the Place de Vendôme was first built, it was square. M.

de Louvois, himself, superintended the erection of the four façades. His plan was to provide house-room for the King's Library, the Cabinet of Medals, the Mint, the various academies, and the grand council, which even now holds its sessions in a rented house. On the day of Louvois's death, the first thing that the King did was to stop the work, and give orders to cut off the corners of the square so as to reduce its size. Nothing that had been planned was done; nothing was constructed but private houses, as we see them today.

Saint-Germain he abandoned; unique Saint-Germain, with its combination of superb vistas and the vast stretches of forest that lie close beside; Saint-Germain, with its fine views, trees, soil and situation, its abundance of springs, its lovely gardens, its hills and terraces, its capabilities that might have been extended to include the beauties and convenience of the Seine. There was a city ready-made, whose site alone provided it with all that man could desire. All this, I say, he abandoned for Versailles, that most dismal and thankless of spots, without vistas, woods, or water, without soil, even, for all the surrounding land is quicksand or bog, and the air cannot be healthy.

It diverted him to ride roughshod over nature and to use his money and ingenuity to subdue it to his will. At Versailles he set up one building after another according to no scheme of planning. Beauty and ugliness, spaciousness and meanness were roughly tacked together. The royal apartments at Versailles are beyond everything inconvenient, with back-views over the privies and other dark and evil-smelling places. Truly, the magnificence of the

The Place Vendôme, about 1705, and the Capuchin monastery at Carnavalet.

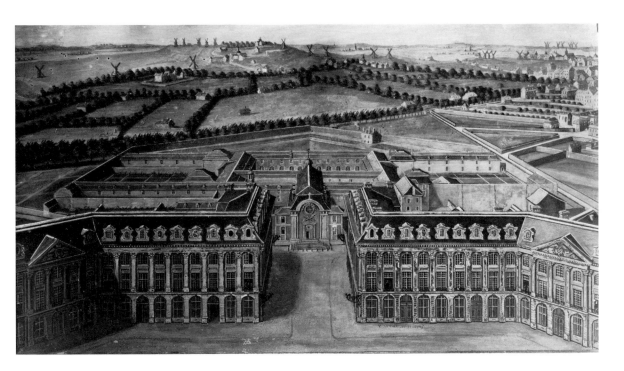

gardens is amazing, but to make the smallest use of them is disagreeable, and they are in equally bad taste. To reach any shade one is forced to cross a vast, scorching expanse and, after all, there is nothing to do in any direction but go up and down a little hill, after which the gardens end. The broken stones on the paths burn one's feet, yet without them one would sink into sand or the blackest mud.

Who could help being repelled and disgusted at the violences done to Nature? Numberless springs have been forced to flow into the gardens from every side, making them lush, overgrown and boggy; they are perceptibly damp and unhealthy and their smell is even more so. The fountains and other effects are indeed incomparably fine, although they require a great deal of attention, but the net result is that one admires and flies.

The glade of the three fountains. By Cotelle.

232

On the courtyard side, the constriction is suffocating and the vast wings recede quite pointlessly. On the garden front, one is able to appreciate the beauty of the building as a whole, but it looks like a palace that has been destroyed by fire because the upper storey and the roofs are still missing. The chapel towers above it because of Mansard's attempt to force the King to add an entire upper storey. As it now is, it presents the distressing appearance of some vast hearse. Everywhere in the chapel the craftsmanship is exquisite, but the design is nil, for everything was planned from the point of view of the tribune, because the King never went below.

But one might be for ever pointing out the monstrous defects of that huge and immensely costly palace, and of its outhouses that cost even more, its orangery, kitchen gardens, kennels, larger and smaller stables, all vast, all prodigiously expensive. Indeed, a whole city has sprung up where before was only a poor tavern, a windmill and a little pasteboard château, which Louis XIII built so as to avoid lying on straw.

The Versailles of Louis XIV, that masterpiece whereon countless sums of money were thrown away merely in alterations to ponds and thickets, was so ruinously costly, so monstrously ill-planned, that it was never finished. Amid so many state rooms, opening one out of another, it has no theatre, no banqueting-hall, no ballroom, and both behind and before much still remains undone. The avenues and plantations, all laid out artificially, cannot mature and the coverts must continually be restocked with game. As for the drains, many miles of them still have to be made, and even the walls, whose vast contours enclose a small province of the gloomiest, most wretched countryside, have never been completely finished.

In the park at the gates of Versailles, Trianon was originally a little porcelain house designed for picnics, and was later enlarged to contain bedrooms. Finally, it was converted into a marble palace of jasper and porphyry, with an enchanting garden. The zoo, that stands opposite, on the further side of the canal, is an exquisite miniature, stocked with the rarest species of beasts and birds. Clagny,[1] also at the end of the park, was built as a present for Mme de Montespan, and was inherited by the Duc du Maine after her death. It, too, is a beautiful château, with gardens, fountains, and parklands. Aqueducts, not unworthy of the Romans, brought water into it from every side. Not Asia, nor antiquity, could show anything more vast, grandiose, and elaborate than these gardens, which were full of precious works of art of every age, marbles, bronzes, paintings, sculptures, all of them perfect in their several ways.

But water lacked. No matter what was done, the great fountains dried up (as they still do at times) in spite of the oceans of reservoirs that cost so many millions to engineer in that sandy or boggy soil. Who would ever credit it? That same lack of water brought about the destruction of the French infantry, for peace reigned at that time and M. de Louvois conceived the notion of changing the course of the Eure between Chartres and Maintenon, so as to bring that river bodily to Versailles. Who could count the gold and the men lost in an

[1] Pulled down by Louis XV.

attempt which was continued for several years? They made a camp at the site of the works, and in the end it was forbidden under heavy penalties to mention the sick, or still worse, the dying, whom the hard labour and exhalations from the turned earth were taking off day by day. How many soldiers wasted long years in trying to recover their health? How many more never did recover? During the whole of that time, not only junior officers, but colonels, brigadiers, and even generals employed there, were forbidden to absent themselves a quarter of an hour, or miss so much as a quarter of an hour's duty on the site. The enterprise finally came to an end with the war of 1688. It has never been restarted. Nothing remains but shapeless mounds to perpetuate the memory of a barbarous piece of folly.

At last the King, growing weary of splendour and crowds, decided that he needed sometimes to have smallness and solitude, and began to search in the neighbourhood of Versailles for a site where he could satisfy this new caprice. He looked at various places, especially among the slopes that lead down from Saint-Germain to the great plain where the winding Seine waters the meadows and rich pastures after leaving Paris. They tried to persuade him to settle on Luciennes,[1] where Cavoye[2] has since built his house, for the view there is bewitching, but he answered that a site so full of capabilities would be the ruin of him. He wanted a mere nothing, and must therefore choose the kind of site that would give him no ideas.

In the end, he lit on a narrow valley with steep and rocky sides that lay behind Luciennes. It was difficult to approach because of the marshes, had no view, was hemmed in by hills on every side and exceedingly constricted. On the side of one of the hills was a wretched little hamlet, known as Marly. The fact that this valley was so much enclosed, without any vista or means of making one, was its chief merit in the King's eyes. The narrowness, which would not allow for spreading, was also greatly in its favour. In fact, he was moved by exactly the same motives as when he chose a minister, a favourite, or a general. It turned out to be an enormous labour to dry up this sewer of a valley, into which all the surrounding country drained itself, and to train the earth to form a new kind of soil. But the King's hermitage was made none the less. It was originally intended for visits of three nights, from a Wednesday to a Saturday two or three times a year, with, at the very most, a dozen courtiers to perform the necessary offices.

Gradually, the retreat was enlarged. Piece by piece the hills were cut away to allow room for building, and a hill at the end of the valley was almost completely levelled so as to give at least one very moderate vista. Finally, with its buildings, fountains, gardens, and aqueducts, so famous, so fascinating under the name of 'La Machine de Marly', with its forests improved and enclosed, its parklands and statues, its precious ornaments of all kinds, there arose Marly, as we now see it, although it has been much despoiled since the King's death.

To provide the forests, many were the tall trees brought from Compiègne

[1] Generally spelt Louveciennes, but pronounced without sounding the 've'. Still later it became the home of Mme du Barry.

[2] Louis d'Oger, Marquis de Cavoye (1640–1716).

234

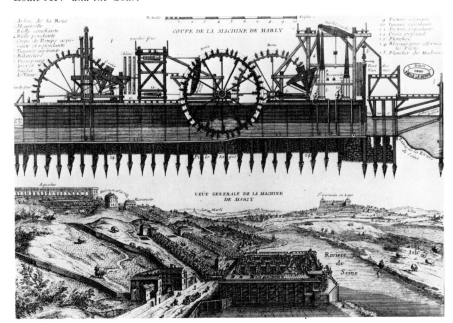

The great machine at Marly, which brought the waters of the Seine up to the aqueduct.

and from even greater distances. More than three-quarters of them died and were immediately replaced by others. Great stretches of thick woodland and dark alleyways were transformed with lightning speed into broad lakes with gondolas at the courtiers' pleasure, and were then changed back to forests so dense that daylight was banished as soon as the trees were planted. I speak of what I saw myself in six weeks, during which time fountains were altered a hundred times, and waterfalls redesigned in countless different ways. Goldfish ponds, decorated with gilding and delightful paintings, were scarcely finished before they were unmade and rebuilt differently by the same artists, and such things were done over and over again. The monstrous machinery for supplying water, which I have already mentioned, with its immense aqueducts, conduits and reservoirs, was intended solely for the needs of Marly, and not to serve Versailles. It is a modest estimate to say that Versailles, such as we see it, did not cost as much as Marly.

If you reckon the expense of continual journeys backwards and forwards to Marly, excursions which became as frequent and almost as crowded as those to Versailles until, at the end of the King's life, it became his usual residence, it would not be too much to say that Marly alone cost several thousand million.

Such was the development of a haunt of snakes and vermin, toads and frogs, that was selected solely on the ground that it would entail no expense. Marly was typical of the King's bad taste[1] in everything, and of the proud pleasure which he found in subduing Nature, from which diversion neither the most pressing needs of war, nor religious zeal, could ever turn him.

[1] Boislisle, however, comments: 'From everything that we know of Marly, its decorations and its wonderful gardens, it must have been a model of good taste and true magnificence. Its disappearance is an irreparable loss.'

235

Mme de Maintenon

We must now pass on to a different kind of love-affair, which astounded foreign nations no less than the earlier ones had shocked them.[1] This time, it was a love which the King carried with him to the grave. From these few words everyone will recognize the famous Françoise d'Aubigné, Marquise de Maintenon, whose reign continued uninterrupted for no less than thirty-two years. She was born in the American Isles,[2] where her father, who may have been of gentle birth, had taken her mother in order to seek their fortunes, and wherein all traces of them have been lost. She returned to France alone, an adventuress, and, landing at La Rochelle, was given asylum out of charity by Mme de Neuillant, mother of the Maréchale-Duchesse de Navailles. Through her poverty and the old lady's avarice, she was there reduced to guarding the keys of the granary and measuring out corn for the horses, until, with the rest of Mme de Neuillant's household, she came to Paris, young, clever, witty and beautiful, but without family or fortune. Some happy chance then brought her to the notice of the famous poet Scarron.[3] He thought her amiable, his friends, in all probability, still more so, while she, for her part, thought it a wonderful and unexpected stroke of good luck to have the possibility of marrying that merry, learned, incapable cripple. Certain people, who may have had more use for a wife than Scarron, incited him to marry, and gained their object by persuading him to rescue from her misfortune this charming damsel in distress.

The marriage accordingly took place, and the bride charmed all the many and varied guests who came to Scarron's house, for he received much company, including some of the very best people in every walk of life. It was the fashion to visit him. Indeed, so many of the most brilliant and distinguished members of the Court and Parisian society came to him that he had no need to go outside his own home for company. His wit, his delightful conversation, the merry way in which he bore his pain, his imagination and pleasant humour, always in the good taste which can still be enjoyed in his works, attracted a continual stream of visitors.

Mme Scarron thus made the acquaintance of a great number of people of all kinds, although, after her husband died, this did not prevent her from being reduced to the charity house[4] of her parish of Saint-Eustache, where she took rooms for herself and her maid[5] on one of the staircases, and lived at first in very straitened circumstances. Her charms, however, gradually relieved her discomforts. Villars, father of the Maréchal, Beuvron (Harcourt's father), and Villarceaux were three permanent supporters, and there were many others. Gradually, they set her up again, introducing her to the d'Albret family, the

[1] In a passage on the King's early love-affairs, Saint-Simon discusses some of the ladies concerned in what he calls the King's 'passades' (his passing fancies). M. Gonzague Truc says that he once began to make a list of them, but found them as numerous as they were unedifying. They included Anne Lucie de la Mothe Houdancourt, later Marquise de La Vieuville, the Princess of Monaco, the Comtesse de Brancas, and many others.

[2] Not true. She was born in the gaol at Niort, where her father was a political prisoner. When she was four he emigrated to Martinique, where he died six years later. His family then returned to France.

[3] Paul Scarron: comic writer and poet, author of *Virgile Travesti, Le Roman Comique*, and other witty and amusing comedies, which paved the way for Molière. During most of his life, he was twisted and crippled with rheumatism.

[4] Les Charités: convents run by nursing-sisters in which many poor young widows rented rooms.

[5] Nanon Balbien.

The King's second (morganatic) wife, Mme de Maintenon, by Mignard. The book and hour-glass suggest her solid worth. The King, in fun, called her 'Votre Solidité'.

Richelieus, and elsewhere, and so she was passed from one to another. In these homes Mme Scarron was certainly not treated as a guest. She did odd jobs, sending for more wood when required, asking the servants when the meals would be coming, or whether so-and-so's carriage had arrived, in fact, all those small services which the use of bells (introduced much later) has rendered unnecessary. It was in such houses, especially in the Hôtel de Richelieu and the Hôtel d'Albret, that Mme Scarron made most of her acquaintances, some of whom were of great service to her, and others whom she afterwards benefited.

The Maréchal d'Albret was of the highest society and party to all the intrigues of the Court, for he was tutor to Monsieur le Prince and M. le Prince de Conti. He lived on terms of intimate friendship with his cousin M. de

Montespan and his wife, but when the latter became the King's mistress, he abandoned her husband and became her adviser, by which means he retained great influence until he died at the age of sixty-two. It was to this close relationship between M. d'Albret and M. de Montespan that Mme Scarron owed the introduction which led, fourteen or fifteen years later, to her incredibly high position.

M. and Mme de Montespan were almost continually at the Hôtel d'Albret, where the Maréchal kept great state, and an open house to which flocked all the most brilliant and exclusive society of the Court and Paris. Mme Scarron's respectful civility, her desire to please, intelligence, and attractions delighted Mme de Montespan, who took a fancy to her. When, therefore, her eldest children by the King (M. du Maine and Mme la Duchesse) were born and concealment became necessary, she suggested making Mme Scarron their governess. This was accordingly done, and a house in the Marais and sufficient means were provided so that the governess might live with them and bring them up with the utmost secrecy. From time to time, the children were taken to Mme de Montespan and shown to the King, until eventually they were brought into the open and acknowledged. They were then established at the Court with their governess, who pleased Mme de Montespan more and more, so much so, indeed, that on several occasions she persuaded the King to make her presents of money. He, however, could not abide her, and what he gave, which was little enough, was done to satisfy Mme de Montespan and with a very bad grace which he did not attempt to conceal.

The estate of Maintenon coming up for sale, Mme de Montespan was tempted by its nearness to Versailles, and gave the King no peace until she had extracted from him a sufficient sum to buy it for that woman, who took the name of Maintenon then, or shortly afterwards. She also obtained funds to repair the château, and teased the King again until he had given enough to restore the garden, which had been left in a bad state.

All this took place during Mme de Montespan's toilette, and was witnessed only by the captain of the guard attending on the King. He happened to be M. le Maréchal de Lorges, my father-in-law, the most truthful man imaginable, who often described the scene to me. At first the King pretended not to hear, then refused, growing impatient because Mme de Montespan, instead of giving up, continued to importune him. Finally he lost his temper, saying that he had done more than enough for that hussy and could not understand Mme de Montespan's partiality, nor her determination to keep her when he had so often requested her dismissal. He then said again, that he could not abide her, but provided that he never saw nor heard mention of her, he would give once more, although he considered that already far too much had been done for that sort of trollop. M. le Maréchal de Lorges never forgot those words, and always repeated them in exactly the same order. He was deeply impressed by them at that time, and much more so later when he witnessed so much that was astonishing and contradictory. He used to say that Mme de Montespan was silent, and appeared distressed at having vexed the King.

M. du Maine was very lame because, or so they said, he had fallen from the arms of one of his nurses. When nothing served to cure him, it was arranged to send him to various bone-surgeons of Flanders and in other parts of the kingdom, and then to certain spas, Barèges among others. Mme de Montespan showed the governess's letters describing their journeys to the King, who thought them well-written, enjoyed them, and gradually lessened in his aversion.

Mme de Montespan's bad temper did the rest, for she was naturally ill-humoured and had never learned to control herself. What is more, her furies were most often directed towards the King himself, who minded them because he was still in love. Mme de Maintenon used sometimes to reproach her for her bad behaviour, and in so doing served him. Others then told him of her good work in soothing his mistress, so that little by little he grew into the habit of telling Mme de Maintenon what she should say, and in the end came to confiding all his sufferings to her ear and asking her advice.

Thus she gradually became the direct confidante of the King's intimate relations with his mistress and laboured so well, turning the position to such good advantage, that by degrees she supplanted Mme de Montespan, who discovered too late that the governess had become a necessity. This having duly been accomplished, Mme de Maintenon began to complain to the King on her own account, telling him of all that she herself had to bear from the mistress who spared him so little. By dint of this mutual complaining about Mme de Montespan, Mme de Maintenon ousted her entirely and made no mistake about securing the situation for herself.

Fate, for I dare not name Providence in such a connection, now prepared the deepest, most flagrant, enduring, unparalleled shame for that proudest of monarchs, by increasing his fancy more and more for that clever woman, so expert in her wiles, which were assisted by the continual jealousy of Mme de Montespan and her frequent, violent outbreaks of bad temper. This is what Mme de Sévigné has described in pretty riddles in her letters to Mme de Grignan, whom she often entertained with the Court gossip.[1]

Fate, I say, the absolute mistress of times and seasons, so ordered things now that the Queen lived just long enough to allow the King's new love to reach its climax, but not so long as to let it cool. The greatest misfortune that could have befallen the King and, as events proved, the State as well, was the sudden death of the Queen at the height of this new attachment, when the ill-temper of his mistress was making her intolerable to him.

The first days of his widowerhood he spent with Monsieur, at Saint-Cloud, and from thence went to Fontainebleau, where he remained throughout the autumn. It was while he was there that absence made his heart grow fonder, until he could no longer bear the pain of separation. On his return, or so they say (for I must distinguish between truth and tittle-tattle), they say, I repeat, that the King spoke more frankly to Mme de Maintenon, and that she dared to

[1] For example, she referred to Mme de Montespan as 'Quanto' or 'Quantova'; to the King as 'the friend', or the 'lord of all'; to the Queen as 'the lady of the house', and to Mme de Maintenon as *'l'enrhumée'* ('Sniffy').

test her power over him, intrenching herself most adroitly behind religion and the impropriety of her present situation. When she saw that the King was not indignant, she preached into him such a fear of the devil, and played on his love and his conscience with so much art that she attained to what our eyes have seen and to what posterity will never credit.

However that may have been, what is very certain and very true is that a few months after the King returned to Fontainebleau, in the middle of the winter following the Queen's death (and again, posterity will scarcely believe it), Père la Chaise, the King's confessor, said mass at midnight in one of the King's studies at Versailles. Bontemps, governor of Versailles and chief and most trustworthy of the four personal valets, served that mass, and there and then the King and the Maintenon were married, in the presence of Harcourt, Archbishop of Paris, acting as diocesan, and Louvois, both of whom extracted the King's solemn promise that the marriage would never be acknowledged. A third witness was Montchevreuil, cousin and friend of Villarceaux,[1] to whom in earlier days he had lent his country house each summer, without removing either himself or his wife. There, Villarceaux entertained that 'queen', as he did in Paris, and paid all the expenses because his cousin was miserably poor. He was ashamed to bring his concubine to Villarceaux and the notice of a wife, whose patience and virtue he respected.

The boredom of respectability, which is so often fatal to marriages of this kind, only served to increase the King's fondness for Mme de Maintenon. Very soon after the wedding, the affair became common knowledge, for she was suddenly provided with an apartment at Versailles, at the head of the grand staircase, opposite to the King's private rooms and on the same level.

Mme de Maintenon was an exceedingly able woman, who had acquired polish and a knowledge of the world from the high society where she was at first tolerated and later cherished. Her love-affairs had taught her the arts of pleasing, and in the different positions which she had occupied she had learned to coax and flatter, to be civil, and always to be agreeable. She was of necessity a schemer, but the various intrigues of one kind and another, which she either witnessed or originated on her own or other people's behalf, gave her a taste for plotting and sharpened her wits. Every action of hers was performed with incomparable grace and ease, for long years of servitude had made natural in her a reserved and modest bearing which marvellously enhanced her own good qualities. When she spoke, it was quietly and correctly, using excellent French, always brief and eloquent. She was three or four years older than the King, so that her best time had coincided with the fashion for witty conversations and elegant gallantries, *Les Ruelles*,[2] as they used to be called. These had so much enchanted her that she never afterwards lost their flavour, nor her pleasure in them. Primness and preciosity added to that old-fashioned air, which had been covered, first with a veneer of self-importance, and later with a thicker veneer of a piety that eventually became her chief characteristic and seemed to absorb every other quality. Piety was, indeed, her greatest asset; she used it to

[1] The Marquis de Villarceaux was supposed to have been the lover of Mme de Maintenon when she was Mme Scarron, and to have possessed a portrait of her in the nude.

[2] It was in *Les Ruelles*, the spaces between the bed and the wall, that the arts of witty conversation and elegant love-making were born. They were, in fact, the birthplace of French wit.

maintain herself upon the heights and, above all, as a means to power, which was her life's ambition, to which she would gladly have sacrificed all else. Truth and frankness ill become such an aim and such success in achieving it; you may well imagine that she could preserve only the outward semblance of those virtues. None the less, she was not so false-hearted as to prefer lies to the truth, but necessity had long since forced the habit upon her, so that, being fickle by nature, she appeared twice as false as she was in reality.

There was no stability in her, except by constraint or force of circumstances. Her natural inclination was to be as changeable in her friends and acquaintances as in her diversions, excepting always one or two faithful old friends of earlier days, whom I have already mentioned. Those she never forsook, and she also clung to some newer friendships that became necessary to her as time passed. As regards diversions, after she began to think of herself as queen, she varied them hardly at all. Where her fickleness was most apparent was in more important matters, and there it did great harm, for she easily became enthusiastic, even to excess, and was just as easily disenchanted. Infatuations, with her, often changed to disgust without rhyme or reason.

The poverty and the abject situation in which she had lived for so long had narrowed her mind and debased her heart and sentiments. She thought and felt so very meanly about most things that as Mme de Maintenon she was actually less of a personality than she had been as Mme Scarron, and was always the same on every occasion. Nothing could have been more boring than such baseness in her glorious position, and nothing more stultifying to any good that might have arisen from it than this fatal weakness for changing friends and advisers.

She had one other deceiving trick. If one had an audience with her and something about one's appearance chanced to please her, she would greet one with amazing warmth that seemed to promise great things, yet a moment afterwards, she might be excessively short and snubbing. One might rack one's brains to discover the causes for her favour and displeasure, both so suddenly displayed, but it would be sheer waste of time. Caprice was her only motive, and her flightiness was unbelievable. You may imagine how thorny was the road to her favour; but, in any case, she was almost inaccessible, by her own desire and the King's preference.

She was so weak as to be influenced by opinions, and welcomed confidences that almost amounted to confessions, but she was easily duped because the life that she led was so narrow and confined. Yet she had an evil passion for administration that cost her what little freedom she might otherwise have retained. It was incredible how much time she wasted over Saint-Cyr, and the affairs of a hundred other convents occupied as much of her leisure. She saw herself as a kind of universal mother superior, especially in spiritual matters, which led her to undertaking the management of the entire diocese. That was her favourite pastime, for she loved to weigh the respective merits of the higher clergy, superiors of seminaries and other schools, as well as those of convents. Thus she developed a host of trivial businesses, all unreal, burdensome, and falsely conceived. There were endless letters to receive and answer, orders to be given to her favourites, and all manner of other such nonsense, mostly ending in nothing, but occasionally leading to important decisions and deplorable mistakes in selection and the appreciation of events.

Mme de Maintenon's heart's desire was always the public announcement of her marriage with the King, and at one point that wish was almost realized. But the King, remembering in time what had happened on that occasion, consulted the famous Bossuet, Bishop of Meaux, and Fénelon, Archbishop of Cambrai, both of whom so earnestly dissuaded him that he put the matter aside for ever. The Archbishop was already in bad odour with Mme de Maintenon, but Bossuet escaped her wrath because he had once unintentionally done her a very great service.[1]

Bossuet was a man in whom honour, virtue, and integrity were inseparable from vast erudition. His office as tutor to Monseigneur brought him into contact with the King, who more than once consulted him on matters of conscience. Bossuet had then spoken out with a freedom worthy of the first centuries of Christianity and the first bishops, and had more than once stopped the King in his immoralities, even venturing to pursue when the King tried to evade him. In the end, he succeeded in preventing all adulterous practices, and crowned his great work by dealing the final blow that drove Mme de Montespan for ever from the Court. Even at the height of her triumph, as she then was, Mme de Maintenon could not have rested easy while her late employer still remained in residence receiving daily visits from the King, for she resented them as so much time and attention stolen from herself. What is more, she could not, with propriety, have avoided treating Mme de Montespan, if not with the respect of earlier days, at least with great civility and the outward semblance of devotion. Such courtesies reminded her only too well of past servitude, as did Mme de Montespan herself, with barbed and exceedingly well-phrased darts, aimed to hurt. Nevertheless, when the King paid his daily semi-public visits to the former mistress, he went between mass and dinner, so as to cut them decently and necessarily short, which provided a most absurd contrast to the lengthy sessions held, also daily, with the former governess, now supposedly neither mistress nor wife, whose apartment had become the stew-pot of the affairs of Court and State. Mme de Montespan's final departure was thus an immense relief to Mme de Maintenon, who realized that she owed it entirely to the Bishop of Meaux.

That also was the period of the perfect harmony and understanding between M. du Maine and Mme de Maintenon, and of her virtual adoption of him, a relationship that became increasingly close and opened the way for him to incredible grandeurs. It would, indeed, have brought him to the throne, had that been within the power of his devoted '*Mie*'.[2]

Having secured the great victory of Mme de Montespan's perpetual banishment, Mme de Maintenon had a further triumph. After failing for the

[1] When he persuaded the King to leave Mme de Montespan. By so doing he paved the way for Mme de Maintenon, with a result which he surely did not foresee.

[2] The Duc du Maine's pet-name for Mme de Maintenon.

second time to declare her marriage, she realized that nothing would be gained by reviving the subject and decided to accept her disappointment sweetly, showing no chagrin at the refusal to make her queen, which made the King feel vastly relieved and grateful to her, and increased his affection, consideration, and trust. In point of fact, she might well have failed under the crushing weight of the rank to which she aspired, whereas in those circumstances, she became ever more firmly established by sustaining the transparent pretence of her position.

It must not, however, be supposed that she needed no skill to maintain herself in power. On the contrary, her life was one long campaign, and that of the King a perpetual delusion. She never received visits, and paid none; there were few exceptions to that rule although she sometimes called on the Queen of England and was visited by her, and sometimes went to see Mme de Montchevreuil, her dearest friend, who came often to her. She never called on the Princesses of the Blood, nor on Madame; but when she had something to say to the King's daughters, which was not often, and almost never except when she wished to give them a good dressing-down, she had them sent for. They used to arrive trembling and nearly always left in tears.

Audiences with her were nearly as hard to obtain as with the King himself, and what few she did grant were mostly at Saint-Cyr, and one had to go at a given day and hour. People would wait outside her apartments when she was leaving or returning to Versailles, those of no account, the poor, and men of quality, all alike. There was not a moment to lose, and a race to catch her eye. The Maréchaux de Villeroy, Harcourt, Tessé, and, in later days, M. de Vaudémont spoke to her at such times, and if she were returning, they would follow her only as far as the ante-room, where she very quickly broke off the conversation and left them. As for me, I never spoke to her anywhere, except as I have described elsewhere.[1] One or two ladies whom the King knew and liked sometimes saw her when he was not present, and very occasionally a few of them dined with her.

Her mornings, which began very early indeed, were filled by interviews with obscure persons concerned with charities or religious administration. Sometimes she saw one or two ministers or, more rarely, generals, when they had something special to report. Fairly frequently, at eight in the morning, or even earlier, she would go to see some minister or other, and very occasionally stayed to dine with them, their wives, and some carefully selected guests. That was a great favour, and made news, but led to nothing but jealousy and a certain amount of deference. The ministers for war and finance were those with whom she had most to do, and it was their acquaintance that she cultivated. She seldom went to others, except for business, very early in the morning, and never dined with them.

Usually, as soon as she rose, she went to Saint-Cyr and dined there alone in her room, or with some favourite nun, gave as few audiences as possible, presided over the convent's internal affairs, ruled the Church outside, read and

[1] In 1710, when Mme de Saint-Simon was made lady-in-waiting to the Duchesse de Berry, Mme de Maintenon congratulated and praised her in public. Saint-Simon was unwillingly obliged to pay her a courtesy-visit but says that he never went again.

answered letters, directed the convent schools in all parts of France, received reports from her spies, and returned to Versailles almost exactly at the time when the King habitually visited her. When she grew old and infirm, she used to arrive at Saint-Cyr between seven and eight o'clock in the morning, and at once go to bed and rest or take some remedy or other.

At Fontainebleau, she had a house in the town, where she often went for the same purposes. At Marly, she had a little room with a window looking into the chapel. She used it as she did Saint-Cyr, but called it 'Le Repos'. It was inaccessible to all, without exception, except to Mme la Duchesse de Bourgogne.

At nine in the evening two maids used to come to undress Mme de Maintenon and, directly afterwards, her butler and a footman brought in her supper—soup and something light to eat. As soon as she had finished, her women put her into bed. All this took place in the presence of the King and the minister in attendance, if one were on duty, or the ladies of the intimate circle. Voices were not hushed and work or conversation continued uninterrupted. By that time it was usually ten o'clock, when the King went to his supper and Mme de Maintenon's curtains were drawn.

It was the same on excursions. She would leave early in the morning with some favourite friend, always Mme de Montchevreuil while she lived, then Mme d'Heudicourt, Mme de Dangeau, or Mme de Caylus. A royal carriage was at her disposal at all times, even for journeys from Versailles to Saint-Cyr, and the equerry in charge of the smaller stables handed her into the coach and rode beside her on horseback. That was his daily duty. On the Court journeys, Mme de Maintenon's own coach took her women and followed behind. She always arranged matters so that when the King arrived he found her comfortably established.

In private, she behaved exactly as though she were indeed the Queen, remaining seated in the presence of the King, Monseigneur, Monsieur, and the English Court. Elsewhere, she was simply a private person, and one of low rank. I have seen her at Marly, sitting at the lower end of the King's table with the rest of the ladies and, in full court-dress, at the Queen of England's apartment at Fontainebleau, yielding up her privileges, drawing back to allow titled, and even otherwise distinguished women to pass. She never allowed herself to be obliged to do so, but did all willingly, courteously, and in all situations was polite, affable, conversational, without pride or ostentation. She seemed intent only on giving consideration to those about her, but for all that, her presence made itself felt.

At all times, she was richly and neatly dressed, in good taste, but very simply, and in a style rather older than her years. On the rare occasions when she appeared after her retirement nothing was to be seen but a black bonnet and shawl. To the King's bedroom she never went, unless he were ill, or on the mornings of days when he took physic, and for much the same reasons she went to the room of Mme la Duchesse de Bourgogne, but never otherwise, not on any account. When the King came to her, they sat each in their armchair on either side of the fireplace with tables before them, she on the side where the bed stood, and the King with his back to the wall, on the side of the ante-chamber door. Two stools were placed in front of his table, one for a minister and the other for his portfolio. On working-days, the King and Mme de Maintenon were alone together only for the short time before the minister entered and the even shorter time after he had gone.[1] The King then went to his chaise-percée, and returned to the bedside, where he stood for a little while, said good night to her, and went to table. Such was the daily life of Mme de Maintenon.

While the work was in progress, she read or did her embroidery, hearing everything that passed between the King and his ministers, for they spoke aloud. Very occasionally, she put in a word, more seldom still, something of importance. Often, the King asked her opinion, and then she would answer with great caution and restraint, never or hardly ever, showing any concern for the matter, still less any interest in individuals. All the while, however, she was secretly in agreement with the minister, who not having dared to oppose her in their private interviews, could do so still less in the King's presence. When the matter concerned some favour or appointment, it was arranged between them before ever it was brought to the King for his decision. Thus long delays occurred, for which neither the King nor anyone else guessed the reason.

She used to send word to ministers when she desired to speak to them, and they dared not mention any subject to the King without knowing her wishes, or until the revolving machinery of times and seasons had given them leisure to come to an agreement. Only then did the minister present his proposals and lists to the King. If the latter paused at the name chosen by Mme de Maintenon the matter ended there, but if he chanced to stop at some other name, the minister would suggest examining the rest, encourage the King to criticize and thus contrive to have them excluded. He scarcely ever directly proposed Mme de Maintenon's choice, but mentioned several other persons, balancing them so nicely against one another that the King would become confused. He would then ask the minister's advice, and he, in turn, would repeat the arguments in favour of a few, finally coming to rest on their nominee. At this point, the King usually demurred, and turned to Mme de Maintenon for her opinion. The lady would smile, play the simpleton, say a word for one of the others and then, as though it were her first thought upon the matter, name the one the minister had suggested, and so it would be settled. Thus, the three-quarters that had to do with favours and appointments, and three-quarters of the remaining quarter of all that took place in her presence between the King and his ministers, were decided as she wished.

In great affairs of state, if Mme de Maintenon desired to make some proposal succeed or fail to go otherwise (which was much rarer for her than interference with favours and appointments), she had the same kind of understanding with the minister, and matters proceeded in much the same way. From this

[1] In a letter to the Marquise de Villacerf, Mme de Maintenon wrote: 'When the King returns from hunting he comes to me. They close the doors and no one enters. I have to sympathize with his troubles, if he has any, his sorrows, and his vapours. Sometimes he is overcome by tears which he cannot master, or he feels disgruntled and there is no conversation. Then one or other of the ministers arrives. . .'

Mme de Maintenon in old age, by Hyacinthe Rigaud.

description, you will perceive that that capable woman did almost all as she pleased, but not all that she pleased, nor when and how she pleased.

There was another ruse for when the King was stubborn. They would prevent his coming to a decision by complicating and prolonging the affair, or changing the subject to some other matter that seemed to arise from it, so that the King became confused and the minister could propose obtaining further information. Thus the first determination would be forgotten, and when they later returned to the charge, they usually succeeded. By such methods or others similar, they made faults to seem greater or less; letters from spies or the secret police were given weight, or glossed over, and ruin or riches might be the result.

That was why working in Mme de Maintenon's apartment was so

immensely important for the individuals concerned, and why it became so necessary for her to make the ministers her slaves. It gave them powerful assistance in rising to high rank and continually increased them in reputation and authority—them and their families, because Mme de Maintenon was ready to cast honours on any dunghill in order to attach such persons to her.

In the short time before they came to work, or after they left her apartment, she took the opportunity to sound the King on their behalf, to excuse or praise them, pity them for their hard labours, extol their merits and, if there were something to be gained for them, to prepare the way, sometimes breaking the ice on the pretext of their modesty, saying that the King's interest demanded that they should be encouraged to further efforts. Thus there arose between Mme de Maintenon and the ministers a chain of reciprocal wants and services of which the King had no suspicion whatsoever.

If Mme de Maintenon could achieve nothing without them, however, the ministers could do nothing without her, much less against her. Directly she saw that it was impossible to retrieve them when they strayed from her ideas, or if they fell out of her favour, their ruin was assured. She never miscarried, although she sometimes needed time, double-dealing and cunning to a great degree, as when she ruined Chamillart, and Louvois before him. Pontchartrain only escaped her because his wit amused the King, because of the thorny financial situation during the war, and because his wife was clever enough to stay in Mme de Maintenon's good books for a very long time. Even he, in the end, was got rid of by the golden gate of the chancellery, that opened for him only just in time. The Duc de Beauvilliers thought that he would be wrecked on two different occasions,[1] and only escaped by a miracle, as I have described elsewhere.

Since the most outstanding ministers and the most distinguished men were on such terms with Mme de Maintenon, you may judge how it was with other sorts of persons, less able to defend themselves or even to realize what was happening. Very many people who had their heads broken were at a loss to understand the cause, and went to much trouble to find out and seek a remedy. But all was useless.

The King's short, very occasional sessions with the generals usually took place in the evening, in her presence and that of the secretary of state for war. Those with Pontchartrain, filled, as they were, with reports from spies, and tittle-tattle of every kind about Paris and the Court, gave her opportunities for doing much good and harm. Torcy never worked in her apartment and she almost never saw him to speak to, which made her positively dislike him, especially as he was head of the post office and had many private interviews with the King over intercepted letters. The King often brought snippets for Mme de Maintenon to read, but there was no continuity; she only learned things by scraps, whenever the King remembered to tell or show her some matter.

As for foreign affairs, they were dealt with at the council of State or, if

[1] In 1698, Mme de Maintenon had unsuccessfully tried to remove the Duc de Beauvilliers from his post of governor to the Duc de Bourgogne, and in 1709, from the King's council.

anything pressed, Torcy took it straight to the King at any hour; there were no fixed times for him. Mme de Maintenon would dearly have loved to have had these conferences held in her apartment, but Torcy was too wise to fall into that trap. He always avoided it by saying modestly that no business of his warranted so much inconvenience to her. It was not as though the King did not tell her everything afterwards, but it was not the same. She felt the difference between hearing regular discussions which she could influence and prepare at leisure, and having to argue with the King herself on the basis of what he alone had told her, or stand up to him alone if she preferred a different course.

At the same time the King was very watchful. It sometimes happened, if they had been less subtle than usual, that he realized it when some minister or general favoured a relation of Mme de Maintenon. Then he would say, half angrily, half-mocking, 'So-and-so has paid his court well. It appears that because he is Mme de Maintenon's cousin, he need not prove loyal service.' Such snubs made her very nervous and cautious when she was driven to speak openly to the King about someone or something, and she always publicly professed that she never interfered on any account, not even in the littlest things.

Le Tellier, in very early days, long before he was Chancellor of France, understood the King's reactions perfectly. One of his friends once asked him to assist in some matter that was coming under discussion, and Le Tellier promised to do his best. This answer did not please the friend, who said frankly that with his position and the King's favour, he might do much better. 'You do not know the circumstances', said Le Tellier. 'Out of twenty matters which we bring before the King, we are sure that nineteen will go as we wish, but equally surely the twentieth is decided against us. The trouble is that none of us can foresee which the twentieth will be, and very often it is the one that most concerns us. This is a trick which the King keeps up his sleeve to show us that he is master, and should it occur on some matter so important that we continue to press our opinion, although that rarely happens, we are sure of an outburst. But in truth, after the reprimand, the King rests content with having put us in our places, and is sorry for vexing us. That is the time when he becomes most gentle and reasonable, and then we can do as we please.'

That, indeed, was how the King behaved all through his reign towards his ministers. He was entirely ruled by them, even by the youngest and most mediocre, even by those whom he liked and trusted least. Always, he was on guard against influences, and always believed that he had been completely successful in avoiding them.

He was the same with Mme de Maintenon, and from time to time flew into terrible passions with her, afterwards congratulating himself for so doing. Sometimes she burst into tears in front of him, and lived on tenterhooks for several days. After she had planted Fagon as chief physician in place of d'Aquin, because she liked to have near her that clever man, to whom she had become attached when she had journeyed to different spas with M. du Maine, she sometimes pretended illness after such scenes and usually ended by turning them to her advantage.

Not that any tricks of that kind, nor even real illness, had power to move the King, for he was supremely self-centred and considered others, no matter whom, only as regarded himself. His hardness was extraordinary. In the times when he was most ardent for his mistresses, discomforts that made travel and tight Court dresses most awkward for them (for until Marly, ladies never appeared otherwise clothed in coaches or at Court) earned them no dispensations. Pregnant, sick, less than six weeks after labour, otherwise indisposed, no matter, they had to be fully dressed, bejewelled, tight-laced into their bodices, ready to travel to Flanders or further, to dance, be lively, attend the fêtes, eat, be cheerful and good company, move about, seem not to notice heat or cold or draughts or dust, and all punctual to the moment, giving no trouble of any kind.

He treated his daughters in the same way. You have already seen how little he was concerned for Mme la Duchesse de Bourgogne,[1] in spite of all that Fagon and Mme de Maintenon could say. Yet for Mme la Duchesse de Bourgogne he felt all the love of which he was capable.

When he travelled, his coach was always full of women, his mistresses, and after their time, his bastard-daughters, his daughter-in-law, sometimes Madame, and some other ladies when there was room for them. But it was only to meets of the hunt, on journeys to Fontainebleau, Chantilly, Compiègne, and on long journeys that such was the arrangement. When he went shooting, or drove out, or slept at Marly or Meudon, he travelled alone in a lighter carriage. He did not care to listen to the conversation of the high officers who might otherwise have accompanied him; they say that Charost, who used to take such opportunities to tell him many things, persuaded him to adopt that attitude more than forty years earlier. The arrangement suited his ministers, who might otherwise have had fresh cause for alarm every day, regarding the exact amount of formality which they must maintain, for the King was most meticulous. As regards women, the mistresses of early days, the daughters who followed them, and the small circle of ladies allowed in his coach, except that attendance was obligatory, the occasions were few and far between and the chatter not greatly to be dreaded.

On longer journeys there was always a vast store of provisions of many different kinds in the King's coach, cold meats, cakes and fruit, for example. They were never more than a quarter of a league on their way before the King asked whether the ladies did not care to eat something. He himself never ate between meals, not even fruit, but it amused him to watch others eat, and eat to bursting point. They had to appear hungry and gay, and to set to with good appetite, and good grace, or else he became displeased and showed his resentment, saying that they were being pettish, nice, or trying to appear refined. Yet those same ladies or princesses who supped at his table on such days, were obliged, under threat of the same reprimands, to produce as much

[1] Pp. 120–1.

249

eagerness as though they had not eaten all day. As for the needs of nature, they could not be mentioned, and in any case, it would have been very embarrassing for the ladies, with detachments of the household cavalry and the King's escort riding before and after the coach, and officers and equerries by the doors raising a dust that covered everyone within. The King liked fresh air, and would have all the windows lowered; he would have thought very ill of it, had any lady drawn one of the curtains against the sun, wind, or cold. One had not to notice that, nor any other kind of discomfort, and he always drove exceedingly fast, and usually with relays of horses. To feel sick was an unforgivable crime.

I have heard the Duchesse de Chevreuse, whom he liked and took with him in his carriage so long as she was able to travel, tell how once, driving with him from Versailles to Fontainebleau, she had been overtaken before they had gone two leagues by one of those pressing emergencies which one feels powerless to resist. The journey was continuous and the King did not leave his coach when he stopped to dine. Her need became even greater, but did not make itself felt at any convenient time, when they dined, for instance, and she might have got down and gone into the house opposite. Unfortunately the meal, although she ate as little as she decently could, brought her to an even worse pass. At moments she thought that she would be forced to confess and stop the coach, and at others she felt near swooning, but her courage kept her up until they arrived at Fontainebleau, where she could hold out no longer. As she set foot to the ground, she happened to see the Duc de Beauvilliers, standing at the King's entrance, and instead of following with the suite, she took his arm and told him that she would die if she did not relieve herself. They crossed the end of the oval courtyard, and entered the chapel, which, luckily, happened to be open, for mass was said there each morning. Necessity knows no law! Mme de Chevreuse relieved herself then and there in the chapel, behind the back of the Duc de Beauvilliers as he guarded the door! I repeat this misfortune to show the discomforts that daily beset those who approached the King most nearly, and those whom he most favoured, for that incident happened in the heyday of the Duchesse de Chevreuse. Such things may appear the merest trifles, and so indeed they are, but they are too characteristic to be omitted. The King himself sometimes felt the needs of nature, and then he did not hesitate to get down from the carriage, but the ladies at such times might not move.

Mme de Maintenon, who detested fresh air and other discomforts, gained no privileges in such matters. All that she obtained, on the pretext of modest reserve and for other reasons, was to travel alone in the manner which I have described. To travel she was obliged, in whatever state of health, and to arrive at the destination as arranged, and be settled and in good order before the King came to her. She made many excursions to Marly in a state in which one would not have sent even a servant, and on one occasion when she went to Fontainebleau, they really thought that she would die upon the road. No matter how badly she might be feeling, the King went to her at his ordinary time, and did whatever he had planned; at the very most, she was allowed to lie in bed. Often she lay there sweating great drops, but the King, who, as I have said, liked fresh air and hated hot rooms, would be amazed at finding everything shut, and would order the windows to be opened, and none left closed, although he saw her state. And this would continue until ten o'clock, when he went to dinner, without consideration for the dampness of the night air. If music had been arranged, neither fevers nor headaches might serve to prevent it, and a hundred candles flared in her eyes. So the King went his own ways, and never inquired whether she were discomfited.

Index